Countertransference

Triumphs

and

Catastrophes

COUNTERTRANSFERENCE TRIUMPHS AND CATASTROPHES

Peter L. Giovacchini, M.D.

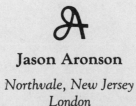

Jason Aronson

Northvale, New Jersey
London

First softcover edition 1993

Library of Congress Cataloging-in-Publication Data

Giovacchini, Peter L.
    Countertransference triumphs and catastrophes / Peter L. Giovacchini.
      p.   cm.
    Bibliography: P.
    Includes index.
    ISBN 0-87668-879-2 (hardcover)
    ISBN 0-87668-284-0 (softcover)
    1. Countertransference (Psychology) 2. Psychotherapy. I. Title.
    [DNLM: 1. Countertransference (Psychology)   WM 62 G512c]
  RC489.C68G56 1989
  616.89'14—dc19
  DNLM/DLC   88-19471
  for Library of Congress   CIP

Manufactured in the United States of America. Jason Aronson Inc. offers books and cassettes. For information and catalog write to Jason Aronson Inc., 230 Livingston Street, Northvale, NJ 07647.

Contents

II
COUNTERTRANSFERENCE
IN SPECIFIC PSYCHOPATHOLOGICAL
CONSTELLATIONS

III
TECHNICAL
TREATMENT PROBLEMS

Preface

Treatment technique and countertransference are insep-
arable. Clinicians who strive to understand the nuances
of the treatment process must understand countertransference. Freud recognized that psychoanalytic treatment
depended on the resolution of the transference. He was,
in essence, referring to an object-relationship quality of
the analytic interaction when he examined the patient's
relationship to the analyst. An object relationship in-

volves two persons, however, and in order to thoroughly understand it as a two-way process, the therapist's feelings also must be
taken into account. Insofar as all feelings have infantile roots,
some of the analyst's reactions constitute countertransference.

The technical factors involved in the treatment of patients,
especially those suffering from primitive mental states, involve
the re-creation of the infantile environment, a process that is
inextricably bound to and revolves around the transference–
countertransference axis. Thus, countertransference as well as
transference elements are in the forefront of any discussion of
psychoanalytic interaction and technical treatment problems.
In this book, I sometimes discuss countertransference interactions and technical maneuvers as if they were synonymous.

Since countertransference is the outcome of a clinical
interaction, I present many treatment vignettes. In fact, this
book contains a series of vignettes as they address various forms
of psychopathology that lead to specific countertransference
reactions. Some of these interactions lead to successful resolutions and others to therapeutic failure.

It is important to understand how the therapist's feelings
and responses fit into the clinical picture. Most clinicians tend to
write about their successes but prefer reading about their colleagues' failures. I believe that there is much to learn from both
situations, although we find difficult and challenging patients
more interesting as we try to work out some of our own problems
with patients. How we handle our feelings determines whether
the countertransference will lead to triumph or catastrophe.

Throughout the years, analysts have become less reluctant
to discuss their countertransference reactions and therapeutic
dilemmas (Boyer 1961, Searles 1953, Volkan 1987). No longer
do clinicians believe that a countertransference response is
always a sign of the analyst's mishandling the patient or a
symptom of a personal disorder that requires further analysis for

the analyst (Freud 1910). There are, of course, harmful counter-transference reactions, and they may be the outcome of the analyst's psychopathology. But because of the emotional inten-sity of the psychoanalytic relationship, a constant, ongoing transference–countertransference interaction is intrinsic to the analytic process. Therefore, an exploration of psychoanalytic treatment must include the analyst's participation in terms of countertransference responses. Treatment, as this book will stress, is not unilateral. It is generally acknowledged that the course of treatment must be understood in terms of the un-folding and development of the transference. To add another dimension that is essential to the study of technical issues from an interpersonal perspective, clinicians must consider the coun-tertransference as a counterpart of infantile factors in the ther-apist with which the patient is getting in touch.

Many of the clinical examples are of my own patients. Obviously, the best way to study countertransference issues is by observing ourselves. To some extent, we are prepared for this type of investigation; having been in analysis, analysts can extend their so-called training analyses by scrutinizing their feelings and reactions to their patients' material. Thus, in order to discuss this expanded framework of the treatment relation-ship, I will have to expose some of my personal feelings and character orientations.

I have noted that many clinical presentations in the psy-choanalytic literature are not particularly clinical. A moderate number of articles and monographs, some of which have been particularly significant to our understanding of psychopa-thology (Hartmann 1939), contain no clinical data whatsoever, despite the fact that they deal with elements of the treatment process. Other articles contain some material about patients, but they also present extensive formulations that go far beyond the clinical data. The opposite also occurs, and the reader is

overwhelmed with a deluge of case material that does not seem
to have a focus.

For the most part, these analysts do not reveal their feelings, nor do they tell us what they actually did. They may tell us
about an interpretation they made, but this, too, is devoid of
any personal element. The interpretation is couched in abstract
theoretical terms; it does not reveal the actual words that were
said to the patient. I have noted similar phenomena in case
conferences in which the therapist reviews countless sessions,
giving the impression that he has just sat through them and said
nothing; still, it is obvious that there was a change in the
material because of the interaction.

For obvious reasons, such as the anticipation of being
judged and criticized, analysts are reticent about revealing what
they do and how they feel about patients. Since Tower's (1956)
paper on countertransference, the tide has turned, and there
have been many papers and some books on the topic of countertransference. There were analysts before Tower who freely
discussed their reactions to patients, but most clinicians felt that
they were taking a risk in revealing themselves.

Perhaps the tide has turned too far. Some clinicians over-
whelm us with discussions about themselves that are either
irrelevant or idiosyncratic. Still, it is a fine line between being
frank and honest and being exhibitionistic. I have tried to limit
my clinical discussions to feelings evoked by the patient; in some
instances, though, I have made gratuitous contributions, because of my personal orientation, that entered the transference–
countertransference interaction for better or worse. I have tried
to indicate these instances in both my own clinical examples and
those of other therapists whose cases are included in this volume.

Most of the patients discussed in this book can be considered as suffering from character disorders. In many instances,

however, we can draw inferences from experiences with these patients that also apply to the treatment of psychoneuroses. Clinical pictures are so varied that precise predictions about treatability, therapeutic course, and, now, the fate of the countertransference are difficult to make or to correlate with the severity of psychopathology. I have tried to establish a rough sequence based on the severity of psychopathology by first discussing patients who suffer from very primitive mental states and then moving upward on the hierarchal scale of developmental fixations and psychopathology.

Depressed patients, in contrast to those suffering from structural psychopathology, are considered to have advanced to a level at which object relationships are fairly intact. They may be ambivalent (Abraham 1927, Freud 1917a); that is, the same object, internal and external, will contain both good and bad qualities. Nevertheless, the depressive position is a much more advanced state in which reality is not acknowledged or related to on the basis of splitting and projective mechanisms (Klein 1935).

I devote Chapter 7 to the discussion of countertransference reactions evoked by a depressed patient. In this chapter, rather than presenting a series of vignettes, I concentrate on a single patient, discussing in considerable detail the development of the therapeutic course. Detailed case reports are usually organized around the unfolding of the transference. I also concentrate on this aspect, but I also *pari passu* trace the unfolding of the countertransference. This represents a microscopic approach, in contrast to the more macroscopic orientation that characterizes the clinical vignette.

In the past, I have repeatedly stated that the severity of psychopathology does not inversely correlate with treatability (Giovacchini 1979a, 1986, 1987). My treatment of a depressed woman further indicates that the depth of illness does not directly correlate with the intensity of the disruption that the countertransference produces. What is perhaps most important is the recognition that, with higher forms of psychopathology, patients may create unmanageable chaos, whereas with some very severely emotionally disturbed patients, their management may not be insurmountably difficult. Still, in general, the more primitive the psychic organization, the more intense the countertransference response. This does not mean, however, that intense countertransference responses hinder treatment or render it impossible.

Direct correlations between countertransference intensity, treatability, and severity of psychopathology cannot be made. A psychoanalytic treatment relationship is highly complex; many variables, some unpredictable, are involved. The human psyche is subtle and malleable. The study of countertransference adds another dimension to the understanding of the treatment process, and the greater our comprehension of the intricacies of the transference–countertransference interaction, the more venturesome we can become in our attempts to engage ourselves therapeutically with a wider spectrum of patients (see Stone 1953).

Peter L. Giovacchini, M.D.

1

The Therapist's Contributions to the Course of Therapy

Clinicians practicing psychoanalysis—or what has been called psychoanalytically oriented psychotherapy—are becoming increasingly aware that treatment success or failure is a complex issue that stresses the irrational parts of both the therapist's and the patient's personalities. Most members of my generation were taught rather simple principles regarding indications for psychoanalytic treatment that referred only to assessments of the patient's character structure. For example, patients had to have good ego strength, a sound sense of reality, sensitivity, and a capacity to profit from insight. They had to be able to form a transference neurosis and work through their basic oedipal conflicts. At that time, nothing was said about the therapist's potential contributions to the therapeutic course. Analysts had to be objective and neutral and not intrude their personal reactions into the treatment setting. In fact, optimally, they were not supposed to have any feelings toward patients other than the wish to understand and analyze them.

Although it was accepted that the treatment course would vary, it was expected that the well-conducted analysis would follow a somewhat predictable sequence. The technical tool of free association would help stimulate a manageable regression, bringing to the forefront specific defenses and resistances that would contribute to the shape of transference projections. After resistances and defenses were analyzed, the oedipal constellation would be reenacted and the analyst would become a parental figure, a situation often referred to as the *transference neurosis*. The termination period of treatment would begin with the resolution and working through of the transference neurosis.

This is a pithy description of an ideal and hypothetical course of psychoanalytic treatment. As I listened to candidates presenting their control cases during clinical seminars, it became clear that the impassive, neutral analyst—or in this case the impassive, neutral future analyst—was a myth rather than a reality. Candidates struggled with their own feelings as well as those of their patients. Perhaps this struggle could be explained by their lack of professional maturity, but many senior analysts were able to empathize with their students and recounted similar episodes in their practices. The orderly course of treatment, such a desirable objective, also seemed to be on the far horizons of our clinical experience.

Psychoanalysis as a treatment procedure represented pure but rarely encountered gold, and clinicians found themselves inundated by copper alloys of modified therapeutic approaches (Freud 1919). The term *psychoanalytically oriented psychotherapy* is often a disclaimer designed to stress that the therapist is not so pretentious or rash as to believe that he is actually conducting a classical analysis. The patient may be lying on the couch, free associating, and experiencing infantile feelings toward the analyst, but somehow what is happening is different from analysis. Thus labeling a procedure *psychoanalytically oriented psychotherapy* is often an apologetic attempt to reassure analysts and other clinicians that what is going on in this particular instance is not really analysis.

Throughout the years, I have wondered why the analytic method has to be separated into two components: the pure, valuable gold and the degraded copper alloy. The analytic ritual and its "predictable" course acquired a mystical and esoteric significance that was reserved for a chosen minority of therapists who had the good fortune to be accepted by a psychoanalytic institute. Because they had been purified by their training analyses, they would deal with their patients in an objective but impassive—or, better stated, neutral—fashion. The therapeutic field would not be contaminated by their feelings.

I am purposely indulging in hyperbole to stress some of the attitudes about the training and practice of psychoanalysis that were prevalent when I enrolled in a psychoanalytic institute several years after the end of World War II, when psychoanalysis had achieved the height of its popularity and prestige. What seems so peculiar today is how we idealized a method that, when carried to its extreme, became a ritual. Furthermore, our fascination with unconscious processes and our dedication to the principle of psychic determinism now seems hypocritical, inasmuch as we turned away from the unconscious, irrational elements of our psyches. Although analysts gave lip service to the acknowledgment of participation of their unconscious in the treatment interaction, it was only to explain the patient's irrational reactions.

What gradually became apparent to me and to many of my colleagues (Boyer and Giovacchini 1980) was that the therapeutic course acquired an independent existence. It became an entity in itself rather than a multifaceted procedure governed by certain principles. Patients had to conform to the demands of treatment rather than the reverse—treatment's being directed to the patient's needs. Even the term *classical psychoanalysis* implies that we are dealing with something tangible, immutable, and pure. The method cannot be modified without losing its status in the realm of psychoanalysis, an idealization of a procedure that has no parallel in the healing arts.

Although the alliance between psychoanalysis and medicine has always been tenuous, it is generally agreed that psychoanalytic treatment has a purpose that, directly or indirectly, will be helpful to the patient. It is not necessarily directed toward the alleviation of symptoms; rather, through understanding and reliving infantile conflicts and traumas, the patient, it is hoped, will gain a firmer sense of autonomy, an increased cohension of the self-representation, and a higher state of ego integration through the acquisition of further psychic structure. These goals were not specifically acknowledged by "classical" analysts, however. In fact, patients who needed such a reformation of character structure would be considered unsuitable for analysis; yet there would be no hope of achieving such reconstruction without, at least, understanding a patient from an analytic viewpoint and using psychoanalytic principles. This dilemma requires clinicians to view psychoanalytic treatment in a broader perspective.

Indeed, the range of psychoanalytic treatment is constantly

being expanded (Boyer and Giovacchini 1980, Giovacchini 1979a, 1986, Stone 1963). Much of the professional literature focuses on the treatment of patients suffering from characterological problems and stresses the fact that therapists can still interact with these patients within a psychoanalytic perspective. Authors have specifically emphasized the better-integrated structure of the analyst's ego (Loewald 1960) as well as countertransference responses and problems (Epstein and Feiner 1979, Slakter 1987). In my opinion, these clinical explorations have opened new therapeutic vistas and widened the psychoanalytic dimension. The metaphor of the pure gold of psychoanalysis being degraded to a copper alloy of modified analysis or of suggestion, as Freud (1919) specifically wrote, is inappropriate. Rather, we are dealing with a valuable therapeutic frame of reference that not only helps us understand psychopathological processes but also invites our participation in a mutually enhancing relationship. Psychoanalytic treatment is not a unilateral experience.

The measuring instrument—the therapist—also has a life of his own. Therapists are not impassive or neutral if they wish to treat the majority of patients who seek their services. Our attitudes about the analyst's technical and emotional participation in the treatment process must be constantly scrutinized. As already noted, much of the professional literature is directed toward questions that stress how we perceive and react toward patients. What was once considered undesirable (Freud 1910) is now in the forefront of clinical assessments; countertransference has become a meaningful counterpart to transference projections as the essence of the analytic interaction.

The inclusion of countertransference response in determining whether a patient is treatable—that is, treatable with a particular analyst—is no longer based on the evaluation of the patient alone. In many quarters, this unidimensional approach has been replaced by an examination of the interaction between both participants in the treatment relationship. Analysts examine their personal responses as well as the patient's defensive adaptations, intrapsychic conflicts, and structural defects. Clinicians attempt to predict potential transference projections and then measure their anticipated responses. The questions frequently asked are whether the therapeutic setting can survive taking into account the therapist's vulnerabilities as well as areas of strength and whether it is possible to construct an effective holding environment (Winnicott 1952, 1956). This does not mean that the course of treatment is, in fact, predictable, as has been discussed by earlier generations of analysts (Fenichel 1945, Waelder 1960).

There is, however, an atmosphere, a feeling tone, often evident even in the first interview, that sets the stage for the future analytic interaction. If this initial feeling is positive, the patient eventually forms a bond with the therapist that is in many ways similar to that described by neonatologists (Brazelton 1980, Emde 1980, Klaus and Kennel 1982, Stern 1985). Such a felicitous response may be the outcome of a feeling of comfortable security and even perhaps familiarity, even though the analyst has never seen the patient before and is unaware of the possibility that a stormy analysis lies ahead.

I have experienced similar feelings when former patients have returned to treatment after having been out of treatment for many years. For example, a 50-year-old man returned to see me after a twenty-five year absence. I immediately recognized him, although he had gained weight and had a beard, which he did not have when I had treated him in the past. I felt that I had just seen him the day before; the passage of twenty-five years was ignored. To me this emphasized the timelessness of the unconscious, as noted by Freud (1915a). We both felt comfortable and warm toward each other, and he commented that I had not changed a bit except that I had dyed my hair white.

I recall another incident in which the patient had a total amnesia about his former treatment with me. I had treated him as a child between the ages of 5 and 7, at which time we terminated because he seemed to be getting along well both academically and socially. I told his mother, herself a mental health professional, that it might be prudent to have her son reevaluated when he reached adolescence. When he reached the age of 15, she suggested he see a psychiatrist. She was surprised that he had no recollection whatsoever of ever having been in therapy. In order to be objective, she suggested some names, and although my name seemed as strange to him as the others, he selected me. He still did not remember me when we again saw each other, but he felt very comfortable and was eager to confide in me and to continue treatment, although he did not feel under any particular pressure. He had some current problems that bothered him, and he wanted some help in making a career choice. He remained in treatment until he graduated from high school and went off to college in another city. We both felt as though we had known each other for many years, but the amnesia for his first treatment with me never lifted.

This patient had undoubtedly integrated his childhood experience of treatment, but perhaps it had become so thoroughly integrated that it was completely absorbed and thereby inaccessible to conscious representation. Whatever the situation, there were certain constellations in his character structure that set the stage for a favorable later treatment relationship. With some new patients, the therapist's psychic structure may have certain qualities that facilitate the treatment process. These qualities may be conscious, unconscious, or both. Granted, this is an impressionistic assessment not as yet supported by a conceptual framework, but, as a phenomenon, it can be explored as we examine countertransference issues.

I will introduce the topic of countertransference by first exploring its negative aspects. This is often the outcome of not being aware of having negative feelings toward patients, which then interferes with the analysis of the transference or causes the therapist to judge the patient untreatable by the analytic method. Unconscious countertransference responses can be disruptive to the treatment and can interfere with the establishment of both a holding environment and the therapeutic bond (Anzieu 1987).

PART ONE

COUNTERTRANSFERENCE
AND
DISRUPTION

2

Countertransference as a Ubiquitous Phenomenon

Freud (1910) first mentioned countertransference in a negative context. He viewed such reactions as disruptive to the natural unfolding of the analytic process and the patient's establishment of a transference neurosis. If analysts develop feelings toward patients other than simply benevolent interest and a wish to analyze them, then something is wrong with the treatment relationship. In such circumstances, Freud recommended that therapists seek further analysis for themselves.

ANALYTIC NEUTRALITY

A personal relationship with patients hinders the therapist's objectivity and interferes with the development of the transference. Freud cautioned against analyzing friends or relatives, but it has been reputed that he analyzed his daughter, Anna (Bertin 1982, Grosskurth 1985). He certainly had many personal relationships with some of his analysands, who became friends and colleagues.

Nevertheless, Freud (1913) suggested that analysts maintain a degree of anonymity toward their patients. This recommendation was supposed to be a technical tool permitting therapists to act as mirrors of the patient's feelings. He extended his concepts of the optimal therapeutic position by using two metaphors. The first was that analysts are similar to surgeons and must be dispassionate in dissecting the psyche. In order not to cause harm, they must maintain a sterile field; otherwise, their feelings would contaminate objectivity. They must be relentless in their pursuit of the unconscious and not let their emotions stand in their way, no matter how much their patients protest and demand responses that are the outcome of their neediness. Analysts cannot allow themselves to stray outside the boundaries of the patient's psyche. Freud also compared analysts to telephone receivers that unscramble messages into a coherent and understandable form. Both metaphors eliminate human elements and concerns that are basic to helpful relationships.

Many analysts find such studied attitudes difficult to cultivate. Reading the reports of some of Freud's analyses (Kardiner

1977), I doubt that Freud himself was able to practice what he advocated. The professional identity that Freud believed was essential for conducting analysis might not be synchronous with the therapist's fundamental identity. The analyst's self-representation might not be able to integrate the detached qualities that Freud described. I also wonder whether analysts who can act like surgeons and who can, without feeling, electronically decipher messages are able to integrate these capacities within their psyches because they lack other qualities that may be essential to reach the deeper recesses of the patient's inner misery. I am referring to constrictions of character that make it difficult to get in touch with primitive feelings and parts of the self (Grinberg 1962).

Still, I believe there is some merit to the technical issues Freud postulated. His relentless pursuit of the unconscious points to an unswerving dedication to the principle of psychic determinism. I have talked to analysts, usually younger analysts, who rigidly adhered to Freud's "classical" principles but who, at the same time, were idealizing the fundamental tenets of psychoanalysis evidenced by their profound respect for unconscious processes. What was missing was their coming to terms with their own feelings. Indeed, they would have felt guilty if they believed that they had any feelings toward their patients other than those related to maintaining a therapeutic perspective (see Reich 1951).

For most analysts, especially because of the types of patients we see, such a neutral stance would be forced. It would be equivalent to constructing a false self, as Winnicott (1960) described. Relating at a false-self level would be experienced as oppressive, and the therapist's attitude toward the patient would be strained. Treating patients under such circumstances could be an exhausting task, and the analytic work would indeed be very difficult. The analyst is paying a heavy price, in terms of expenditure of psychic energy, to preserve a classical, idealized modus operandi of therapeutic efficacy. Maintaining a pose day after day would certainly support the view of analytic work as an "impossible profession" (Freud 1925).

Perhaps the orientation of analytic neutrality is not always a pose. It may be compatible with some personalities. I believe, however, that in many instances it is a pose, and that, in itself, such a stance represents a countertransference obstacle that may be disruptive and catastrophic to the treatment alliance (Greenson 1960, Sharpe 1930).

I do not believe that the mirror, telephone, or surgeon analogies represent stances that would be useful in treating most of the patients who seek analytic help today. Perhaps it was helpful for Freud's patients, but I doubt it, inasmuch as his patients were not significantly different from those we see today (Meissner 1984–1985, Reichard 1956).

We assume that we know what is meant by analytic neutrality. Its obvious purpose is to help us be objective in understanding the patient. This means that we must not side with either aspect of the patient's ambivalence. We do not ally ourselves with any particular element of the patient's psyche, such as supporting the ego against the superego or vice versa. Thus, neutrality stresses that we weigh and value all the components of the personality equally. To be neutral indicates that we are nonjudgmental and that we respect all layers of the mental apparatus. It does not signify noninvolvement or emotional distance. At the most, as A. Freud (1965) stated, it refers to maintaining equidistance between various parts of the mind; it does not mean, however, that we have to be distant from the patient as a person. On the contrary, to achieve such an equidistance in the realm of psychic structure requires considerable involvement with and feelings for patients.

In general, it is considered desirable that analysts reveal as little as possible about their feelings or personal lives. This helps facilitate the development of transference. When analysts stray from this reserved position, they are exhibiting the counter-transference feelings that Freud (1910) believed were detrimental to therapy. It is unwise to generalize when discussing psycho-analytic treatment. In view of the diverse personality types we encounter, it is best to maintain some flexibility. Revealing our personal feelings and attitudes could be helpful in some in-stances (Boyer 1983, Giovacchini 1979b, 1986, Searles 1965).

VALUE AND TYPES OF COUNTERTRANSFERENCE

In the twenty-three volumes of the *Standard Edition* of the works of Sigmund Freud, the word countertransference appears only four times (Guttman et al. 1980). Today, the situation is vastly changed: Books that comprise collections of articles by various authors have been devoted exclusively to the topic (Epstein and Feiner 1979, Giovacchini 1975). Nevertheless, the negative eval-uation of countertransference feelings has been a dominant orientation up until the last two decades, especially in the United States.

In England, Heiman (1950), Little (1951), and Winnicott (1949), and Racker (1953, 1968) in Argentina, felt that therapists could learn much from countertransference reactions that would help them to understand the transference interaction and to effectively analyze the patient. Until relatively recently, how-ever, these analysts have had very little impact in the United States. Rather, A. Reich's (1951) ideas, though not necessarily attributed to her, dominated our thinking. She argued vehe-mently that countertransference reactions were generally harmful and could not in any way be analytically useful.

Some analysts have divided countertransference issues into two components:

1. The existence of countertransference feelings, which A. Reich (1951) and Freud (1910) believe is, in itself, a sign of a disrupted therapeutic setting and perhaps indicative of the analyst's psychopathology,
2. The communication of such feelings to the patient. Both Little (1951, 1981) and Searles (1965) rather freely communicate their feelings to their patients.

Thus it may not be a sign of a serious disruption for therapists to have countertransference feelings, depending on what the analyst does with such feelings; it may not be at all prudent for therapists to burden patients with their personal reactions. The therapist need not remain uninvolved, as Freud and Reich recommended, meaning there are no countertransference responses. It is accepted, after all, that the analyst is human and will have personal reactions. They may have to be contained, however, and not allowed to invade the therapeutic relationship.

Little and Searles believe that countertransference is ubiquitous and that, under certain circumstances, it can be beneficial to share it with patients. Freud (1912a, 1914, 1925) asserted that transference is a universal phenomenon. If this is so, it is more than likely that countertransference is generally encountered. It does not necessarily follow that it is also ubiquitous, but it is highly probable that it is. If therapists are devoid of feelings and are truly uninvolved, as Reich recommends, then clinicians such as Little and Searles, as well as Racker and Winnicott, would question whether such a reserved stance is not, in itself, indicative of psychopathology or a sign that there are difficulties in the analytic interaction. Thus, some clinician's thinking has gone full circle. The absence of countertransference may be a warning signal that there are problems between therapist and patient that go beyond the patient's psychopathology.

Although there may be situations in which it appears to be absent, I nevertheless wish to stress the ubiquity of countertransference. There are also clinical encounters in which there seems to be a lack of transference. Some analysts have referred to this phenomenon as a defense against the transference (Gill 1979, 1983), or as a defense transference, but these are types of transferences, with corresponding countertransferences.

In these instances, the patient or therapist is repeating an infantile defensive adaptation, such as withdrawal, and is seeking protection against frightening, sometimes terrifying involvements. Noninvolvement is an infantile mode of relating, or nonrelating, that protects the psyche from what might be an annihilating fusion. Infantile adaptations emerge in the therapeutic setting as the treatment interaction stimulates regression. Despite their manifest form, whether they consist of positive or negative affects and lead to involvement or withdrawal and seeming noninvolvement, they are still transference reactions simply because they are infantile reactions and adaptations that have been transferred to the analyst. The analyst's noninvolvement is frequently a response to the patient's transference; that is, it is a defensive countertransference reaction. On other occasions, the analyst's noninvolvement may not be a direct reaction to the patient's withdrawal; it may, instead, be the therapist's characteristic method of maintaining distance because of his own unresolved infantile conflicts. We might say, then, that the analyst, because of his psychic structure, is forming a transference toward the patient, but logistically it is less confusing to call it countertransference.

Although these issues had been discussed in the literature as far back as forty years ago, they were not seriously considered, at least in Chicago, until Tower presented a paper on countertransference to the Chicago Psychoanalytic Society. She is a respected teacher and had, and still has, a reputation of being a conservative analyst. Her paper had a significant impact on our group, especially on the younger analysts, although some senior analysts became very much involved with her ideas. Her paper was then published in the prestigious classical *Journal of the American Psychoanalytic Association* (Tower 1956). Briefly, Tower was questioning traditional views about countertransference and was exploring how it could be used to best advantage in psychoanalytic treatment.

I believe that the dissemination of Tower's ideas led to a more relaxed attitude among analysts, both older and younger, about countertransference. Although Boyer (1961) and Searles (1953) in the United States had expressed similar views, the fact that these ideas were coming from an analyst identified with the Establishment helped considerably in bringing the subject out into the open. It even helped many of us in discovering Racker's writings and the so-called English school. During my days as a candidate at the Chicago Institute for Psychoanalysis, I never once heard a mention of Winnicott or Melanie Klein or any of her followers. After Tower's presentation, we became sufficiently bold that we could discuss our feelings toward patients without the fear that we would be attacked or ostracized.

* * *

Countertransference reactions extend over a broad spectrum ranging from positive to negative feelings. The therapist's feelings may vary from finding some patients very attractive to loathing and hating them. Indeed, some patients are appealing and likeable and others may be obnoxious and intrusive, and having some reaction to them is only natural. Most analysts can merge such responses with their clinical interest and concern, however, and their attitude becomes observational rather than critical. They need not pass judgment as they subject the patient's character traits to analytic investigation. On occasion, however, this benign clinical viewpoint is submerged by disturbing feelings that could become disruptive to both patient and therapist.

Despite considerable discussion about countertransference over the last three decades, no general consensus has been reached as to its definition. What is countertransference? Some analysts consider it a response to the patient's transference projections. For example, Racker (1968) wrote about what he called *concomitant* countertransference. This represents the analyst's resistive and oppositional response to the patient's projections. The therapist feels uncomfortable as the receptacle of such projections and, he therefore resists them. He may feel angry, upset, and disrupted. These may not be consciously perceived responses, but they will, nevertheless, have an undesirable effect on the equilibrium of the treatment process.

By contrast, Racker also discusses what he refers to as *concordant* countertransference, which consists of the analyst's identification with the patient's infantile feelings and vulnerabilities. This identification generally leads to a positive treatment interaction inasmuch as the analyst feels empathically in tune with the analysand. It has been argued that such an orientation represents an optimal therapeutic attitude and need not be included under the rubric of countertransference. This viewpoint would limit the concept of countertransference to only damaging and negative attitudes. It ignores the various levels of the analyst's personality that are participating in the final determination of responses toward patients. In the instance of concordant countertransference, although it may lead to sensitive and empathic understanding, it still involves getting in touch with primitive parts of the analyst's character as they resonate with similar levels of the patient's psyche. This may be an optimal therapeutic response, but it is still very much a personal one.

Concomitant countertransference is not simply a response to the patient's transference feelings, nor are other types of responses, whether helpful or harmful. It is not always easy to determine what stimulates analysts' feelings. The fact that these stimuli may not be entirely determined by elements in the analyst's infantile past has led to attempts by some clinicians to separate countertransference from noncountertransference reactions.

I prefer not to distinguish between countertransference and noncountertransference responses, any more than I would want to separate transference from nontransference reactions (Giovacchini 1987). All the therapist's responses contain countertransference elements, in the same way that all the patient's feelings and thoughts contain some degree of transference. Everything we experience contains, in varying degrees, elements from all levels of our psyches. The contributions of the deeper primitive levels as they are directed toward an external object, either the analyst or the patient, can be referred to as transference and countertransference, respectively. Countertransference is thus determined by the infantile elements of the analyst's background rather than being just a response to the patient's infantile feelings. The analyst's countertransference may be stimulated or precipitated by transference projections, but it can also be determined by other factors of the therapeutic relationship that can cause therapists to get in touch with the deeper parts of their psyches.

This viewpoint about the ubiquitous nature of countertransference is based on the principle of a structural hierarchy. It represents a way of observing subjective material and placing it in its proper structural perspective. This type of evaluation does not tell us how significant the countertransference element is to the analytic process. Similarly, the recognition of transference feelings does not mean that we can always make a transference interpretation. The transference contribution—that is, the participation of primitive levels of the personality—may be so minimal that it would sound far-fetched to the resistive patient to explain fairly complex behavior on such a basis. If a patient is late to a session because, as she claims, she had a flat tire, it may be futile and counterproductive to interpret her need to control the analytic relationship as a hostile negative transference. This interpretation may very well be accurate, but to make it in such a context does not lead to the assimilation of insight. Under these circumstances, the introduction of the intrapsychic focus seems absurd to the defensive patient, who places the sources of behavior and feelings into the external world.

Furthermore, to make the patient responsible, even in the most qualified and indirect way, for the analyst's feelings—that is, his countertransference—may in some instances lead to serious treatment impasses. Of course, analysts usually do not place such responsibility on their patients, but they may still wish to explore the extent of the patient's contribution. This does not mean that therapists ignore what stems uniquely from themselves. There is a balance between what the patient stimulates and what emerges, in a sense, spontaneously from the analyst.

Because of this balance, I prefer to divide countertransference reactions into two general categories determined either by their universality or by their being the outcome of unique characterological configurations and intrapsychic conflicts. I label the first *homogeneous countertransference reactions* and the second *idiosyncratic countertransference responses* (Giovacchini 1979a). Homogeneous reactions, as is true of all responses, have infantile elements, but they are minimal. They are average expectable reactions that will cause most of us to react in a similar fashion. For example, certain types of behavior are generally objectionable, an extreme example being the dangerous patient who threatens the therapist's life. When a patient took the letter opener from my desk and brandished it in front of my face, I was both frightened and angry. I peremptorily ordered him to give it to me without being at all concerned, at that moment, with the intrapsychic sources or transference implications of his behavior.

In other instances, the analyst may react in an exaggerated or unique fashion to a situation that most therapists would consider innocuous. I call this type of transference idiosyncratic because the therapist's reactions are idiosyncratic. For example, an analyst felt very uncomfortable during an initial interview with a woman patient. He was puzzled, because she seemed to be intelligent, well-bred, psychologically minded, and eager to be analyzed. As she was telling the analyst when she could be available for appointments, he found himself dreading the prospect of seeing her again. He was certain that he would not be able to work with her, so he referred her to a colleague. Later, he pondered his not wanting to treat her and finally, to his astonishment, realized that she strongly resembled his mother. He was not aware of it at the time he was seeing her. Only later could he relax enough to understand why he felt so strongly that he did not want to treat her. This highly idiosyncratic situation would not have occurred with another analyst.

As I have indicated, countertransference reactions may have their transference parallels. Gitelson (1952) believed that if the analyst appears in the first dream in an undisguised fashion, then the analysis is doomed. He predicted that a strong transference would develop that could not be resolved. Gitelson attributed this potential impasse to what could be considered an idiosyncratic transference response. Apparently the analyst, because of his manner or appearance, bears a strong resemblance to an emotionally significant figure of the patient's infantile past. Consequently, the patient is not able to maintain an intrapsychic focus because the current analytic interaction cannot be separated from an actual relationship. The undisguised appearance of the analyst in the dream would mean that the patient will be unable to deal with the analyst as a displacement or symbol; he will relate to him only as a real and concrete person. There is some question as to whether such predictions about treatment can be made from the manifest content of the first dream. However, this type of impasse can be explored in terms of both transference and countertransference factors.

In any analysis, I believe there will be elements of both types of countertransference, homogeneous and idiosyncratic. Hopefully, most of the therapist's responses are of the homogenous variety, but it is crucial to recognize the contributions of idiosyncratic elements.

As long as we are dealing with countertransference and transference, inasmuch as these are feelings that stem from infantile settings, we can question whether all such reactions are basically idiosyncratic. Freud (1912a, 1914) stressed the universality of transference, but he also viewed it in terms of its connection with psychopathology. Thus, he recognized the idiosyncratic element of transference as playing a crucial role in analytic treatment, but the fact that it is ubiquitous and occurs outside the therapeutic relationship would indicate that some transference projections can also be homogeneous.

The distinction between homogeneous and idiosyncratic stresses the significance of infantile elements. Both transference and countertransference are based on archaic, infantile feelings and constellations. Patients present to their therapists the unique and idiosyncratic aspects of their personalities through their transference projections. These projections are the outcome of their character structure and particular psychopathology. A feeling, impulse, or attitude is not necessarily idiosyncratic just because it has an infantile source. It has to be involved with conflict or trauma, and to the extent that it is, it is idiosyncratic, as it is the case with patients' transference projections. Of what does homogeneous transference, as a counterpart of homogeneous countertransference, consist? I believe that the patient's dependency on the analyst and the security and soothing that the holding qualities of the analytic setting provide could be considered infantile in nature and represent a homogeneous transference—the satisfaction of infantile needs that are at the moment of gratification not experienced as traumatic or conflictual.

Perhaps part of the analytic task is to convert idiosyncratic transference to homogeneous transference. A similar process occurs in the analyst with countertransference feelings, but it is not exactly a parallel process. Idiosyncratic transference feelings dominate the treatment process, especially at the beginning of treatment. Later, as the analyst can provide a holding environment, the patient can allow himself some gratification without feeling anxious or conflicted.

In the sphere of countertransference, this sequence is reversed. Analysts, at the beginning of treatment, should have only minimal idiosyncratic reactions toward the patient and should feel relatively calm and comfortable regarding the emotional problems presented to them. Their infantile responses are both minimal and, for the most part, nonconflicted. This type of response is probably what Freud (1910) considered to be free of countertransference, whereas I prefer to include countertransference elements to all responses; but in this instance, the responses would be of the homogeneous variety and could be useful in facilitating the therapeutic alliance. Later, however, these same infantile elements can become involved in trauma and conflict, being converted to idiosyncratic countertransference, which can be disruptive to treatment. This conversion may have been precipitated by the patient's transference projections (Racker's concomitant countertransference), or the analyst may find the patient's regression threatening to both the patient's and analyst's survival. The movement from homogeneous to idiosyncratic countertransference can be stormy, disruptive, and difficult to contain, but it may also lead to precious insights and resolutions, as will be discussed throughout this book.

In defining various types of countertransference, I find another distinction to be important: Is the countertransference disruptive, or nondisruptive. Freud and Reich, when they viewed countertransference negatively, were apparently discussing disruptive countertransference. It is almost a matter of definition that if something is disruptive then it is harmful to the treatment process. As many clinicians have indicated, however, this is a short-sighted view. What may at one moment be disruptive can, through analysis and working through, become a valuable part of the analytic process. Disruption and nondisruption are variables that must be placed in their proper perspective. Both homogeneous and idiosyncratic countertransference can be disruptive. The homogeneous variety can also be nondisruptive, and idiosyncratic countertransference can, in some instances, become a valuable asset to the therapeutic process.

3

Disruption of the
Therapeutic Process

Clinicians occasionally encounter truly catastrophic situations in the treatment of patients with primitive mental states. The combination of the patient's behavior and the therapist's responses often creates a crisis in treatment that seriously threatens the stability of the relationship. The therapist may feel massively attacked and intruded upon to the degree that he cannot maintain his professional stance and decorum. I am referring to intense countertransference reactions, but, in view of the patient's intrusive, obnoxious, and irrational demands, such reactions on the part of the therapist are understandable and can be considered largely homogeneous. I stress, however, that countertransference responses must be evaluated on a relative basis; it is a matter of degree as to how many idiosyncratic elements are involved. There is always some balance between the two, but the situations I am about to describe can be accounted for primarily on the basis of homogeneous rather than idiosyncratic factors.

MACROSCOPIC ASSAULTS

The violent, assaultive patient destroys the treatment relationship because the therapist becomes disrupted to the degree that he can no longer function as an analyst. To preserve the setting and his own integrity, he may have to respond forcefully, authoritatively, and prohibitively. In situations in which interpretation is ineffective in containing the patient's rage, little can be said or done from a psychoanalytic perspective. The countertransference is dominated by anxiety, and the analyst cannot continue in a calm, introspective manner. The analysis may have to be abruptly terminated, perhaps with the hope that enough can be salvaged to enable the analyst to feel secure enough once again that the analytic relationship can be reestablished. Fortunately, direct attacks on therapists are infrequent, and it is rare that patients who have been in treatment regress to the point of assaultiveness. These are gross situations, and the ensuing disruption can be considered macroscopic as the treatment frame collapses.

Although further analytic treatment may be impossible, at

least with that particular analyst, it may be helpful for the analysts to examine what they may have done to have provoked a catastrophic explosion and an unmanageable, violent regression. Perhaps there was an initial error in diagnostic judgment in that the patient was so volatile and his ego boundaries so fluid that he should never have been subjected to analysis in the first place. Such situations undoubtedly occur, but I not believe that this extreme situation is common without the analyst's having made some contribution to stimulating the violence. In the various clinical seminars and workshops I have attended throughout the years, I have detected what seems to be a trend. I am struck by how the same analysts have a number of unruly patients, whose behavior ranges from verbal abuse to hurling ashtrays and throwing pillows at them, while other analysts, who maintain a benevolent, calm, authoritarian dignity, have patients for whom such behavior would be unthinkable. Can you imagine a patient throwing an ashtray at, or even raising his voice to, Sigmund Freud?

Although I stated at the onset that we are dealing with a homogeneous variety of countertransference responses, I am now questioning the significance of idiosyncratic factors. The analyst's response to the attack is, in my mind, a variety of homogeneous countertransference, but the analyst's participation, if any, in stimulating or provoking the disruptive incident is idiosyncratic and perhaps the outcome of defensive adaptations. In view of the severity of the patient's psychopathology, it is sometimes difficult to discover how the analyst helped to bring about therapeutic chaos.

The whimsical speculation that patients did not dare act out in such an unruly manner toward Freud may be countered with the rejoinder that patients, at least in terms of impulse control, were different in a mid-Victorian milieu, and that Freud simply did not or would not see the patients we treat today. This is possible, but I conjecture that Freud's brilliance and autonomy created a treatment setting, a holding environment, that clearly spelled out the tolerable limits, and that this was reassuring to the patient. He certainly worked with some very disturbed patients (Freud 1918).

Regarding disruptive idiosyncratic countertransference reactions that are subtle in expression, I can recognize at least two types that undermine the patient's psychic integration and contribute to the loss of impulse control. The subtle and covert quality of the analyst's provocation is often responsible for the intensity of the patient's reaction, although more overt provocations can also have catastrophic consequences.

The reaction I have heard of most frequently has occurred with supervisees, although some colleagues and I have reacted, at times, in a similar fashion. The therapist feels confused and anxious because he does not understand what is going on. He is anxious because the patient is demanding relief from overwhelming misery and tension. Such patients sometimes blame their therapists, holding them responsible for their inner turmoil. The analyst, in turn, feels helpless and frustrated and is overcome by the impulse to do something. He struggles, out of his anxiety, to give himself and the patient relief.

The function of interpretation in these difficult clinical circumstances is not to expand understanding and release constricting inner forces that hamper autonomy. Rather, interpretation is designed to make the analyst feel better and to halt the patient's protestations and manifestations of psychopathology. Thus the analyst makes a forced interpretation bathed in his anxiety. The patient, instead of feeling understood, only senses and receives the anxious parts of the interpretation and feels betrayed. I do not believe it is the incorrectness of the interpretation; indeed, it may even be correct, but it, nevertheless, foments chaos. The analyst has abandoned the patient because he is not able to survive the patient's psychopathology. Some patients have experienced similar situations as children, when their mothers abandoned them because of their psychoses, anxieties, or depressions. The repetition of the infantile setting is unbearable for such a vulnerable patient.

The second type of countertransference response that can have catastrophic, and sometimes even tragic, consequences involves a direct verbal attack on the patient. On the surface, it does not appear to be an attack. Often it is considered a confrontation, with the therapeutic intent of encouraging patients to face the facts or of setting limits so that treatment can proceed in an organized fashion. The purpose of such confrontations is to establish order, but they frequently achieve just the opposite. I have heard analysts speak about how childish and immature their patients are. These were not clinical evaluations. Rather, as evidenced by their tone, they were critical appraisals that were communicated to their patients as exhortations to grow up. The therapist might have been disdainful and sarcastic or, in other instances, intrusively managerial.

The actor–actress couple of Mike Nichols and Elaine May provide us with a humorous, pithy example of such an interaction. Nichols plays the part of the patient and is telling his analyst, played by May, how busy and harassed he has been all day. As an aside, he mentions that he had had a hot dog and a Pepsi-Cola for lunch, when his analyst, in a thick Yiddish accent, abruptly interrupts him and says, "A Pepsi-Cola and a hot dog! What kind of lunch is that?" This strikes the listener as funny, but in an actual analysis, the results of such interactions can be quite grim, as they were in the following case.

A young woman in her 20s had just begun seeing her third analyst. She had liked her first analyst, and he had apparently liked her. In fact, he had told her that he considered her a friend. Although she found that gratifying, she really needed an analyst, not a friend. After approximately a year of treatment, she told him that everything in her life was fine, and she terminated therapy on good terms. She then sought another analyst, who, according to the patient, refused to take her seriously. Reputedly, he told her Jewish jokes. She found this amusing, but again, this was not what she wanted from treatment. Thus, she found a third analyst.

This avid patient was a fairly good actress. She had the capacity to change her voice to fit a mood or a particular stage of life. After several months of analysis, she felt as if she were a little girl and started using what she later called her "baby voice." During such a session her analyst stopped her and said, "Is that the way a grown woman should talk?" whereupon she got up from the couch, walked out of his office, and never returned.

She then came to see me, and I wondered how, after so many bad experiences, she still had faith in the analytic process and wanted treatment. The last episode was experienced as a direct assault, a betrayal, because she was attacked for revealing the infantile part of herself. She saw this as a violation of the analytic contract.

She was in analysis with me for many years. It was a gratifying analysis for both of us inasmuch as it helped her in dealing with her world, eventually marrying, and having children. I learned a good deal from her. It was not an easy analysis, however, and there were many stormy moments when I was verbally assaulted. Perhaps her previous therapists had sensed that there would be some very painful encounters and in their own way manifested their refusal to accept her as an analytic patient. This is, of course, mere speculation. It was interesting that once she learned that I was delighted to listen to her different voices as barometers of various ego states, she stopped using them.

Her previous therapists had clearly breached the analytic

frame. The first two had probably decided that she needed something besides analysis. By contrast, the third analyst believed that he was conducting analysis. She was lying on the couch and had been instructed to free associate. Then he confronted her by equating free association and regression with disruptive acting out. He was apparently trying to set the analysis on a proper track, but instead he created total disruption and destroyed the treatment.

All the clinicians who have heard me talk about this patient immediately agree that the third therapist was manifesting some type of idiosyncratic countertransference. This seems rather obvious, but there are other clinical encounters in which the distinction is far from clear between confrontation as an attempt to set limits and establish organization in order to preserve therapy and confrontation as the outcome of the analyst's fear that he cannot survive the patient. In other words, some regressions, as is the situation with the assaultive and violent patient, are unmanageable and have to be halted, but, as already discussed, we must never lose sight of the therapist's probable participation. We are faced with a paradox in which attempts to establish order often boomerang and make the situation more unmanageable. In some instances, the therapist may have been motivated by something other than idiosyncratic countertransference elements that are eventually manifested in a destructive confrontation (Jacobs 1986).

* * *

I wish to emphasize again that the distinction between idiosyncratic and homogeneous countertransference is not precise. Some momentary annoyance may be magnified out of proportion by the hypersensitive patient. A mild reaction toward an extremely vulnerable patient might have a destructive effect on treatment, whereas a similar response toward another patient might not even be noticed. It is this balance of sensitivities between patient and analyst that must be studied; for a particular patient, a countertransference response might be experienced as an idiosyncratic assault. Are some patients so sensitive that anything the therapist says is felt as a massive assault?

A middle-aged man described himself to me as having a "very thin skin." His infancy had been highly traumatic in that he had been subjected to considerable violence. His mother had probably been psychotic, and his father frequently beat all members of the family, especially the patient. He had also been sexually violated by his father.

Currently, the patient was almost constantly overwhelmed with rage, and he was always afraid that he would not be able to control his feelings. He had seen several analysts before me, leaving them because he found them to be managerial and to have "drowned his autonomy." He had heard that I valued autonomy, so he thought I might be able to treat him.

I very carefully monitored my feelings and interventions. In fact, I tried not to think in terms of intervention, a word that seemed too strong for this particular patient. I preferred thinking in terms of sharing of insight and tried to relate exclusively to his feelings.

Because I did not want to impose anything of my own onto him, I was very sparse in the frequency and content of my interpretations. I was also very tentative, wanting to avoid dogmatic pronouncements, so I introduced my statements with "possibly," "maybe," or "as you just said." The patient seemed to accept the analytic decor I created for about six months, the longest period of treatment he had ever sustained.

He then complained about my long periods of silence, insisting that I did not care about him and had abandoned him.

During childhood he had frequently been abandoned by his taciturn, psychotic mother, who had periodically been institutionalized. Unlike the countertransference dilemma I discussed in which the analyst withdrew from the patient because he was anxious and confused, I understood what was happening and, as far as I could tell, did not feel anxious. I wanted to respect his autonomy and not trammel on his sensitivity to intrusion. I tried to respond to his need for more feedback without burdening him with viewpoints that were not immediately connected to his current experience. I had been relatively successful in doing this when I made only infrequent interpretations, and although I knew that our relationship was tenuous, I felt comfortable.

I tried to monitor my activity so that it would conform to his needs—although I do not believe that it is always prudent or possible to respond to infantile needs. I did not want to create an analytic ambience that resembled the infantile milieu. Patients ordinarily, through the repetition compulsion (Freud 1920), try to bring their infantile orientation and object relationships into the consultation room, but the analyst has created a different decor within the confines of the holding environment. The holding environment is significantly different from the infantile milieu, and it is this difference that is essential to the working-through process (Freud 1914a). My patient failed to see this difference, and, inasmuch as he was unable to make such a distinction, he was exhibiting a psychotic transference.

I was not able to find the correct frequency of interpretations that would help form a holding environment that could be recognized as distinct from his abandoning infantile world and still not be felt as intrusive; I could not seem to establish a situation that could be separated from the assaultive elements in his childhood. This was, for me, an impossible therapeutic course to chart. The patient felt, even with my most objective interpretations, that it was still *my* mind that was shaping *his* material and *my* voice that was communicating it. Therefore, I was putting parts of myself into him. He called this "mind fucking" and experienced my "interventions" as assaultive. Several months later, he terminated treatment on fairly amiable terms. He acknowledged that I had tried to analyze him but, like everyone else, I was unable to deal exclusively with his mind without interjecting elements of my own.

I discuss this patient because I do not know whether his psychopathology is of such a nature that even an entirely nonintrusive setting (if such a setting exists) would be able to hold him in treatment. It is also possible that because of the dilemma I faced, which can be summarized as being caught in the polarity of too much or too little, I might, in fact, have attacked him through my interpretations as a retaliation for the disruption I felt. I am fairly certain that the content of my interpretations was not hostile, but I cannot be absolutely certain about how I conveyed them to him; perhaps my mood or tone of voice might have indicated some annoyance.

Indeed, there are many clinical situations in which countertransference reactions are subtle and practically indiscernible. In these marginal instances, the two types of responses I have discussed (the therapist making interpretations because he feels anxious and wants to calm himself rather than the patient, or the therapist criticizing and attacking the patient with interpretations that are actually prohibitions) blend with each other. I believe that such a combination of countertransference reactions exists in all such treatment impasses, because confusion and anxiety often lead to anger. In most instances, though, one type is clearly more prominent than the other.

Analysts who use a professional frame of reference to attack their patients have reconstituted themselves or are, at the moment, reestablishing their psychic equilibrium. They are moving away from the anxiety and disorganization created by the patient's regressed state. This makes the situation even more difficult for patients because the therapist who is formidable and strong is more of a threat than one who is vulnerable and confused. Furthermore, using a therapeutic interaction as an assaultive weapon rather than as a soothing instrument is often experienced as a ruthless betrayal. The patient feels both help-less and outraged and may respond in an intense fashion (Little 1981).

My patient, who was criticized by her therapist for using a baby voice, impulsively got up from the couch and bolted from his office, never to return. In other instances, the patient's reaction may be considerably more intense and violent.

* * *

I was once asked to do a consultation with a patient who had shot and killed his therapist. He was a middle-aged man who showed enough loosening of associations to classify him as schizophrenic. It was especially interesting that when he turned to the topic of his treatment, he became organized and spoke quite coherently. He had many things he wanted to tell me about his former therapist.

From the beginning of the relationship, the patient had felt very warm toward his therapist. He found him to be a nice, nonthreatening, friendly person, and they were on a first-name basis. I asked him if he considered whether this degree of friendliness might not have interfered with the establishment of a professional relationship. He replied that he had not thought so at the time, but now he definitely felt that it had. Later in treatment the patient began to believe that maybe his analyst disapproved of him, although he had not said anything that would confirm such a suspicion. I wondered whether this was a retrospective reconstruction. I had the feeling that the patient was correct in his appraisal, but he was not then consciously aware of such attitudes toward him. Much later in the relationship, this disapproval became painfully obvious.

I learned from the chart and the attending psychiatrist that the patient was a self-defeating character type. He worked at jobs that were far beneath his intellectual capacities, and even in these nondemanding positions he did poorly and often managed to get fired. He created self-humiliating encounters. His brother, who tried to look after him, would become infuriated with his asinine behavior. To compensate for his feelings of foolishness and to build a macho self-image, he would provoke fights—which he invariably lost. When he started treatment, he had no job and was virtually nonfunctional. His brother paid for his treatment and was responsible for his complete support.

After three years of therapy, the patient believed that he had made significant gains. His brother still took care of him financially, but the patient felt that he was better able to relate to people, and he did not end all relationships by making a fool of himself and then becoming reactively violent. I asked him if he could remember specifically what topics he had dwelled on at this point in treatment and what his feelings toward his therapist had been, as well as what he believed his therapist's feelings were toward him. He reported that the atmosphere was tense and that every time he presented something that sounded like a minor success, his therapist would "debunk" it. Nothing positive seemed to count until the patient found work and supported himself. The analyst made a final interpretation that the patient had passive homosexual feelings toward his brother and that he would have to discontinue treatment until the patient could pay for it himself. The payment-for-treatment demand was confirmed by the brother, who was disturbed by this edict because he knew that the patient could not accede to it, and yet treatment had been vital for him.

In the context in which it was given, such an interpretation was an attack and indicated disapproval of the patient's behavior and a demand that he change it. The patient was devastated and felt betrayed in that the friendly first-name relationship, to him, proved to be a sham. He described feeling as if the floor had been pulled out from under him. Rather than rage, he felt frozen, and then he added that he felt frozen in time. He had not remembered anything that happened for the next several days.

When he regained consciousness, so to speak, he had found himself sitting in his bedroom with a revolver in his lap. He had no recollection as to how he had acquired the gun. The last thing he remembered was being dismissed from treatment, but he was not feeling anything about it. In fact, he had no feelings about anything. He reported that past and present came together and there was no future. Events that had occurred years ago seemed to be part of his current experience. Nothing had happened; everything was happening.

He pocketed the gun and walked to his therapist's office. The consultation room door was open and his former therapist was alone, sitting in his chair, reading. Without saying a word, the patient shot his therapist three times in the chest and then slowly walked away. Before he left the building, he was apprehended by several security officers, but he did not resist. He allowed them to take him to the police station, where he was arraigned for murder.

A review of the extensive background material collected by social workers revealed a pattern of childhood relationships in which an older brother (not the one who was supporting him) would encourage him to become proficient in sports and would even play with him and teach him the fundamentals. Then, when he was becoming proficient, this brother would attack and ridicule him for being inept and clumsy. On several occasions the brother had beat him severely; once, he was hurt so badly that he had to be taken to the hospital. His other brother, the one who was supporting him, was also disdainful but for reasons of his own needed to be his brother's keeper.

His infantile relationships had apparently been reenacted in the treatment. His analyst, like his brother, was initially friendly, even beyond what might have been professionally optimal, as evidenced by the first-name interaction. And then he became critical. The patient no doubt experienced this as an assault. I believe this is another example in which the analyst unwittingly took over the role of a person of the past who was abusive and assaultive. The therapist re-created the traumatic infantile environment, which had been rejecting and violent. The rejection by his analyst, and the way in which he was rejected, was too intense an experience because it was too real; that is, he felt swallowed up by his infantile world, having lost hope he could find a more benevolent setting in the present. The past precipitously overthrew the present, and he was over-whelmed by destructive and self-destructive feelings.

The patient's psychic equilibrium was shattered, but do these circumstances explain the intense, drastic reaction of killing his therapist? He reported being in what might have been a fugue state. He had lost contact with current reality as he moved in the delusional setting of the infantile world. In such a setting, the act of killing becomes equated with the impulse and wish to kill. The fragmentation of his ego at the time of the murder was so great that both his rage and his reality boundaries were obliterated. He could relate only in terms of blind action.

The foregoing formulations must be accepted as speculative because they are derived from the data of two interviews and a

rather lengthy chart that included extensive psychological testing. Still, the nuances of the transference–countertransference
axis must, in large measure, be inferred. Assuming that these
formulations have some validity, we can wonder further about
the essential source or causes of this tragedy. How much can be
ascribed to the therapist and how much of our explanation can
be derived from the patient's unique violent background and
psychopathology? One might expect intense reactions from such
a patient, but do they have to lead to such a fatal extreme as
murder?

On the other hand, the therapist's constribution seems to
be obvious in that he converted the past infantile setting into
the real current milieu in the consultation room, but this has
occurred in many other clinical situations without such fatal
consequences. Perhaps the congruence of the therapist's response and the patient's psychopathology was an unusually
explosive fit, but I believe that there was more involved in the
therapist's responses that could have been studied from the
countertransference viewpoint. We do not know what factors in
the therapist's character structure accounted for his ultimatum—factors over and above the patient's projections and
apparently successful attempts to re-create the infantile ambience. The therapist's unique—that is, idiosyncratic—contribution is important to understand. Unfortunately, in this incident
it is difficult to discover.

By a curious set of circumstances, I was able to gather some
further information about this analyst and his impact on some
of his medical colleagues. His office was in a medical building,
and after he was shot, his body had been brought to the adjacent
hospital on a stretcher. Another physician, who happened to be
a patient of mine, saw the body being wheeled away. He felt
immense hatred at the time and later wondered why, because he
hardly knew this analyst. That night my patient dreamed that

he was on an escalator that was going up. He was dressed like a gladiator and carried a trident. He next saw the analyst on the same escalator above him, but he was walking down toward my patient. The analyst approached him and embraced him, trying to kiss him on the lips. My patient pushed him away and stabbed him in the chest with the trident, making three distinct, bleeding puncture holes. The dream assumed the qualities of a nightmare, and the patient awakened. The day residue for the dream was the patient's seeing the body on the stretcher with three bullet holes in the chest that were still visible in spite of the massive amount of blood that covered the whole body.

My patient's associations went back to approximately two weeks before the shooting. He was going up on the elevator of his building with one of his medical partners when the analyst joined them. He looked at the two physicians, chuckled, and then asked, "Do you two go together?" They both felt extremely uncomfortable, and my patient believed he blushed.

My patient knew this psychiatrist socially and was also acquainted with many of his psychiatric colleagues. The analyst was known for his keen intuitive grasp of the unconscious mind of his patients. He could be crass and undignified, however, and he offended both patients and colleagues. He apparently used his sensitivity in an insensitive fashion.

My patient demonstrated that when a person senses the content of another's unconscious and then uses this insight to deride and humiliate, such behavior is capable of stimulating murderous rage. The patient who killed his therapist had a primitively oriented, easily fragmented ego. He lost all boundaries and blended the past with the present. Then he imposed his dream-like state into the external world. By contrast, my patient was able to contain his rage by elaborating it into a dream. His ego was rather well integrated and cohesive, so he had fairly firm boundaries that kept the inner world of his mind separate from the external world. The murderer did not have this capacity, and he acted out the dream my patient had had. Of course, there was no actual connection between the two patients. I am simply stressing Jung's (1909) formulation that the schizophrenic's behavior is the outcome of dreaming while awake.

MICROSCOPIC DISRUPTIONS

In the previous section I discussed circumstances that had traumatic impact on the therapeutic setting as a whole. These were situations that made treatment impossible and led to a tense and forceful termination. Here, I refer to microscopic, in contrast to macroscopic, interactions because even though the difficulties created might lead to the cessation of treatment, they were not originally conceived as assaults on the general setting. Rather, they have their initial impact on some circumscribed segment of the analyst's psyche. Again, I emphasize that these are not precise distinctions. The analyst's personality is always involved, as I have discussed, when formulating the concept of idiosyncratic countertransference. In the clinical examples that follow, we can observe how specific areas of the psyche are involved by presenting a microscopic scrutiny of various ego subsystems. These clinical observations emphasize intrapsychic factors rather than a direct attack on the analytic setting (Bleger 1967, Kernberg 1965).

Disruption of the Professional Ego Ideal

Analysts sometimes feel uneasy when they begin to believe that the treatment is not following a specific course. In spite of our more flexible ideas as to what constitutes analytic treatment, many analysts have incorporated certain classical therapeutic principles into their ego ideal. Some nonconforming patients represent a special threat for these analysts in that they do not follow any course, but they are especially irksome because their attitudes and orientation are perceived as potent attacks on the therapist's value system. The analyst is not consciously aware that he feels compromised in his professional integrity, but this makes the situation even worse.

A single man in his early 20s sought treatment because he felt he was not making any progress in his life. He initially presented himself as a failure in all areas: sexual, social, vocational, and academic. He was still going to school, a local community college, but it seemed highly unlikely that he would ever graduate unless he made some drastic changes in his study habits. Although he occasionally dated, very few women would go out with him a second time. He had no friends, and he lamented about finding some area of work in which he might excel. Perhaps he could be a writer, but an instructor in a creative writing course told him that he had no talent whatsoever.

The manner in which he detailed these accounts of his ineptness and lack of accomplishment was strange. He was not depressed or self-condemnatory, as might be expected. On the contrary, it almost appeared as if he were boasting, as if he were talking about achievements rather than failures. He was arrogant and covertly blamed the world for not appreciating him. For months on end he spoke of innumerable failures and gauche behavior within the context of self-aggrandizement. He seemed to exemplify the oxymorons of *victorious defeat* in his behavior and *valuable failure* as the hallmark of his personal ideal. His orientation and attitudes were clearly bizarre, but rather than viewing them as interesting aspects of his psychopathology, I felt mildly annoyed.

He then began to talk about what he valued most in life. He was an avid believer in astrology and spent many sessions discussing the subject with religious fervor. He considered himself an expert astrologer, believing that he could predict the future with unerring accuracy. He was always beginning to write horoscopes but, as was characteristic of all his endeavors, he never finished any. He also had some complex ideas about food, megavitamins, and fad diets. Furthermore, he had some intricate feelings about Oriental religions and was fervently involved with a group of mystics who believed in soul travel and telepathy.

I continued feeling annoyed with him and wondered why, since, quite obviously, this was a very disturbed young man who was desperately trying to cling to a semblance of self-esteem. This should not have provoked any untoward countertransference reactions. To understand whether there was something peculiar about my feelings, I asked permission to tape-record an interview so that I could let some colleagues and residents hear it. He magnanimously granted my request, feeling that others would find the interview both instructive and interesting. In the long run, he proved to be correct. The interesting part was that everyone who heard the tape—whether a clinically inexperienced resident or a veteran clinician—felt an immediate antipathy toward the patient. I felt somewhat reassured that my feelings were, at least, shared and not too peculiar. After this "experiment," I was able to listen to him with a less critical attitude, but it did not last long.

I realized that it was not the combination of abysmal ineptness and devotion to grandiose systems and movements that disturbed me. I recognized that he was struggling with problems of self-esteem and serious defects in the ego's executive apparatus. If anything, an analyst might feel some compassion for such an emotionally crippled person. I discovered that he was, at first subtly and later more openly, trying to convert me to his viewpoint. Furthermore, he wanted to abandon my orientation as I encompassed his.

He discussed astrology as if it were the ultimate scientific system that would render psychoanalysis obsolete. His pronouncements were dogmatic and, at times, displayed a certain devious logic that would have been cumbersome to refute. I knew he would not listen to me if I tried to argue with him, and he was incapable of a scientifically consistent discourse. Nevertheless, I had an urge to attack his wild premises and sweeping generalizations—an urge that I kept in check with considerable difficulty. I gradually realized that what bothered me most was his blatant misunderstanding of the fundamental hypotheses of psychoanalysis and his tendency to overthrow them with the grandiose predictions of astrology. The fact that some of his proselytizing had a semblance of logic made matters worse. If he were obviously irrational or delusional, I do not believe he would have provoked any particular reactions.

* * *

As therapists, we are not put off by patients who display their delusions openly. Although they may try to involve us in them or enlist us in supporting some aspect of their psychotic system, we can maintain our psychic equanimity as we recognize how far removed they are from reality (Giovacchini 1979b). This patient was especially confusing because his psychopathology was presented as if it were part of a rational, reality-oriented, scientific system. Only after careful scrutiny of his material did it become apparent that it seemed rational if one listened only superficially and did not pause to ponder the connections between his dogmatic assertions.

In this connection, I can recall other patients who spoke quite freely and seemed to be revealing important aspects of their psyche. After careful reflection, however, or after taking detailed process notes, I realized that they had said nothing meaningful. This patient was making understandable statements that had no basis in reality, nor were they reasonable inferences derived from particular phenomena. Most disconcerting, however, was his insistence that I accept his pseudoscience as the fundamental, true science and give up psychoanalysis and admit that it is a pseudoscience. This was a direct attack on my professional integrity, and as long as I was not aware of his attempts to subtly undermine my ego ideal, I felt annoyed and uncomfortable. My colleagues and residents apparently had similar responses.

My patient displayed his character defects in overcompensations that were couched in reality elements rather than in bizarre, delusional distortions of reality. This confused me and made me question what was founded on solid reality and what was not. This doubt eventually had some impact on my ego ideal and made me irritable toward the patient, interfering with my capacity to understand him on his own terms. The following incident helped reestablish my analytic equanimity. I at first found the incident disturbing, but a hidden delusion finally emerged, an event that took the edge off my countertransference disruption and reestablished the solidarity of my ego ideal.

The patient became very upset because he had slept with a woman who turned out to be a lesbian or, at least, had had sexual relations with women as well as men. He insisted that I should have warned him about her and stopped him from acting out what he considered to be a catastrophic indiscretion. I was confused and somewhat indignant: How could I have been so omniscient as to know that she was a lesbian, and besides, what difference did it make? He seemed to be making a relatively trivial incident into an earthshaking event. Everyone would have contempt for and cast ridicule on him. This idea seemed bizarre in view of the combination of ineptness and grandiosity that really did make him look ridiculous and absurd.

To give some credence to his viewpoint, I acknowledged that he came from a prominent family with an illustrious history of achievement, and that such a tawdry encounter would compromise their exalted status. Perhaps there might be some snickers and raised eyebrows at their exclusive country club, but it was difficult to understand that there would be anything more drastic than that. In a negative sense, his belief that such a casual encounter would alter the course of history was, once again, grandiose. The discrepancy between his sexual behavior and the anticipated consequences indicated that there must be other, unrevealed connected thoughts that might make his attitude somewhat understandable. I was able to adopt an investigatory perspective, and I regained my therapeutic orientation.

Finally, he confessed that it was not that his escapade would have been so significant for an ordinary person, but like Caesar's wife, he had to be above reproach. He believed that he was the Messiah and that his disciples were in his immediate vicinity, but the time had not arrived when they could come to him. They had to wait for the moment when he would receive a message from God to reveal himself. Having submitted himself to such carnal lust, especially with a lesbian, he would lose his exalted status in the eyes of his disciples.

He revealed the basic psychosis that was the foundation of his grandiosity, and it had many paranoid elements. Until these revelations, his psychosis had not been easily recognizable, because many of its paranoid features were imbricated with situations in the external world that obscured the delusional element. The fact that he believed himself to be the Messiah caused him to try to obliterate any value system that lacked the omnipotent factors to sustain his divinity. I had felt the impact of his destructiveness on my ego ideal. Being able to appreciate the extent of his psychopathology made its manifestations bearable.

Disruption and Existential Crises

Some countertransference difficulties stem from what therapists perceive as attacks on the cohesiveness of their self-representations. I have just discussed countertransference reactions to assaults on the integrity of the ego ideal. The identity sense, or the self-representation, which for the purpose of this discussion I consider to be identical, contains the ego ideal. The therapeutic interaction that will be described next is in many ways similar to those in which the ego ideal is threatened. This is understandable because the ego ideal is a component of the self-representation. Because the total identity sense is involved, however, countertransference difficulties are globally disturbing and analysts are more likely to lose control of their feelings. In the previous example, I felt annoyed and irritated, but I was, nevertheless, able to monitor the expression of my feelings.

The patient, a young physician in his middle 30s, sought treatment because he was not satisfied with his relationships with women and was unhappy about remaining in his specialty. He had had some residency training in psychiatry and was ambivalent about whether he should seek admission to a psychoanalytic institute.

From the very beginning he was disdainful of the treatment procedure. Rather quickly he started attacking psychoanalysis, as had the previous patient. Unlike the other patient, however, his arguments were tightly reasoned and he was not altogether certain as to what theory and treatment might be better. He finally settled on Gestalt psychology, but the substance of his argument did not seem to be devastating to basic psychoanalytic principles. In fact, I read Perls's book and in many ways I found it compatible with the basic tenets of psychoanalysis. The patient, nevertheless, seemed to feel that the two systems were very far apart, antagonistic to each other, and he continued his litany against psychoanalysis. I was not particularly perturbed, although I wondered if he was so dissatisfied with psychoanalysis, why he did not seek out a therapist whose primary orientation was that of Gestalt psychology? We both knew several therapists who had this qualification. Nevertheless, I was neither tempted nor sufficiently irritated to confront him with such a challenge, and he apparently did not want to take any action based on his antipathy toward psychoanalytic treatment.

His acting out was, in retrospect, rather humorous. I was seeing him four times a week. After each session he had an appointment at a nearby gymnasium, where he took judo lessons. He felt that he was getting better, but he attributed this to judo, not psychoanalysis. I did not respond to any of his deprecations, sometimes feeling a mild irritation at the unending litany but also wondering what underlying psychic factors were responsible for his constant criticism.

Thus I was surprised when he began a session with an expression and tone of furious anger. He raged that I had been rude and sarcastic during the previous session. It was nothing that I had specifically said: It was my angry mood and disdainful demeanor that had offended him. He had not said anything at the time because he was "shocked" and he had not felt the full impact of my behavior until later. I was taken aback: I had no recollection of having behaved in a hostile and deprecatory fashion. Nevertheless, I felt that I should give credence to what he felt and that we should investigate the matter further. I indicated to him that, despite my being unable to remember having been rude, his observation was of crucial interest. Inasmuch as our relationship was predicated upon being as open as possible with the unconscious recesses of the mind, I would be faithful to that principle and would be willing to look into my own hidden psychic processes. He was satisfied with my reply.

As we reviewed the events of the previous session, we were able to reconstruct the following sequence. The patient, in his usual fashion, had been extolling the virtues of Gestalt psychology. Then he mentioned the name of a psychiatrist, quickly adding that he knew I did not like this man. I believed that I had an opportunity to make an effective interpretation because I had never heard of this psychiatrist. I do not recall the content of my interpretation, but it was related to the patient's having projected some attitude of his own into me. After I had made my interpretation, I remember feeling uncomfortable and irritated with him. It seemed that the patient's accusation that I had been rude was correct, because I was definitely angry.

While pondering this sequence, I had a fantasy. I pictured the patient talking into a tape recorder. He was talking about Gestalt psychology and then mentioned the name of the psychiatrist whom I reputedly disliked. When I started to make my interpretation, he shut off the tape recorder. He let me talk without interruption. When I finished, he turned the tape recorder on again and continued talking. When the tape was played back, the listener would not be able to tell when the machine had been shut off. The continuity of the patient's material was in no way affected by my intervention. What I had said was completely obliterated. I could now more easily understand the source of my anger and was able to connect it to some elements of the patient's childhood environment and relations.

The patient's mother was an intellectual woman who valued art, music, and other cultural activities. She was socially active and ambitious. Consequently, she felt ashamed of her uneducated, ill-bred husband, who spoke with a thick accent and who embarrassed her because of his poor manners when they were forced to be in public together. She treated her husband as if he did not exist, and she constantly derided him to her son. At the same time, she praised her brother whenever she could, elevating him to an exalted status. However, the patient did not meet his uncle until he was 8 years old.

The uncle turned out to be a ne'er-do-well who had borrowed a considerable sum of money from his father and had never repaid it. The patient felt betrayed and devastated when the uncle who had been presented as a role model was suddenly shattered as an ideal. He still had a depreciated view of what he considered to be a nonexistent father. In the course of treatment, however, he developed a somewhat different view of him. Although his father was uneducated, he was successful in business and provided his wife and son with material comforts. He was able to pay for his son's education up through college and medical school, and he even contributed to his support during his residency. It became apparent that the patient did not know with whom he could identify in order to consolidate a masculine identity.

Throughout his life, and certainly during treatment, the patient had sought causes, situations, or systems that he could idealize and others that he could depreciate. This tendency reflected the dichotomy his mother had created between his uncle and his father. In treatment, the patient maintained this polarization by pitting Gestalt psychology against psychoanalysis. It became clear, however, that he had no real sense of conviction. Who was the villain and who was the hero? The hero turned out to be a fake, and his depreciated father was able to provide well for him and for his mother. He was confused, and his confusion extended to doubts about his orientation. He wondered about his identity and about the purpose of his life. To a large measure, he suffered from an existential quandary that had expressed itself in his symptoms at the beginning of treatment.

His behavior was largely overcompensatory. He knew what was right and he took great pride in his appearance and physical prowess, especially as he became more proficient in judo. He strove for both intellectual and physical superiority. Nevertheless, he felt weak, vulnerable, and empty, and there had been earlier periods in his life when he had experienced symptoms similar to those Erikson (1959) described as characteristic of the identity diffusion syndrome. During those times, he felt that he was nonexistent—an empty void. Much of his behavior and many of his attitudes were designed to achieve a sense of being, to give him a sense of existence.

Returning to the session following the expression of my annoyance with him, the patient conjectured that I had reacted to a reverse oedipal situation; as an older man whose resources were waning, I was jealous of and competitive with his youth and vigor. I was threatened by his accomplishments. I felt that possibly he was correct in his assessment, but somehow it seemed to miss the mark. It was too glib and limited an explanation. Instead, I thought more about the fantasy of the tape recorder and concluded that the patient had projected aspects of his self-representation onto me.

In other words, he had succeeded in getting me to absorb the emptiness and nonexistence that he felt and that he so vigorously defended himself against. He could resort to the defense of reaction formation as he projected his vulnerability into me. Rather than oedipal competitiveness, I was experiencing something much more primitive, an existential crisis, and

I reacted to my inner disruption by attacking him. I discussed this interaction with him, and it became the central theme of the analysis for several years, during which time he was able to relax his overcompensatory defenses and give up judo.

This obliteration of my sense of identity can be viewed as belonging to a spectrum that includes patients who attack the analyst's ego ideal. The first patient created countertransference problems that were the outcome of vulnerability of a circumscribed area of the psyche. The physician, on the other hand, encompassed a larger segment of my personality: the self-representation. There was, at least for me, a direct proportion between the intensity of disruptive countertransference reactions and the extent of the psychic area involved. It would seem obvious that compromising the sense of existence would provoke much more severe reactions than an intrusion into one's value system, especially a circumscribed aspect of a value system — the professional aspects of the ego ideal (Thorner 1985). There are other aspects to the patient's intrusive behavior that must be discussed, however, because they contribute in a subtle and complex manner to our reactions, which, in turn, will be significant to the analytic interaction.

PART TWO

COUNTERTRANSFERENCE IN SPECIFIC PSYCHOPATHOLOGICAL CONSTELLATIONS

4

Countertransference Reactions to Primitive Mental States

A major problem in writing a book on countertransference is the difficulty in correlating various responses with particular types of pathology. Specific cause-and-effect relationships are not easily established because such observations are phenomenological and could be produced by a variety of psychic states, transference projections, and defensive postures. The intrusive patient, for example, can be represented by many psychopathological types. From a subjective viewpoint—that is, when the analyst experiences the patient as intrusive—analysts' reactions can vary widely, depending on their character structure, without necessarily being idiosyncratic.

The personality structures of the participants in the therapist–patient dyad and the manifest transference–countertransference reactions are not linked to each other in a fixed, immutable fashion. Furthermore, the analyst may be more comfortable with some elements of the patient's character structure and regression and may react adversely to others. Because of the multitude of variables involved, etiological sequences are neither specific nor predictable. Thus the therapist's reactions to the patient, or to the patient's projections onto the analyst, are not necessarily indicative of particular psychopathology or a specific phase of the treatment process.

Our countertransference feelings contribute to our perceptions of patients, which, in turn, lead to clinical and diagnostic assessments. If we attempt to categorize patients on the basis of observable character traits, our subjective responses will determine the qualities that we emphasize and to which we will react, either favorably or adversely. What may be experienced as intrusive by one therapist may be viewed differently by another. The patients presented in the previous chapter could be thought of as intrusive inasmuch as they attacked or intruded into specific parts of the therapist's psyche. Still, it was my sensitivity that made them instrusive.

Although I will be discussing intrusiveness as an essential feature of certain types of character structure, it is also true that whenever our countertransference feelings make us uncomfortable or cause us to feel disrupted, we find patients to be intrusive. This is, at times, a blurred issue because we have to understand whether we are disturbed because the patient is intrusive or whether something within ourselves has caused us to perceive the patient as intrusive. Perhaps it is our own feelings that are intrusive as they interfere with our therapeutic equanimity. Because the patient has in some way stimulated such feelings, we feel that the source of intrusiveness resides in the patient's transference reactions and character structure.

These distinctions are not absolute; that which comes primarily from the therapist is often difficult to distinguish from that which is precipitated principally by the patient. In some instances, it may not make any difference to the outcome of the therapeutic course, especially if the analyst can create a holding environment in which various patient–therapist interactions can be nonjudgmentally examined (Winnicott 1952, 1963a).

Although, as stated, it is difficult to correlate psychopathology with homogeneous countertransference responses and to list various categories of connections and interactions between patient and therapist, I believe that some correlations can be discovered if we concentrate on psychic processes and relate to the patient's infantile world. As we become more familiar with those areas, countertransference issues and the patient's intrusiveness are highlighted, and this intrusiveness must be understood from both the patient's and therapist's viewpoints.

For patients suffering from primitive mental states, wanting to intrude and feeling intruded upon are universal character traits and reactions that developed in the infantile setting. We must understand as much as we can about this early ambience, because patients attempt to re-create it in the consultation room, and it is enacted around the transference–countertransference axis (Jacobs 1986).

For many patients, the act of being born is viewed as a *primal intrusion*. The infant is thrust into a world that does not want him. He is treated as an intruder who upsets the psychopathological equilibrium that had been established by his parents. These children may be rejected, assaulted, ignored, or treated as nonhuman objects.

I have described a large group of patients who were treated by their parents as transitional objects (Giovacchini 1986). These parents have used their infants as receptacles of the unwanted, hateful parts of themselves, and their children have not learned to distinguish what is truly their own and what has been intruded into them. In the most extreme instances, these children never recognize any parts as their own and live a subhuman existence. Others have adopted various defensive strategies to cope with their traumatic environment and object relations. These adaptive techniques are used in their daily lives and will invade the analytic setting. The patient's intrusiveness is often a defensive attempt to invade others; the alternative is to feel assaulted and violated by an intrusive parent who manipulates and exploits the child into a state of nonexistence. In a paradoxical fashion, the intruder role is the only approximate cohesive identity these patients have ever known. Their intrusions in and assaults on the outer world protect them from being swallowed in a nonhuman anonymity and from becoming a transitional object with no feeling of being alive (Searles 1963, 1965).

PASSIVE INTRUSION

As previously stated, many psychic interactions are not necessarily associated with particular action sequences. We generally think of intrusion as an active invasive process, a violation of our privacy and autonomy. There are situations, however, in which patients succeed in entering our psychic domain and disturbing our tranquility, and yet they appear to be passive and withdrawn. They are not directly impinging on our psyches, but the effect they produce in the therapist can be catastrophic. It may seem strange that a patient who is shy and withdrawn can evoke within us such disturbing feelings. This situation is especially interesting because these patients have imperfectly developed feelings and sometimes practically no feelings at all.

The patient with the type of character disorder I am discussing suffers from a maldevelopment of feelings related to an inability to form endopsychic registrations of gratifying, nurturing experiences. Winnicott (1963b) distinguished between privation and deprivation, the state of privation being the most traumatic and primitive. The infant who has known privation has, in a relative sense, never had a satisfactory nursing relationship and therefore does have a memory and introject of a gratifying experience. This is not absolute, of course, because no one could live with a total absence of gratification. The children Spitz (1941) wrote about approximated total privation, and none of them lived beyond infancy.

Most children who have experienced privation have very little affect and remain withdrawn, not moving into the external world. They also do not feel frustration, again a relative lack of feeling, because in order to be frustrated one must have had some gratifying experiences that have formed what I call a *nurturing matrix* (Giovacchini 1979a, 1986). Infants ordinarily form memory traces, or mental representations, of being gratified. Later nongratifying experiences run counter to the expectation of gratification that is created by the nurturing matrix. Thus, these children, and later adults, know the feeling of frustration, whereas those who have suffered privation do not.

From a countertransference viewpoint, we would expect some significant reactions on the part of both patients and therapists when a patient who has not developed the capacity to feel gratified is confronted with a therapist who has such a capacity. The analyst wishes to provide a gratifying environment for the patient. The analyst, at some level, "feeds" the patient with interpretations, which, like food, are supposed to nourish and promote integration and development—in this instance in the realm of the psyche rather than just the body. The good mother's ministrations, however, are also directed to the attainment of psychic stability. The treatment relationship, especially with patients suffering from primitive mental states, is in many ways similar to the mother–child nurturing interaction. The mother and child form a bond, and as the infant enjoys being fed, held, and comforted, the mother is also gratified. With good bonding, a positive feedback sequence is established. In a manner of speaking, the infant fuels the mother as well as the reverse, and both are involved in a mutually rewarding growth experience. Something similar occurs in a good therapeutic relationship as the analyst provides nourishing interpretations and establishes a holding environment (Winnicott 1952, 1956).

It follows that to the extent that there are deviations from this optimal relationship, or insofar as it is unattainable, there will be technical difficulties that will be expressed in the transference–countertransference interaction. The patient does not provide the necessary feedback that the analyst may need in order to be able to function effectively or to feel secure in his professional acumen. I grant that I seem to be putting the burden of responsibility on the patient's shoulders to soothe what may be an overly sensitive analyst. Still, these situations occur and must be recognized and made explicit if there is any hope for the treatment to be effective.

The analyst, when feeling disrupted, may not be aware of his expectations of the patient. Even when the patient is withdrawn and makes no overt demands or attempts to penetrate the therapist's ego boundaries, the analyst may still feel intruded upon. Sometimes the patient's mere presence is felt as intrusive.

* * *

A 40-year-old man complained that his previous experiences with analysts had never "gotten off the ground." He could not describe exactly what had happened. He knew something was missing, but he could not be any more definitive. He added that his wife had had the same problem with her therapists, but that was as far as he could go with his description. I was struck by his flat affect and dull demeanor, but it did not seem to be part of a depressive constellation. I also noted that although the patient spoke loudly at times, there was very little feeling attached to the increased volume. He wanted treatment, but he doubted that analysis would do him much good. He anticipated another failure, but he lacked the desperate quality usually associated with hopelessness.

At first, I believed that the patient was fairly psychologically minded. He spoke freely and brought in meaningful dreams that could be understood. Exploration revealed certain fundamental paradoxes; the patient's mental set was far more concrete than had first been apparent.

Early in analysis, he brought two dreams that were prototypical of many other dreams he had throughout the treatment. These later dreams were variations and embellishments of the themes presented in the earlier, considerably shorter dreams.

In the first dream the patient was on a small island, totally isolated from the outer world. He was sitting nestled on the side of a hill next to a cave and feeling, as much as he was able to, contented. He described a sensation that resembled warmth, although it was difficult to determine exactly what he felt, since he reported not having feelings as most people do. What was startling in the dream was that this island was an iceberg and he was enveloped in ice. The experience was comfortable, or more precisely stated, nonthreatening. He was literally being hugged by ice, and he derived some satisfaction from this situation. Coldness and isolation (as depicted in the drifting iceberg) were the norms that characterized his infantile environment, and they were paradoxically gratifying. These qualities seemed bizarre in the context of the current milieu, in which warmth and a sense of belonging and being loved are the means of obtaining gratification and security.

In the second dream, he was again alone. He was in a space capsule somewhere in the "outer limits of the universe." He was floating in a vast empty space. The inside of the capsule was stark, with white walls and neon lights. The patient was aware of his breathing and felt peaceful. The atmosphere that surrounded him consisted of carbon dioxide instead of oxygen, but he believed that was what he needed. Again, the dream is an obvious paradox. He was taking in carbon dioxide instead of oxygen, the reverse of how one ordinarily breathes. What are waste products for all of us were his source of sustenance. He was able to thrive on what is poisonous to everyone else. The setting of the dream, like that of the first dream, emphasized the stark, colorless quality of both his inner life and his relationships in the outer world. He was an isolated as could be, but he was not sad. He felt relatively comfortable and had a modicum of security.

Later dreams depicted the impact of analysis. The space capsule dream was recurrent, for example, but he added to its structure. He attached a small oxygen-filled compartment to the capsule. He could not breathe the oxygen because it would have been toxic to his lungs, but, over the years, he was finally able to breathe it for limited periods of time. His associations indicated that oxygen represented the analytic interaction. He dreamed of his therapy in this impersonal, nonsubstance-like fashion, and it was many years before he could include me as a person as he explored the therapeutic process.

He had to maintain distance between us because he could not integrate intimate relationships. It seemed that a good deal of his life was spent in avoiding significant attachments. He was married, but his marriage seems as barren as the iceberg and the space capsule. He described many situations in which he felt that any overture, no matter how tentative, made toward him was an intrusion. Unlike the patient I described in Chapter 3 who described himself as having a "thin skin," this patient did not feel assaulted by interpretations. On the contrary, I found him to be intrusive, but there were no active or obvious incursions into my psychic space. He did not overtly complain or make unreasonable demands, but I reacted to him as if he did.

The first year of treatment seemed to be comfortable for both of us. He occasionally commented about the hopelessness of the prospect of improvement, but as was the case with everything he said, there was no intensity or conviction to his statements. He often commented about being unable to feel. He revealed that he never felt joyous or happy, but then he never felt depressed in the sense of being sad or miserable. He also had very few discrete somatic sensations. All inner stimuli felt the same. For example, he experienced neither hunger nor satiety, so he could eat enormous quantities of food or he could go for an indefinite period of time without eating. He ate at specific times; he ruled his eating habits with the clock because otherwise he could not tell when he needed to eat. Similarly, he could not discriminate between the need to defecate or urinate. He just experienced some vague sensation that signaled to him that he should go to the toilet. He was able to tolerate fairly wide extremes of temperature because he seldom felt particularly warm or cold.

I stopped thinking in terms of intrapsychic conflict, repression, and inhibition. Rather, I gradually began to view him as having imperfectly developed drives and defects in the sensory apparatus, especially that part of the sensory system that registered inner sensations. Therefore, I should not have been surprised or irked when he did not respond to my interpretations.

I perceived the patient as needy, although during the first two years of treatment he never directly asked for anything. He was simply disappointed with me and never seemed to understand my interpretations. I finally realized that my descriptions of psychological processes were falling on deaf ears, because even though he heard what I said, it was as if I were speaking a foreign language or just uttering nonsense syllables. His reactions to my attempts to help him understand the inner recesses of his mind were not examples of active rejection. I became convinced I was trying to penetrate a stone statue, not a stone wall. His psyche was made of impenetrable stone; it was not just surrounded by a fortress. He was not keeping me out; rather, he was constitutionally unable to let me in.

I believe that two factors were involved in creating this impasse. Impenetrability is characteristic of the concrete and difficult patient (Giovacchini 1979b, 1986). This patient proved to be not at all psychologically minded, as I had initially assumed, but was the outcome of a false-self organization (Winnicott 1960). He used words as if they expressed feelings and were symbolic expressions of psychic states. But there were no underlying feelings. His behavior and surface orientation had a distinct as-if quality (Deutsch 1942, Giovacchini 1984), being the outcome of transient introjections of the psychologically minded milieu that surrounded him. He and his wife worked closely with mental health professionals. He was able to take on some of their mannerisms, opinions, and thoughts, but this was not a true identification. Rather, he was dealing with his environment at the surface of imitation, and his apparent psychological mindedness was not an integrated and established character trait. It was not a part of his true self. Actually, his basic approach to life was rigid, literal, and nonintrospective. He looked for the sources of his behavior and limited feelings in the outer world. He also had a limited concept of psychic determinism.

Concreteness is frequently associated with privation. The patient's early environment had related to him only at a minimally sustaining level. This privation led to his relative absence and maldevelopment of feelings and his inability to use potentially helpful experiences in the outer world. His lack of a nurturing matrix prevented him from incorporating—or even recognizing—positive, growth-promoting relationships. The resultant inability to be gratified created disruptive countertransference reactions.

I experienced his incapacity to be gratified as intrusive. Inasmuch as I could not get the patient to "receive" my interpretations, I felt as if I were pounding a stone wall. Yet I did not feel that I was being actively repulsed. I felt frustrated as I faced a patient who had only a limited capacity to feel frustrated. My frustration took the form of feeling intruded upon. His inability to accept my frame of reference made me feel that the patient was imposing his concrete world of privation into the consultation room.

The therapeutic world was invaded by the patient's infantile milieu. Once I became aware of this interaction and recognized the extent of the patient's privation, I was able to relax and wait for him to develop some degree of receptivity, hoping that the holding environment would create a secure, trusting therapeutic ambience. I regained my equilibrium as I further understood the quality of the interaction, and for a while I did not perceive the patient as intruding into my space with his concrete world. I decided that the patient only appeared to be intrusive but that, in actuality, his general demeanor was characterized by a passive orientation. Although the patient's passivity had an invasive quality, I did not continue to perceive it as intrusive once I recognized the passive, concrete nature of the patient's character.

Gradually the patient's demeanor changed. Instead of being quietly hopeless and unreachable, he now began subtly complaining. He commented that I never gave him anything and that I never made any attempt to understand him. At first these thoughts came up as vague insinuations, and their meaning was unclear. After several weeks, he became more explicit. I felt bewildered because, I had been trying very hard to understand what was going on, and although my interpretations were not overly abundant, neither were they sparse. It was difficult to determine the optimal frequency of interpretations. Indeed, the attempt to make such a determination is absurd since there are so many complex variables to the analytic interaction. Still, the patient was beginning to accuse me of never saying anything. I did not react particularly to this material, and I maintained the therapeutic frame of reference by trying to look at the relationship through the patient's eyes. From the patient's viewpoint, not saying anything meant not saying anything meaningful.

The patient's mood continued to be flat and his demeanor remained passive in spite of the increasing clarity of his comments. They were, in fact, comments rather than complaints, and once I had a better grasp of the material, I no longer felt resentment toward the patient.

The patient continued in this manner for over a year and then began to embellish the passive feeling of hopelessness that had been present since the beginning of treatment. To him, treatment had failed. In his concrete way, it was either a success that cured him or a failure that did not help him. Treatment was something outside of himself, and because I personified the treatment, I had failed him. At first I was able to work with these reactions as manifestations of the maternal transference—the mother who had failed her son. After several months, however, I began to feel annoyed and once again intruded upon. I found it difficult to accept the patient's transference projections—in this instance, to accept the role of the inept, failing mother.

The patient, as usual, was impervious to my interpretations. He did not understand what was meant by a transference projection. He saw no connection between the therapist and his mother. I had failed him, and that was a fact that had nothing to do with his past. It also had nothing to do with him. Again, his concrete orientation prevented him from taking any responsibility for his treatment. I tried to explain that his feelings about failure were the outcome of a repetition of the infantile failure in the therapeutic interaction and, as such, were an inevitable feature of the treatment process. The patient agreed superficially, but I knew that, as usual, he did not accept a single word I said. The patient could not see the equation of the therapist with the failing mother.

Consequently, it became even more difficult to accept the patient's projections. The countertransference was once again dominated by the feeling of intrusiveness. To represent the failing mother in treatment as a therapist was an acceptable therapeutic phenomenon, but to be a failing therapist in the present, without any connection to the past, upset the analytic setting. Actually, rather than being perceived as symbolically failing him, the patient created a concrete reality that intruded into my psychological perspective and disrupted it. As discussed in the previous section, it also ran counter to the professional ego ideal, which values making successful interpretations that lead to creative integrations.

As I have frequently felt with other patients suffering from primitive mental states, my main task was to survive. In order to do so, I had to maintain an intrapsychic focus and not respond to the patient in terms of the content of the material. Keeping the principle of psychic determinism in mind, I had to remain in another frame of reference, on an observational platform, and try to avoid directly confronting his character defects. (I will further discuss these technical factors in the next section.)

This patient remained in treatment for several years, and we discussed his privation and his need to relive the infantile maternal failure in the transference context. This was only partially accurate because it was the only way he knew of relating; thus it was not actually a reliving. In time, however, he was able to see some similarities between the past and the present, and he began to view his attitudes and reactions as reliving. He related that life in general was better for him because of treatment, but that in many ways he was still handicapped.

* * *

Because of his concreteness and incapacity to make symbolic connections, this patient might be considered incapable of forming a transference. Nevertheless, he dealt with me as he had with the infantile environment. More precisely, his subjective response to me was the same as that which he had experienced during infancy and childhood. His vision was so narrow that he could not see any other world than the one that had created the privation. Privation—that is, the inability to be gratified and to assimilate helpful experiences—in turn prevented him from moving into a world different from the infantile world. His mode of relating was based on an ego state that had a poorly synthesized nurturing matrix.

As his dreams indicated, even his minimal means of achieving satisfaction would not be understandable for a person who lives in the ordinary world. He was held by cold, hard ice rather than warm, soft arms, and he breathed the respiratory waste product carbon dioxide instead of life-sustaining oxygen. Whatever gratification he achieved was paradoxical because the normal sources of nurturance, soothing, and sustenance were the antithesis of his. Thus even if I had been able to get the patient to accept what I offered, his response would have been unfavorable. The patient would have been harmed by such ministrations, at least in a psychic sense, if the interpretations of the messages conveyed by his dreams were correct.

This situation caused further countertransference difficulties, I felt intruded upon in this context as well. To face such a paradox—wherein that which is ordinarily harmful is perceived as gratifying and that which most persons find gratifying is perceived as harmful—is disturbing because the analyst's ego executive system lacks the adaptive techniques to relate to such a foreign situation. The patient's expectation of being gratified in a paradoxical fashion is experienced as an imposition since the analyst feels that he is being covertly asked to give up his sources of gratification. That which he is asked to integrate into his ego is not capable of being integrated and, therefore, is felt as an intrusion. The patient need not be openly demanding; his mere expectations can have a tremendous impact on the analyst. The analyst's main task is to survive the patient's attempts to bring him into his paradoxical world, which also means that he has to remain in his own analytic world without causing unmanageable turmoil. The latter may be difficult, and in some cases impossible, to accomplish.

In a sense, this paradoxical world is delusional. It is not obviously delusional in the ordinary sense of the term, but it is constructed along the same axes. Rather than involving gross distortions of the environment, which are replaced by parts of the self, this delusion is far more subtle because there are no such projections. The distortion of reality relates to the paradoxical satisfaction of needs. The world that nourished my patient is grossly different from the one in which we live, and for him to have expected me to gratify his needs in the bizarre fashion he required would be tantamount to demanding that I participate in a delusion. This demand usually has a significant impact on the therapist and can be disturbingly intrusive, as I have described elsewhere (Giovacchini 1979b).

* * *

There are other cases in which patients suffering from privation do not evoke these particular countertransference feelings, nor do they create delusional worlds characterized by paradoxical types of gratification. Engel's (1954, 1968) famous patient Monica illustrates these phenomena. The way in which the world related to her might indicate a different, perhaps positive, countertransference if she had been in treatment. I believe, however, that even a positive countertransference would have led to a treatment impasse.

* * *

During the first months of life, Monica was hospitalized because of an esophageal atresia. She could not receive nourishment because of an anatomical defect that prevented food from reaching the small intestine. Thus Monica was literally starving to death. At first the surgeons constructed a fistula, an opening that extended from the external abdomen into the stomach. She was then fed through a tube passed through this opening. Later, reconstructive surgery was done on the esophagus and Monica was able to eat in a normal fashion.

In her earliest months of life, Monica had obviously suffered from privation. She literally could not be fed. Ostensibly
this was due to a somatic obstruction rather than to the unavail-
ability of a gratifying, nurturing relationship. Whatever the
reasons, however, Monica did not receive nurturance; presumably this would have led to the lack of formation of an endopsychic nurturing matrix.

Engel showed films of Monica lying in her crib several
months after her final surgery. She seemed somewhat apathetic
and hypotonic, inattentive to the toy that lay nearby. She
seemed to derive little gratification from the toys offered to her
or from the considerable attention the staff gave her. Her
interactions had an anhedonic quality and a lack of joyful
anticipation. Nevertheless, the staff persisted in trying to get
through to her, and one particular psychiatrist (Reichsman)
became especially devoted to her (Engel and Reichsman 1956).
Monica was followed by the psychiatric clinic for many years—
at least until she was in her 20s. Slowly, over a long period of
time, Monica was able to relate to the staff members on a
relatively pleasurable basis, and she made some friends in the
outside world and managed to graduate from high school.

Monica was very dependent on the staff of the psychiatric
clinic and formed a special bond with Dr. Reichsman. The
formation of these relationships would indicate an achievement
in that she was able to receive dependent gratification. It would
mean that she had been able to form some kind of nurturing
matrix.

From the films Engel showed, it was apparent that Monica
was extremely dependent. For example, she was shown entering
a room, most likely one used for occupational therapy. Easels
were set up. As she came into the room, she walked up to a male
staff member. She twisted her body, permitting him to reach
over and take her coat off. He then hung it up. She went to the

easel and started to paint. During the lunch break, Monica was shown sitting at a table next to this same staff member. Someone set two wrapped hamburgers in front of them. The staff member proceeded to unwrap them and hand one to Monica. Almost reflexively, she took the top of the bun off and handed the open sandwich back to the staff member, who quickly salted it and returned it to her. Both the removal of her coat and the hamburger incident occurred so smoothly that I doubt that either Monica or the staff member was consciously aware at the time of the dependent nature of the interaction. In the film, Monica did absolutely nothing by herself except to smear some paint on a canvas, but no one seemed to care or notice.

Her passivity and dependence were highlighted in a tape-recorded interview. The interviewer wanted to be nondirective and, in essence, asked her to free associate. He asked her to tell him anything that came into her mind, to spontaneously choose a topic. Monica asked what he would like to discuss because it did not matter to her. He again exhorted her to be spontaneous, but she kept putting the burden of choosing the direction onto him. The interview was perfectly calm and indicated no annoyance whatsoever on the part of the therapist about Monica's recalcitrance. As they bantered, he suggested that perhaps she would like to talk about a certain topic. She replied that she would be glad to, if that was what he wanted, and then the interviewer took over the discussion. It seemed as if the interviewer was not aware of having been manipulated into determining the content of the discussion. He did most of the talking.

Monica apparently could not be spontaneous, and her dependency, her need to be taken care of, was all-pervasive. Most remarkable was her skill in weaving her dependent orientations into all areas of her life and the fact that others reacted favorably to her. They seemed to want to take care of her, and in some instances it appeared that they were not even aware of the extent of their caretaking activities. For example, a high school teacher spent an inordinate amount of time with Monica in addition to her classroom hours. She helped Monica complete assignments, but she neither felt imposed upon nor resentful, even though Monica frequently called her at home. This teacher was always glad to respond.

Monica is now married, and her husband seems to have a strong need to take care of her. He attends to almost all of the household chores and works to support his family.

Because of the constant care and devotion she received postsurgically in the hospital and afterward throughout her life, Monica, I conjecture, had been able to construct some type of nurturing matrix. Prior to surgery, she could not be fed, and she was not able to endopsychically register gratifying experiences. The internalization of ordinarily satisfying nurturance occurs early in the neonatal period and ultimately leads to bonding. This apparently did not occur in Monica's early infancy; only later was she anatomically able to receive nurturance, and whatever psychological internalization took place must have begun some time in the second six months of her life. She seemed to have established a nurturing matrix, as evidenced by her capacity to be dependent, but it was not securely integrated into the ego, nor could it have been stable or cohesive.

I believe that the nurturing matrix was unstable because Monica was so completely dependent and passive. It seems as if she had to reassure herself that she could be gratified. She had to reinforce the mental representation of a nurturing experience by being constantly nurtured, in the same way that a person who lacks evocative memory cannot maintain the internalization of a mental representation unless that person is actually present (Fraiberg 1969).

From a countertransference viewpoint, it is interesting that everyone responded positively to Monica. It is difficult to say whether such a positive attitude could have been sustained in an analytic relationship. Perhaps she could not have been analyzed, as indicated by her refusal or inability to free associate. Still it is fascinating that in her everyday relationships, no one experienced her as intrusive, whereas others, such as the patient I have just discussed, were disruptively invasive despite their passivity. The difference might be due to the fact that Monica had had a more cohesive, integrated nurturing matrix (although it was weakly established) than persons similar to my patient.

I believe, however, that Monica did not feel that she was an intruder, nor was she treated like one, as she entered the world. She could not be nurtured, but this was due to an anatomical defect rather than to rejection. Her inability to take in sustenance was organically, rather than emotionally, determined. Consequently, later in life she had to be reassured that she could receive, but this was not a reactive, defensive need to repeat a primal intrusion. The latter would have created disruptive countertransference problems, whereas passive receptivity alone is much more tolerable. Still, even with Monica, there is a balance between emotional and organic factors—that is, between feeling like an intruder and being unable to be gratified. It is highly likely that Monica would have had emotional problems, regardless of the esophageal atresia.

Some very passively dependent persons cannot become engaged in a psychoanalytic treatment relationship. If by some circumstances they begin analysis, it soon becomes apparent that they will not free associate. (Whether they will not or cannot may be impossible to determine.) This may be annoying to the therapist, but he will not necessarily feel threatened. He or the patient may choose to discontinue treatment, or the analyst may decide to modify his technique. For the therapist, these are usually autonomous decisions and not the result of intrusive coercion.

AGGRESSIVE INTRUSION

Clinicians who deal with structural psychopathology must face a large group of patients who are aggressively intrusive, a quality that evokes strong and disruptive countertransference responses. The global situations described in Chapter 2 were examples of treatment situations in which the patient was forcefully intruding into the analytic space and disrupting the process. I repeat that certain phenomena cannot be equated with specific forms of psychopathology. The psychopathology that we will now explore, and that causes the patient to be aggressively intrusive, has unique features that make intensely disconcerting demands of the therapist. I believe that the nature and consequences of such a therapist–patient interaction are typical in the treament of a particular type of patient. The therapist feels intruded upon in a characteristically identifiable fashion even though, as is so often the case with disruptive countertransference feelings, the features of the patient's impact may not be at all recognizable at the moment it is being felt. The intrusiveness of these patients is most often attributed to obnoxiousness. This is not a professional or charitable appraisal; nevertheless, therapists occasionally feel this way about some of their patients and, as is the case with all untoward responses, it is better to acknowledge them than to let them remain hidden (Kernberg 1965, Pick 1985).

The patient, a middle-aged married woman, was, in many respects, similar to other patients I have described. She intruded into my psychic space and threatened various aspects of my personality, such as my professional self-representation, but she did it in a specific context, and I had failed her in a special way (Giovacchini and Boyer 1975, 1982).

She was depressed because she felt generally useless. Her feelings were typical of an involutional depression. Her children were grown up and did not need her anymore, and her husband, who was enjoying huge business successes, was too busy to spend time with her. She suspected that he might be having an affair.

Her husband's success had been achieved relatively recently, and she dated the onset of her depression to that time. Prior to his meteoric rise, he had provided a bare subsistence and was frequently ill with gastrointestinal problems. He was once diagnosed as having ulcerative colitis and was very seriously ill. His wife had diligently looked after his every need. His psychiatrically oriented internist had suggested psychoanalysis, and with some reluctance, he accepted the suggestion. After two years of treatment, he changed his vocation, started a business, and was an immense success. He no longer needed his wife to take care of him, and this, compounded by the last child's having left home, precipitated my patient's depression. She apparently needed to care for and protect her husband and children, a not uncommon situation with patients who succumb to depression. Rather than discussing the rather familiar psychodynamics underlying this type of decompensation, I will focus on a defect in early nurturing and its contribution to an intrusively disturbing countertransference.

To emerge from her depression and to push herself back into the external world, she set up a boutique with her best friend, also a housewife of about the same age. The boutique did not do very well, but, with a small subsidy from the patient's husband, it was able to barely survive. Its purpose was to give her something to do rather than to bring in substantial profits. For a while she was satisfied with the status quo. As the months went by, she began complaining about her friend and partner. At first she suspected that she was not accurately reporting the sales. The vehemence of her suspicions gradually increased, and finally she was convinced that she was being exploited. The evidence she produced to substantiate her accusations was not presented in an organized or convincing fashion, so it was difficult to conjecture about the validity of her claims. Her agitation was extremely intense, however, and it was clear that she was approaching a psychotic decompensation.

Her accusations acquired a definite paranoid quality and intensity, but they were not directed only against her friend. She started attacking me. She insisted that I should have foreseen that the enterprise would turn out to be a debacle, and inasmuch as I had done nothing to stop her, I was to blame for the catastrophe. However, this situation was different than the one created by the patient I described in Chapter 3, who blamed me for not having stopped him from committing an indiscretion that would impugn his divinity. I did not believe that this woman had an underlying organized delusion, although her rancor and indignation strained the boundaries of reality.

She seemed to reach the height of irrationality when she accused me of being responsible for all the pain she had suffered throughout her life. She also reviled me for not caring for her, for having been so removed that I was indifferent about what would happen to her. I would abandon her to a devouring world and not lift a finger to protect her. I was letting her venture forth unprotected as she faced innumerable dangers, paying no attention to her helplessness and vulnerability. She frequently alluded to a story in which a Russian family in a troika is trying to outrun a pack of wolves. To slow the wolves down, they throw one baby at time to them. She felt as if she were a babe in the woods and as if everyone thought only about his own welfare, not giving her needy and weak self a second thought.

Her anger could not be contained, and in a furor, she fled from treatment. I had been drawn into the all-pervasive affective turmoil, and during our last session I lost my temper as she kept hammering at me with her accusations. I tried to understand her rage in terms of her intrapsychic conflict and her infantile background, but it was difficult to maintain a professional orientation in the face of the intensity of her attacks. After she left, I was finally able to regain my composure and to further understand her behavior as the outcome of certain childhood experiences and ego defects.

Her father had been a volatile, unstable man whose behavior was bewildering and unpredictable. He could one moment be peaceful and loving and then incomprehensibly lose his temper, sometimes physically abusing his wife and children. There was also some question of sexual abuse of the patient when she was 2 or 3 years old. He often got drunk and could not remember what he had done when intoxicated. The mother was totally ineffectual and offered the patient no protection from her father. When he became violent, the mother would run out of the house, abandoning her children to him.

The fantasy of throwing babies to the wolves seemed an apt description of the mother's abandonment and failure to protect the patient. Because of her needs, it was not enough that I remain in the intrapsychic domain. She insisted that I step into her life and protect her from dangerous situations. It was also inevitable that I fail her, as the dominant element of the repetition compulsion was that her mother actually had failed her. It is difficult to conjecture whether the fiasco with her business partner was unconsciously manipulated, but it was easy for her to perceive the experience as another example of an abusive, exploitive situation in which she was assaulted and her vulnerability and helplessness exposed.

I began to understand our interaction on the basis of the reenactment of the infantile milieu—that is, her father's unpredictable abusiveness and her mother's abandonment. I experienced her complaints about my lack of involvement with her business activities as an attack on my professional orientation, and I experienced her demand that I change my modus operandi as disruptively intrusive. My feelings must have contributed to the intensity and ultimate chaotic degeneration of the treatment relationship. At this point, we could not view these events in terms of the transference–countertransference interaction, and the transference had reached psychotic proportions.

What I could not understand, and what seemed to be manifestly delusional, was her making me responsible for all the pain she had ever felt. Recognizing that every paranoid delusion has a reality core, I acknowledged, at least to myself, that from one viewpoint she might be right. I remembered that there had been little color or feeling in her life prior to treatment. True, she had been depressed, but this was manifested by a blunting of feeling rather than by pain. Certainly there was no joy. In treatment she had developed some capacity for experiencing affects; she could now feel a minimum of pleasure and intense pain. Inasmuch as the treatment was instrumental in creating these sensory experiences, she was, in a sense, correct in blaming me. The first time she had experienced organized pain was when she was in analysis; her feelings became sufficiently discriminated that she could distinguish between pleasure and pain, whereas previously she had been enveloped in a veil of sadness.

Several months after her abrupt departure, she called me. She said that she had missed her analysis and asked if I would let her return. I was delighted to hear from her again, and my attitude had mellowed considerably after I understood what had transpired as a manifestation of the repetition compulsion and her lack of development of feelings. Like the patient I experienced as passively intrusive, she had underdeveloped feelings but not to the same extent. Her lack of discrimination applied chiefly to the separation of pleasure and pain and did not involve more specific sensations such as hunger and excretory pressures. Pleasure and pain are related to feeling gratified or frustrated, a distinction that she had had difficulty making prior to therapy.

She had established a nurturing matrix, but as was the case with Monica, it was poorly established. In contrast to Monica however, gratification was associated with intrapsychic conflict. Her ambivalence toward both parents, especially her father, made her fearful of allowing herself to feel closeness and intimacy and to have expectations. To be dependent and to receive was dangerous since her father might capriciously attack her and her mother precipitously abandon her, leaving her in a state of unprotected, exposed vulnerability. She seemed never to have had the protective shield, the *Reizschutz*, that Freud (1920) described. He had emphasized that an important aspect of the mother–infant interaction is the mother's forming a stimulus barrier to protect her child from potentially disruptive external stimuli.

In treatment, this lack of modulation of stimuli in infancy has intense repercussions. The stimulus barrier, Freud postulated, maintains a state of psychic equilibrium for the child. The mother not only provides nurturance, but she also produces a state of comfort and calm. The nursing experience is especially gratifying when the child is held and soothed. Thus, soothing is part of the mother–child interaction and leads to a sense of security and feeling protected. Similarly, in treatment, the therapeutic process consists of two components: nurturing interpretations and the soothing holding environment (which will be discussed further in the next section). Without a soothing component, interpretations cannot be integrated. My patient, by re-creating the past, had upset the holding environment and, instead of feeling soothed, relived the infantile state of unprotected vulnerability.

Prior to her affective explosion and regression, the patient had been able to feel some soothing because the treatment had provided her with a fairly comfortable holding environment. The repetition compulsion represented a direct assault on the holding environment and upset the treatment equilibrium. She could no longer be soothed or feel protected. Her inner feelings had overwhelmed her, but she projected internal dangers, introjects of the unpredictable, abusive father and the unprotecting mother, into the external world. The disappearance of the holding environment had its effects on me as well. With its sudden disruption, both the transference and countertransference became unmanageable.

Nevertheless, the patient had missed the analysis after she left, meaning that she had missed the soothing qualities it had held for her prior to its collapse. When she returned, she was initially shy and meek. She was wary, fearing that I might get angry, as I had during our last session. Nevertheless, she broached the same subjects she had been emphasizing before the collapse of treatment, but her tone was mild rather than directly accusatory. She gently remarked that I had been rude prior to her leaving. I acknowledged that I had been, and then I apologized for having lost my temper. The patient was momentarily surprised and relieved and then emboldened to proceed further. She added, again in a mild tone, that I had failed her. Again, I agreed, but I did not go any further. Once more she was surprised, but she noted that this time I had not apologized. Having gone this far, she asked for an apology. I replied that I would not apologize, because her feeling that I had failed her was an inevitable feature of the treatment relationship. In nontechnical terms I explained how the infantile environment, through the repetition compulsion, was reenacted in the transference; later, I briefly explained my behavior on the basis of disruptive countertransference reactions.

She quietly listened to my explanations and decided not to

pursue the topic further. She said something to the effect that if what I had said made me feel better, then it was acceptable to her. In any case, she was gradually able to discuss the various traumatic elements of her past and to understand how she relived them in the present and in a transference context. The treatment endured for several years.

* * *

Various factors contributed to the intensity of my countertransference reactions. Like all countertransference responses, they can be explained in terms of which aspects of my ego were specifically threatened. Certainly the professional sense of identity is usually involved, but there are various elements that may be more or less threatened by different patients. In addition to finding it provocative to be accused of failing her and of being insensitive and unempathic, I found that the most disturbing element of our interaction was her insistence that I give up my modus operandi. She demanded that I move from analyzing intrapsychic phenomena to managing her life. She then vehemently reprimanded me for not having done so, for not having taken over the role of an infantile object and becoming the protective mother, a mother she had never had and could not create through her transference projections. In other words, I was being blamed for trying to analyze her rather than taking over a protective function that would have been appropriate in infancy rather than adulthood. Basically, I felt that she was trying to destroy me as an analyst. As she continued attacking me, I became functionally paralyzed by the intensity of her intrusion.

This patient's impingement on my analytic functioning was the outcome of a specific infantile constellation. Although she was generally intrusive, which could be considered a character trait, the essential core of her traumatic past took time to emerge, and its full impact was not felt until a fairly solid treatment base had been established. The analytic relationship became stormy and was nearly destroyed, but it survived. I had to learn that when she was the most agitated and disturbed, she was presenting me with the essence of her psychopathology. I had to recognize this and survive the onslaught. This was an example of a psychoanalytic paradox that I will describe more fully in the next section. Other patients may be similarly disruptive and intrusive, but their behavior is not necessarily a direct expression of reactions to infantile traumas.

In some respects, these patients may be more difficult to treat than the woman I have just described. They also demand that the analyst change his modus operandi, or they do not permit him to introduce the analytic procedure at all. Freud (Breuer and Freud 1895) would probably have considered these patients to be exhibiting massive resistances that rendered them unanalyzable (Freud 1911-1915). There are many reasons that patients resist getting in touch with the unconscious parts of their psyches, and these reasons will be instrumental in stimulating countertransference reactions.

The patients I will now discuss are irksome, but they are not as catastrophically experienced as those who pervade the consultation room with their traumatic infantile milieu. The treatment is threatened, but the analyst may not feel so personally involved. The level of the patient's personality that is in the forefront of the transference is an important factor in determining the amount of devastation caused by the transference–countertransference interaction. If the clinician is dealing primarily with defensive surface adaptations, he may not feel much turmoil in maintaining the analytic setting.

Some patients need to set their own conditions for treatment in order to be in control and to protect themselves from vulnerability. The control issue can create an impasse (Giovacchini and Boyer 1975, 1982), but such a need for control is related to surface layers of the patient's personality and will not, as a rule, threaten the integrity of the professional self-representation. The analyst may become annoyed at protestations designed to coerce him to conduct himself as the patient demands. The therapist feels intruded upon, but the intrusion does not penetrate very deeply. Nothing fundamental is disrupted, although there may be considerable tension and anger in the consultation room. Anxiety usually is not acutely experienced, however, as it has been with most of the patients I have already discussed. Resentment prevails, especially if the analyst feels betrayed.

* * *

The patient, an attorney in his early 30s, was eager to begin analysis with me. He had read some of my works and knew several persons whom I had analyzed. Consequently, he seemed genuinely disappointed when I told him that I had no time on my schedule but would be glad to refer him to a colleague. He refused the referral and insisted on calling me again in several months to see if I might have some time open. I discouraged him, urging him not to wait, but he was adamant. He had waited for over a year when I finally saw him. I might have seen him earlier for a consultation, but he was very explicit in indicating that what he wanted was analysis.

He began by giving me an obsessionally organized history. He completely filled the first session, rarely letting me satisfy my curiosity by asking an occasional question. He went into minute detail, determined not to omit anything. He continued in a similar fashion during the second session, when I finally firmly interrupted him in the middle of his litany. I told him that I believed I had enough information to have a general orientation about him. I then briefly explained the principle of free association and suggested he lie down on the couch. He was visibly perturbed about being interrupted and not being allowed to finish what I was convinced would go on forever. Nevertheless, with some protest, he did lie down and began to talk in a random fashion.

As he entered the consultation room for his next session, he moved toward the chair. I stopped him by motioning him toward the couch. He angrily grunted but reluctantly lay down. He then proceeded to talk in a somewhat associative fashion, but he also interwove historical data into his material. Part of the time he free associated, but he also organized his thoughts into various categories and sequences.

Midway through the session he abruptly sat up, faced me, and asked me to summarize what had happened in the treatment up to this point. He also wanted to be "briefed" as to our goals and our progress thus far toward attaining them. Stunned, I was momentarily speechless. Such behavior in a patient who had assiduously pursued being analyzed by me for over a year was astonishing. All I could do was to tell him to get back on the couch. He was very angry as he complied with my request, and he remained silent for the next ten minutes. Then he continued with his history.

He started the next session by stating that he wanted to sit up. I was mildly irritated, but I firmly resolved not to give in to what amounted to a demand. At that moment, I felt it would have been wrong for me to give in, so I told him that whatever he wanted to say had to remain within the context of treatment. He would have to lie down. I could not let him compartmentalize the therapeutic relationship into a "sitting up" and a "lying down" part. He acquiesced, but he was angrily silent throughout most of the session. Toward the end of the session, he repeated that he wanted an evaluation and summary. I said nothing. The following interview was similar. He was on the couch, and his demands became increasingly intense. He was working himself into a rage. It was difficult for me to continue to believe that my lack of response was a therapeutic technique, an analytic silence designed to maintain an observational frame of reference. I visualized a tug of war: He was pulling at one end with his prosecuting-attorney staccato of questions, and I was pulling in the opposite direction by remaining silent. My silence had become a weapon to defend myself against his angry barrage.

This was an annoying situation, but it was in no way overwhelmingly disturbing. Like other patients I have discussed, he was demanding that I change my modus operandi. He wanted me to "brief" him, to answer his questions, and to be allowed to sit up. I also realized that my analytic silence had been reduced to a defensive weapon and that to continue using it would result in a breach of the analytic frame. I decided that I would define the analytic setting and then let the patient decide whether he wanted to be analyzed or not. I felt secure when I realized that I was not going to change my modus operandi and succumb to his ever-intensifying demands.

I finally spoke. I said that my only interest was in learning about his mental processes and in helping him understand them. I did not see myself as a therapist who answers questions on demand, provides summaries, or gives progress reports. If that was what he must have, then I would be glad to refer him to a therapist who would accept these conditions. I, however, did not intend to compromise my analytic autonomy, as I wished to enhance his. This cleared the air for me, and he begrudgingly accepted my resolve: He did not want the referral and decided to continue with me. Displeased and angry, he complained about my rigidity, but now I was able to view his protestations in an analytic context and still not necessarily respond directly to them. I had lost the urge to argue with him.

We were eventually able to understand the defensive adaptive nature of his attempts to derail the analytic setting and to replace it with the familiar strategy of the courtroom. He was protecting himself from feelings of vulnerability by wanting to be aggressively in control. As the treatment unfolded, his underlying dependence and passive homosexual feelings emerged in the transference interaction. It became clear that his controlling, demanding behavior protected him from what he feared would be passive surrender. As mentioned, this patient had insisted that I change my modus operandi, and I felt sufficiently threatened that I believed that I could not continue functioning as his therapist if I were to give in to his demands.

* * *

In other situations, it might be possible to modify some aspects of the analytic setting without destroying it. The intensity of our negative countertransference responses are determined by the extent to which the patient expects us to deviate from our own norms. My patient wanted me to change my therapeutic style completely. I did not see how I could survive as an analyst in such circumstances. In other clinical situations, the therapist may be able to modify some elements of the treatment setting without compromising his analytic integrity.

It is not simply a question of analytic integrity, however, which might be viewed as rigid insistence upon clinging to a particular professional stance. The clinician is primarily concerned with the patient's needs within the treatment context rather than with strict adherence to abstract therapeutic principles. As analysts, we want to help our patients achieve maximum autonomy; our goal is not to get them to change their adaptation to the external world in order to make their relationships with reality and external objects more gratifying and symptomatically unconstricted. Certainly we hope that they will function more adaptively, but that is a choice they will make; it is not a primary therapeutic goal. Analysis is more concerned with internal change than with focusing directly on the external world. As long as our technique does not abandon the intrapsychic focus, a certain amount of flexibility is allowed so that the patient does not flee from treatment because of overwhelming anxiety.

My patient's demands would have destroyed the intrapsychic focus and introduced a different frame of reference in which reality would be the central emphasis. It turned out that his need to conduct treatment on his terms was not so intense that he could not eventually adapt himself to the analytic ambience. His behavior represented an adaptive defense, but it was not vital for his psychic survival. He had other adaptations that helped him maintain psychic equilibrium, and he was able to exercise his need for control in his profession and in other relationships.

Other patients have even stronger feelings of vulnerability and are not able to suspend their reactive defenses to adapt to the conditions required to conduct analysis. The analyst then has to decide how far he can bend in order to keep the patient in treatment. With my patient, I chose not to alter my technical style and refused to develop a relationship that was antithetical to my professional orientation. To a large measure, my not wanting to enter his frame of reference was determined by my unfamiliarity with his terrain. I really did not know *how* to function therapeutically at the level he demanded. Perhaps with another patient I might have been able to become involved in a supportive psychotherapeutic relationship, but this patient had initially presented himself as desperately desirous of psycho-analytic treatment. I suspect, in retrospect, that he basically did want analysis and that, to some extent, he knew what that meant. His desire for analysis was an unconscious wish that conflicted with the parts of his personality that were designed to control both his inner and outer world. What he had demon-strated when he pursued me as an analyst was genuine and prevailed, in the sense that he responded to my challenge by reluctantly agreeing to accept my minimal conditions for anal-ysis. Another patient might not have been able to continue in treatment.

With these kinds of impasses, the analyst has to make a choice. After I made mine, the patient could decide whether he would remain in analysis with me or seek the type of treatment he felt he needed elsewhere. I have known situations in which the patient did, in fact, leave. In some instances the patient returned soon after termination. Others returned many years later. I reasoned that even though the patient did not want or could not tolerate analysis at the moment, I would nevertheless preserve the analytic setting, a setting to which he could return later if he wished.

It is important to distinguish between modifications that destroy the analytic setting and those that do not, because, as previously mentioned, this distinction is a significant deter-minant of countertransference reactions that are potentially harmful. The analytic procedure comprises various elements, some of which are fundamental and others of which are conve-niences that facilitate the process but that may be discarded if indicated by the patient's psychopathology. The former are basic in that they comprise the intrapsychic focus and follow the principles of psychic determinism. The latter can be considered the formal elements of psychoanalysis; examples are having the patient lie down on the couch, usually not answering questions, and not intruding personal information or opinions. Some patients may be able to continue to view events from an intrapsychic perspective but may not be able to abide by these formal elements. If the analytic relationship is conceptualized in terms of the patient's needs and these two components, the relinquishing of some of the formal elements of analysis may not evoke disruptive countertransference responses.

Patients can also be divided into two categories of psychopathology as they impinge on the analytic process. The patients who cannot tolerate the formal elements of the procedure often display a lack of ego cohesion, which renders them especially vulnerable to the regressive pull of the analytic process. Because they lack basic trust, they find it difficult to accept the supportive aspects of the holding environment that a therapeutic relationship attempts to create. Like patients suffering from privation, these patients are often unable to avail themselves of potentially helpful experiences in the outer world. Although these patients display more severe psychopathology than the patient I have just presented, the reactions they evoke when they try to breach the therapeutic frame are not as intense.

The other group is characterized by my attorney patient, who had a fairly well integrated ego. His behavior, as I have stressed, was the outcome of manipulative, defensive adaptations, but his ego was fairly well integrated. Although it turned out that my patient also had ego defects, they were less conspicuous and severe than those found in patients who object to the formal elements of analysis. Such patients may, paradoxically, be easier to treat—at least at times—than those patients who are better integrated and yet are capable of totally disrupting the treatment relationship. I am distinguishing between patients who suffer from character disorders and those who have fairly intact characters but, in the tradition of the psychoneuroses, also have considerable intrapsychic conflict.

Before proceeding to discuss the more severely disturbed group of patients, I wish to point to another group that falls somewhere between the character disorders and the intrapsychically conflicted patients. Clear-cut diagnostic labels can seldom be applied to actual patients. Most patients present combinations of features found in various nosologic entities. The patients I am about to discuss have features of both groups. These commonly encountered patients can be irksome and annoying.

In some ways these patients are similar to the young attorney I presented. He wanted me to discuss his analysis up to the time he had been in treatment. I experienced this request as ridiculous, especially in view of the very short time he had been in treatment. The patients I am now describing also make requests, but they are delivered in the form of questions. Instead of talking about themselves, they talk and ask questions about the analytic process. They ask, for example, what the purpose of free association is, how and why their problems have unconscious sources, and why the loss of identity causes pain. Their innumerable questions deal with the rationale of treatment technique and metapsychology. These are not just intellectual reflections; there is usually a driven, desperate quality to their questions and ruminations. They may also present a dream or a curious event in their outside lives and then, without any associations, demand an explanation.

If the therapist ventures an interpretation with so little material upon which to base it, he is usually reacting to the patient's pressure for answers. The patient is insatiable, however, and an answer will lead to another question indicating that the interpretation needs clarification or is a subject for debate. They create a frenetic atmosphere and behave like little children who are constantly asking why.

They do not directly ask the analyst to change his modus

operandi, but in constantly talking about analysis, they create a situation in which the analyst cannot "do" analysis; their behavior, a disruptive resistance, becomes difficult to tolerate. This type of aggressive intrusiveness causes the therapist to feel functionally paralyzed.

* * *

I experienced one of my patients, a successful middle-aged businessman, as intrusive because of his tendency to ask constant questions without revealing anything about his inner thoughts or feelings. At most, he would introduce a feeling in the form of a question such as "Why do I feel this way?" or "Why do I have such thoughts?" Although he was lying on the couch, I felt as if we were involved in "meta-analysis" rather than analysis.

I decided to treat his questions as material, a hybrid form of free association. I did not want to be caught in the same power struggle that was created in the treatment of the attorney patient. Consequently, I told him that I might or might not answer his questions as I saw fit. I defined the purpose of analysis as a focus on the intrapsychic and explained that I would deal principally with hidden motives and not necessarily with the content of his material. I added that his questions represented, among other things, a resistance to getting in touch with inner feelings. He accepted my comments without rancor and was able to curtail his "meta-analytic" approach.

From time to time, as might be expected, he would return to it, and at other times he intruded in a subtle fashion. For example, he would express an opinion or tell about his reaction to an event and then ask whether I agreed or would have felt the same way. At other times he would wonder about some of the bizarre events in his life; he would ask, "Doesn't this seem strange?" or "Why does this happen to me?" or "Do other people have the same problems?" There were sessions in which I felt annoyed: every sentence he uttered was a question. The sessions also had their humorous moments. I remarked during a particular session that he had not made a single declarative statement; all of his remarks had been questions. He seemed somewhat startled and then replied "They have?" We both laughed as he recognized that what he had said actively validated my observation. Such episodes made his behavior more tolerable.

It became apparent that his questions represented resistance, but it was a type of resistance that is typical of the concretely oriented patient. I am referring specifically to the type of questions that were directed toward my reactions and toward events in the outside world. He was trying to draw my attention to external situations and thereby move away from an intrapsychic perspective. In fact, he was trying to cling to the view that the sources of his reactions, feelings, and behavior resided in the external milieu. If he felt frustrated, depressed, or angry, it was as if he had nothing to do with the creation of those feelings. His reactions were caused by external traumas or lack of gratifying opportunities. This attitude was clearly a resistance since he was ignoring the principle of psychic determinism, but once explored as such, the resistance became incorporated into the psychoanalytic dialogue.

This patient's character structure was fairly concrete, but he was aware of psychological processes. He operated on a fine line; he was not particularly psychologically minded, but he was able to listen to my explanations and interpretations and, to some extent, understand them. His concrete outlook caused him to externalize but, inasmuch as it was also used as a resistance, it could be dealt with in the analytic framework. Because of his rigid character, it was difficult to get him to look inward, but it was not impossible.

His partial accessibility distinguished him from the paranoid patient. Attributing the sources of feelings to the outside world is an intrinsic aspect of projection. If what is happening is painful and traumatic, and if some person or event in the outside world is blamed, then we are dealing with paranoid projection. My patient blamed the milieu for his distress and, to that extent, he was paranoid, but he did not display the rigidity and the intractability of the typical paranoid patient.

As mentioned, this "meta-analytic" patient, whose concept of etiology is limited to the external world, is commonly encountered, especially among young, upwardly economically mobile adults. They have the superficial appearance of being intellectually curious, interested in art and music, and they profess an interest in fine dining. They go to the opera, to symphonies, and to gourmet restaurants. Basically they are narcissistic personalities who are fairly distant from their inner lives, and their attachments and interests are shallow and transient. They are afraid of intimacy, and their professed emotional involvement is part of a false-self orientation (Winnicott 1960). The latter quality may be used to therapeutic advantage, however. For example, my patient, because of his false-self organization, needed to comply with my wishes as to how to conduct the analytic procedure. Instead of protesting, as the attorney patient had, he professed to go along with my ideas about therapy, and he treated them like instructions. It was not a true involvement, but it made it possible to continue treatment without any particularly disruptive impasses.

The countertransference dilemma often consists of a vacillation between feeling intruded upon and feeling comfortably complacent about the process, inasmuch as the patient seems to be producing fruitful material. These patients are often inventive and charming and are able to amuse their therapists and to seemingly give them what they want. The analyst has to understand the defensive nature of many of the apparently constructive and positive moments in treatment, as well as the intrusive facets of the patient's material. Although these defensive tendencies are character traits in these patients, many of them can eventually relinquish, or at least, partially relinquish, their defenses and adaptive modes enough to get in touch with or begin to construct a true self (see Part III). Sometimes they leave treatment before getting started; often, though, a certain amount of therapeutic work can be accomplished and, in some instances, the results can be gratifying.

Again, these patients do not refuse or protest the conditions the therapist prescribes for analysis. They accept such requirements but then do not bring in material about themselves. In contrast, another group of actively intrusive patients are quite willing and anxious to talk about themselves, but they cannot accept the formal aspects of analysis. They are usually frightened and refuse to lie down on the couch, and most analysts sense their fragility and their disruptive underlying tension. Their basic ego weakness may be apparent despite a determined, aggressive stance about what they expect from treatment and how they want it conducted. They make it clear that they will require feedback; they need to be locked in with the therapist, and they will not tolerate a nonparticipant analyst. Many of these patients do not comment about the couch until the analyst brings it up, and then they refuse to use it.

It seems that I am describing an imperious and perhaps arrogant person, and this is often an accurate appraisal. I have felt momentarily taken aback by some of these patients, but with the passage of time my impression changes and my feelings for them soften. This is because I have sensed their fundamental helplessness and realized that their behavior is reactive and designed to maintain a precariously organized self-representation. Without their facade, these patients could not maintain ego cohesion and would regress to panic, with a severe loss of ego integration. The analyst faces the quandary of deciding whether to modify his technique in view of the patient's lack of ego strength or to remain firm in establishing a traditional analytic setting in order to overcome what might be an obstructive resistance. The latter assumes that the resistance can be overcome without creating an unmanageable transference, an assumption that is often difficult to make.

Many therapists (Boyer 1982, Giovacchini 1979a, 1986, Searles 1987) believe that the analytic setting can be supportive for patients who have a tendency to undergo severe regression. The holding environment provides the patient with security, and although the patient regresses, he maintains sufficient organization so that the regression is not disruptive. The patients I am now describing insist on determining the construction of their holding environment, and this might require the sacrifice of some of the formal elements of analysis. Without their specific type of holding environment, they cannot survive the experience of analytic treatment.

Sometimes the analyst does not immediately recognize the patient's underlying precarious ego organization and treatment may be broken off before it has begun. The analyst may be impessed with the structured aspects of the psyche. Such was the case with the patient we will now consider.

* * *

An internist referred an attractive woman in her middle 40s for analysis. He did not tell me much about her except to note that she occasionally had short episodes of anxiety and mild depression, for which he had been prescribing small doses of alprazolam (Xanax).

The patient presented herself as poised, sophisticated, and competent. She was stylishly dressed and spoke with an air of confidence and assurance. She related her history in a calm, coherent manner, emphasizing her various accomplishments. She came from an aristocratic family of prominent socialites. Her mother was a famous hostess, and the patient was also known for her gracious, fashionable parties. She was reputedly eager to be rid of her symptoms, and she stated that she understood how emotional factors could be responsible for creating them. She had discussed this issue with friends who had been analyzed and with her internist, who was psychologically minded. She seemed to be well integrated and a reasonably good candidate for analysis. She had expressed a wish to be analyzed.

After she had sat in a chair for two sessions, I explained to her the principle of free association, which she said she had known about from her friends and from some of her readings. I then asked her to lie down on the couch. Her friendly, cooperative demeanor abruptly changed, and she became visibly anxious. She became pale as she hesitantly approached the couch. She lay down with her head at the other end of the couch so that she was facing me. I explained that the traditional position was the opposite of hers, and that one purpose of lying down was that she could free associate without having my image intruding into her thoughts and forcing them to be socialized and reality-bound. The patient agreed, turned herself around, and started talking in a tremulous voice. I was astonished at the dramatic change and the complete breakdown of her self-assured, charming, cooperative demeanor. She remained lying down for about ten minutes when she suddenly sat up, screaming that she could not stand it any longer. She then politely excused herself and left, adding that she would see me at our next scheduled appointment.

She called to cancel our next interview, stating that she had an incapacitating cold. We scheduled another appointment, which she neither kept nor called to cancel. I called her, but no one answered her telephone. I called again at various times of the day, but I never got a response. Finally, her internist told me what had happened to her.

He told me that she was an uncontrollable drinker, an alcoholic, who would frequently go on binges. He referred to her rather short respites between binges as her "lucid periods," and I had apparently seen her during one of them. After her session with me, she had gotten drunk and had remained that way ever since. She did not answer her telephone because she had either turned it off or had passed out. Her husband was thoroughly exasperated with her and was threatening divorce. The internist suggested that he persuade her to return to see me. The husband coerced her with the threat of divorce and forced her to call me for another appointment.

Now I understood how vulnerable she was and that her poise and sophistication were part of a facade designed to hold together a helpless, dependent, masochistic self-representation. She did not say anything about her alcoholism and drunken sprees, preferring to present herself as an aristocratic, charming socialite. She kept herself engaged in innumerable activities because, basically, she felt useless. There was no purpose to her life, and there was very little that would contribute to her self-esteem. Although her husband, on the surface, seemed to want her to give up drinking and to feel secure and comfortable with herself, he did everything possible to undermine her and subtly urged her to drink. He needed someone toward whom he could feel patronizing, condescending, and contemptuous (Giovacchini 1958).

I had to examine my countertransference reactions. I realized that at first I had been a little put off by her charming-hostess facade. She seemed to have everything in such perfect focus that I wondered why she sought such an arduous procedure as analysis. I was not altogether aware of my feelings, but, in retrospect, I recognized that I felt demeaned, that she was treating me like a servant who was hired to look after her needs, and I experienced this as intrusive. Perhaps my asking her to lie down on the couch had been a reactive gesture on my part to make a dent in her subtly arrogant, faintly condescending manner. If so, this was a misuse of psychoanalytic procedure in that I was using the accoutrements of psychoanalysis as a weapon. On the other hand, using the couch is a formal element of analysis that I usually advocate. Perhaps the way in which I introduced it was especially threatening for this very vulnerable patient. Lying on the couch could have represented a situation in which she felt demeaned and assaulted, an abrupt stimulus to release what became uncontrollable masochistic impulses.

As I became increasingly aware of what lay underneath her aristocratic self-representation, I saw how necessary it was for her psychic organization. When she returned to treatment, she sat down in a chair, and I accepted the fact that she was unwilling to lie down. I decided not to make an issue of a procedural matter. For her, my insisting on the couch was equivalent to forcing her to prematurely relinquish a defensive adaptation. I knew she could not do this and that therapy would be impossible if I persisted. She seemed grateful that I did not push the point.

She remained in treatment for many years and we were eventually able to face the inner terror and fear of masochistic dissolution that was the basis of her core personality. As the years passed she became increasingly able to free associate and brought in dreams to analyze. She gradually became what we might consider a good analytic patient, but she continued sitting up throughout her treatment. This was a subject that she did not want to discuss, and as time went on it did not seem to matter. I relinquished the formal requirement of using the couch. She also did not want to analyze her refusal. I suspect that some fundamental and powerful ego defect did not allow her to distinguish the couch as a symbol of defenselessness from the couch as a concrete representation of vulnerability. I did not feel it was necessary to pursue the matter further since she had established a fairly stable psychic equilibrium, and the referring internist had reported that she had stopped going on drunken binges. I felt that an insistence on a "complete" analysis would have been the product of an idiosyncratic countertransference.

* * *

Something similar happens with some homosexual patients who want to be analyzed but do not want any encroachments on their homosexuality. It is an adaptation that serves them and prevents them from facing certain conflicts. They are able to maintain a degree of fragmentation that isolates the ego defect or intrapsychic conflict and still permits them to reach higher levels of ego integration in other areas of the psyche. Eissler (1958) discussed the way in which an area of the mind can contain an encapsulated psychosis, and yet the remainder of the psyche can function at the highest level of creative integration. Such was the case with Goethe. This is a risky balance, however, and splitting defenses sometimes become ineffective, in which case the patient may severely regress or psychotically decompensate. Nevertheless, Goethe, despite definitive paranoid traits, led an illustrious, creative life. Similarly, my patient is now relating to the world at a much more integrated level and no longer has to regress to states of alcoholic stupor.

In discussing countertransference feelings of being intruded upon, I am referring to our reactions to a group of patients who, for various reasons, cannot adapt themselves to the formal elements of analysis. Such noncompliance, if understood in terms of the patient's underlying precarious organization, should not evoke disruptive countertransference responses. The analyst may initially feel uneasy and resentful, but once he understands that the patient's refusal is based on constructing a pathological false self that maintains psychic survival, he should be able to relax his concerns about psychoanalytic ritual and protocol. The patient's needs must remain in the foreground until a holding environment is established and analytic work can be accomplished. As long as the latter takes place, analysts should not feel that their professional styles are being compromised or that they have made concessions that are at variance with their professional self-representations.

More than patients with other types of severe psychopathology, this group of patients are in need of a setting that will, if not support, at least not threaten their precarious adaptations. It generally is not clinically useful to support psychopathologically constructed defenses. This is where analytic neutrality enters the picture (see next section). Analytic neutrality transcends judgments about the manifestations of emotional disturbance. Actually, such a nonjudgmental perspective is the outcome of comfortable countertransference reactions and helps create a soothing holding environment.

Because of the constant reliability of the treatment setting, the patient may feel secure and soothed, maybe for the first time. In some instances, however, the analyst may wittingly or unwittingly upset some element of the holding environment; thus interrupting the constancy of the therapeutic frame and possibly stimulating uncomfortable and resentful transference feelings. Usually, only minor breaches of the holding environment are involved. Nevertheless, any change of the setting upsets these sensitive patients and causes them to become acutely aware of nearly imperceptible impingements on the holding environment. Their tenuous ego organization does not blend itself easily in the treatment setting, and they will cease to feel soothed and supported if there is any shift in the analytic ambience. The analyst may not at first even be aware of such a change, or, if he is, he may feel that it is so insignificant, it is inconceivable that anyone would react to it. The fact that the patient does react may be experienced as an unreasonable and unexpected intrusion, and may create reactions in the therapist that are as out of proportion as those of the patient.

Many patients react to some concrete change in the setting. The analyst may remove a plant or rearrange the furniture. Patients who, after initial resistance, have finally accepted the couch, may be unusually sensitive to any change in it. I recall violent reactions when I had to replace the pillow because the old one wore out. On several occasions I had to get a new couch, and it has always been an unpleasant experience for these patients. The new couch is either too hard or too soft. It is unfamiliar and simply not comfortable. One patient had the illusion that she owned the couch, and that I had deprived her of an important part of herself.

If analysts view their offices as belonging to them and as parts of their professional self, as many do, then the patient's claim to ownership becomes a challenge. These analysts feel intruded upon because they feel that their patients are trying to control their space. Since the incidents are manifestly trivial, it is especially important to monitor both the patient's and the therapist's reactions, which will clash with each other. Freud

(1919) referred to such clashes as the outcome of the narcissism of minor differences. The patient feels that the analyst has intruded into his space, and the analyst, in turn, resents the patient's attempts to encroach on his freedom and autonomy, which, in these instances, is represented by the concrete elements of the therapeutic environment. It is not an equal struggle, however, because the patient's reactions are the outcome of the deepest layers of the psyche, whereas for the analyst, only the surface elements of his adaptations should be involved.

Despite the apparent superficiality of some of these incidents, the outcome is often catastrophic, because the analyst tries to transcend his annoyance and irritation by treating the situation as if it were trivial. The impasse is created because the incident seems unimportant to the analyst, but for many patients it is deadly serious. The problem is further compounded because nothing can be done about the dilemma. Certainly most analysts are not going to change the furniture or other concrete aspects of their professional environment because of a patient's seemingly capricious complaints. To do so would no doubt evoke such resentment in the therapist that it would interfere with his analytic objectivity. For patients, however, these preferences are not whimsical; they represent attempts to reestablish a supportive holding environment or to secure their place in the consultation room, something they have never had in the real world.

* * *

I know of some colleagues who, in a limited way, have tried to accede to the patient's demands. One analyst finally responded to a patient's insistence that he remove from his wall a painting that she considered ugly. After he had removed the offending painting, she wanted him to hang a picture that she had painted in that same spot. With great reluctance he accepted her painting and hung it. He believed that if he did not, he would lose the patient. The analyst was uneasy about this arrangement, and he did not even like the picture.

There were several repercussions. Most of his other patients immediately noted the change and took an intense dislike to the painting. They sensed that it was out of harmony with the general decor, but more than that, they sensed that it was alien to the analyst's personal style. They felt that it was not part of him and believed that it was out of synchrony with the general mood of the consultation room. It had a jarring effect. To make matters worse, the patient's need to intrude herself into the treatment setting remained unabated. She insisted on bringing in her own pillow, and she took the blanket that was on the couch with her at the end of her sessions. Although she would return it the next day even if she did not have a session, it was gone much of the time and other patients noticed its absence. The situation had clearly gotten out of hand, especially since this patient was creating havoc for other patients who needed a constant, reliable holding environment.

At first, the analyst did not take seriously the patient's wish that he get rid of his painting and replace it with hers. From a reality viewpoint, the idea seemed preposterous, but then he did not intend to deal with it on any level except the intrapsychic. In this case, however the analyst's insistence on remaining at the intrapsychic level was experienced by the patient as demeaning and as a refusal to seriously acknowledge what to her were important, even vital, needs (McDougall 1979). The analyst then realized how miserable and vulnerable the patient felt, and he was afraid that she would either leave treatment or have a psychotic break if he did not accept her painting. He was aware, even then, that his acceptance was partly motivated by guilt in that he had initially treated her demands as superficial, not having recognized how truly desperate she was.

Nevertheless, the situation became increasingly serious for both the analyst and his other patients. He did not like the changes she had intruded into the consultation room, and she would not accept the formal conditions of analysis as presented by the existing therapeutic ambience. She had to mold it to suit her idiosyncratic needs. She also had to maintain control by dictating how the concrete setting should be constructed, but, most important, she had to make her presence felt. She had to make an impact. Unfortunately, her impact penetrated many boundaries, including those of the analyst and several other patients. The dilemma seemed irresolvable, but the analyst had no other course than to restore the setting the patient had rejected.

The analyst returned the painting and, to be consistent, told her that she could not bring her own pillow nor take the blanket home. He explained in detail how he had to create a therapeutic setting in which he could comfortably work. He went on to explain that he had felt threatened in his autonomy, and that the changes in the office threatened the integrity of other patients. The patient angrily responded that she always had to be concerned about the feelings of others; no one cared about her except to use her as a vehicle to soothe themselves. She then angrily terminated treatment. The therapist regretted this hasty, impulsive, premature ending, but he had not known how else to handle this episode while still retaining his composure and maintaining the treatment of his other patients.

The patient sought other therapists, but none of them was able to keep her in treatment. They rejected her demands, although in some instances she did not voice them until she had been in treatment for almost a year. After two years she returned to her former therapist and reluctantly accepted the setting without insisting too much on altering it.

* * *

It is not always possible to learn something definitive from a transference–countertransference dilemma that will help us deal with similar patients. With this patient, one can immediately ask whether the therapist should have initially refused to change paintings. That is what I would have done and, thereby, would not have been entrapped by my countertransference reactions. I would have had some reaction to her insistent demands, but as long as I did not take action, I believe I would have been able to deal with this interaction on an intrapsychic level.

This patient was presumably unable to tolerate being refused or having her demands analyzed instead of immediately met, as evidenced by her experiences with therapists after she left the analyst she had been seeing. She returned to him, perhaps because he had tried to meet her conditions whereas other therapists had summarily rejected them. Does this mean that his supposed error in responding to her wishes was really "correct" in that she was able to return to treatment? If this decision were technically appropriate, it is not likely that the analyst would wittingly allow himself to become involved in such an arrangement again; thus the treatment process would, of necessity, be disrupted. This means that what might technically be required is generally impossible to achieve—an irresolvable conflict.

In the next chapter, I will describe clinical impasses that occur as the outcome of a specific structural defect: the inability to form and hold a mental representation. The patient I have just described is similar in many respects, but, unlike the patients to be discussed later, she had some capacity to maintain internal representations of external percepts and experiences, although she had an extremely precarious and friable self-representation. She was sufficiently structured, however, that she was able to move into the external world and seek from other therapists what she felt she needed.

This patient is similar, in a very subtle sense, to those patients I described earlier in this chapter who have to relive infantile failure. They have to create a situation in which the failure is experienced in the analytic setting. This patient was different from the patient who felt unprotected in that she did not attack the analyst for failing her, nor did she express any disappointment in the treatment prior to registering her demands. In fact, she was able to be gratified and to express appreciation for what the treatment had provided. She had been able to push herself into the setting to the point that, at some level, she felt she owned it. It was learned that she had to constantly push herself toward her parents in order to get them to acknowledge her existence; according to the patient, they never did. Much of her behavior could be understood in terms of such a struggle, which in essence consisted of her marking her territory and then being evicted from it by her parents. They did not take her seriously and invested their energy in projects and social activities.

The situation with her analyst was based on a delicate balance. To some extent, he was in a state of grace, as the patient later stated, when compared with her interim therapists. First, his ability to give her some gratification had made her feel that he was accepting her as she really was. Then she tried to possess the analytic setting and make it her territory. It was inevitable that she would fail, and she found this repetition unbearably painful and frightening. I surmise that because the analyst had already established a fairly satisfactory relationship with her, she was able to return to treatment despite her utter desolation at his refusal to continue to go along with her.

She did not have such a base with the other therapists, who must have sensed her threat to their milieu and thus, were unable or unwilling to form a bond with her. Her analyst learned that she had intruded on her subsequent therapists from the very earliest sessions by giving them books and articles to read so that they could understand her better. She taped descriptions of her dreams, and she wanted to play the tapes rather than talk about the dreams. She also read poetry and notes she had written to them. Some of her therapists had stopped her and others had gone along with her. She terminated immediately with the former therapists and became more intrusive with the latter by making demands similar to those she had made on her first analyst.

Again, these patients may create irresolvable impasses based on their need to re-create and then change their infantile environment in the analytic setting. They attempt to construct a holding environment based on overcoming infantile rejection. In order to achieve this, they have to assault some of the formal aspects of the analytic setting; yet, in the repetition, they create conditions that the therapist must necessarily reject. This rejection is then experienced by the patient as a reflection of the infantile rebuff. If the therapist attempts as much as possible to relate to the patient's needs, even though he will eventually fail, the patient might be able to tolerate the constriction inherent in the analytic relationship. As occurred with the patient described, building such tolerance might require occasional interruption of treatment.

5

Countertransference and Specific Structural Defects

Countertransference responses and treatment impasses often depend upon the particular psychopathology with which the clinician is dealing (Giovacchini and Boyer 1975). Patients with character disorders evoke a variety of disruptive reactions that, in a manner of speaking, overlap; that is, they are not characteristic of any particular diagnostic category, either alone or in combination (Bleger 1967). For example, as we discussed, intrusiveness and concreteness are not confined to specific diagnostic boundaries. These traits are found both in neurotic patients and in patients suffering from the character disorders (structural psychopathology) (Giovacchini 1979a), although they are more conspicuous and rigid in the latter group. Countertransference responses will vary, but the basic disruptions that analysts feel also have some homogeneous qualities.

These countransference disturbances can be grouped into three overlapping and interrelated categories. Certain patients invoke threats to 1) the analyst's professional self-representations, 2) the analyst's mode of operation, and 3) the analytic setting. These three categories are aspects of the treatment setting and of the analyst's professional orientation. Other elements of the therapist's psyche may be drawn into the maelstrom of technical complications and disruption but these are usually related to the various aspects of the professional ego ideal.

Countertransference disturbances brought about by attacks on the therapist's professional orientation are often evoked by patients with particular types of structural psychopathology that are commonly encountered but often go unrecognized. The fact that they are unrecognized contributes significantly to the magnitude of the technical difficulties. These structural defects transcend diagnostic boundaries but are restricted to the character disorders, including schizoid states, borderline personality disorders, and character neuroses (Giovacchini 1979a, 1986). The clinical material that follows emphasizes the role of a specific defect as a disruptive therapeutic influence. The type of disruption created is not particularly different from those discussed in previous chapters. As stated, the disruptions are the outcome of attacks on the analyst's professional orientation, but the unique features of the disruptive interaction are determined by specific ego defects (Blum 1986) and affect both therapeutic style and the analytic setting.

DEFECTS IN SELF-ESTEEM REGULATION AND MENTAL REPRESENTATIONS

These patients share with previously described patients the lack of a cohesive self-representation. It follows that they would have difficulty maintaining self-esteem, sometimes to the extent that they cannot function. These patients have severe character disorders that are accompanied by a variety of ego defects. The inability to form and hold mental representations is prominent and is reflected in the tenuous construction of the self-representation, which, in turn, determines the instability of the identity sense (Erikson 1959).

Unlike the alcoholic hostess discussed in Chapter 4, these patients usually openly manifest the primitive features of their psychopathology. However, some have adopted overcompensatory defensive stances that make them appear to be better integrated than they actually are. At best, this is a transient, unstable false-self organization that rarely obscures the primitive, vulnerable underlying psychic state. In contrast, there is a group of patients who can maintain a somewhat cohesive false self and thereby produce spurious self-esteem as long as they can replenish emotional supplies with intense contacts with the external world. The latter constitute sustaining narcissistic replenishments (Kris 1983).

A housewife in her late 40s sought therapy because she was unhappy and vaguely dissatisfied with life. She had never felt comfortable with herself, but after menopause, her world became grey and markedly unsatisfying. Her husband had been her great admirer, but now he was unresponsive and indifferent to her.

When I first saw her she was quite distraught. Her speech was agitated and accelerated. At the same time she had an imperious, demanding quality, which was in sharp contrast to her obvious insecurity. She made it clear that she was not the type of patient who would tolerate analytic silence and that I would have to actively participate in the relationship. I felt a mild wave of resentment at her attempt to dictate how I was to behave toward her, but this reaction was considerably mitigated by her obviously desperate, needy demeanor.

During her youth, she had achieved a modicum of success as an actress. She was not a national celebrity, but she was well known in local acting groups and had starred in many productions at nearby theaters. She was a fairly good dancer and reputedly had a pleasant singing voice. After she formally left the stage, she continued to use her talent in various actors' clubs and in charity and country-club productions. She received considerable praise, and most of her friends and associates thought of her as attractive and charming. She was socially active and very much in the limelight.

Despite her ostensibly exciting, fulfilling life, the patient exhibited much insecurity. She had become very aware of feeling vulnerable and helpless. In retrospect, she recognized many desperate elements in her activities with friends and colleagues. She realized that she could neither be alone nor tolerate peace and quiet. She had to be constantly on the move and in the midst of people. Her weekends were planned months ahead of time and she had scheduled New Year's Eve parties for at least five years in the future. Each morning she would check her appointment book for information about which of her friends would be home at particular times. It was as if she had to have several people available in case she felt the need to call them. She usually did not call, but she had to know that someone was there. She did not know why she needed them to be there, but if there was no one she could contact, she became quite agitated and anxious, sometimes to the point of panic. This seldom happened, however, because she was usually able to find at least one person, and often more, to be on hand. Her large group of friends included not only her acting colleagues but also many physicians and psychoanalysts.

She was a promiscuous name dropper and directed this propensity toward me by speaking of the many prominent analysts who were part of her intimate social circle. My annoyance was mild and fleeting, because I eventually concluded that this was less an attempt to be condescending and patronizing and more an appeal for admiration. As I learned about her past, I understood why she needed to be surrounded by admirers.

An extraordinarily pretty child, she had been hired as a model. She was the star of school performances. Her parents, especially her mother, basked in her glory. Because of her modeling, she made a considerable amount of money. Her mother often asked her daughter to perform for guests, who were apparently delighted to watch and responded with much applause and praise. The patient described her childhood as blissful: She was always at center stage, the recipient of praise and admiration. She believed that everyone loved her. She continued to be surrounded by an adoring audience through high school and college, where she was the star of some rather elaborate productions. She was noticed by talent scouts and became a member of several theater groups.

She met her future husband in one of these acting groups. After making him wait several years, she finally accepted his ardent proposal of marriage. He gave up the stage and became moderately successful in business. She continued performing with her local groups and blamed her husband for pinning her down with a house and children so that she could not become a famous celebrity. Later, in treatment, however, she ruefully wondered whether she really had the kind of talent required to achieve worldwide acclaim. Now that the world, especially her husband, had, in a relative sense, stopped being an enthusiastically appreciative audience, her narcissistic equilibrium was disrupted and she felt vulnerable and anxious. Menopause was also threatening in that she could no longer maintain an image of herself as a sexually desirable young woman. Losing her youth was extremely traumatic, and she went to great pains to appear young. She even had plastic surgery.

In my office, she presented a mixed demeanor of a narcissistic, self-contained woman and a pathetic, abandoned little girl. Her superior, histrionic, self-admiring stance seemed to be a compensatory pose to defend against her basic sense of loneliness and isolation. It was as if she were desperately seeking to continue viewing the world through rose-colored glasses. This attempt dominated and dictated her approach to therapy. When I asked her to lie down on the couch, she vehemently refused. On the surface, she was angry because I had expected her to lie down, but it was also apparent that she was frightened at the prospect. I sensed her fear and felt only momentarily irritated at her adamant refusal. I rather quickly adjusted to her sitting up and decided that I would try to analyze her even though she was not on the couch.

Throughout the course of analysis, the patient revealed her intense insecurity; in spite of all the acclaim she had received, she had extremely low self-esteem. She had unconsciously learned that in order to be acknowledged, she had to perform. She had to be admired; it was the only way she could be reassured that she existed. On the surface, she appeared to be a classic narcissistic personality, but as is often the case with such character defenses, she felt basically empty. Her self-representation was amorphous, and when she was not in the spotlight, she felt dead. Only by performing could she be reassured that the external world would relate to her and give her a sense of being. Otherwise she would feel abandoned, worthless, and ugly.

The initial treatment impasse that caused her to refuse to lie on the couch was due to her inability to view the infantile ambience as separate and distinct from the current world, which included the treatment situation (Boesky 1983). This occurs to some measure with all patients, but her incapacity to make such distinctions was greater than usual. In extreme situations, this inability constructs a psychotic transference (Gill 1984–1985).

The patient did not realize that her refusal to lie down on the couch was the outcome of an infantile adaptive pattern designed to maintain a cohesive self-representation and to compensate for an ego defect. Inasmuch as she demanded of me the fixed, constant, and intense admiration that she required to exist, she was viewing me strictly in terms of an infantile object relationship. She experienced lying down as a danger and not as a reaction that should be analyzed. She did not perceive her refusal as a transference phenomenon. This inability to distinguish between transference and reality is sometimes referred to as a transference psychosis. This patient was not psychotic in the traditional sense, however, in that her reality testing was generally intact. I emphasize that it was *generally* intact because her ego defect caused her to have idiosyncratic perspectives about some segments of the external world.

This patient demonstrates specific absences of various structural configurations. In order to maintain self-esteem and a cohesive self-representation, she needed external reinforcement.

Similarly, she could not form or hold a mental representation without the presence of an external object (Boesky 1983). She did not require an actual presence; as long as she knew that a friend could be reached by telephone, she could maintain a mental image of that person sitting by the telephone. She had to keep me within her visual sphere; otherwise I would disappear. Not having developed object constancy, she demanded eye contact (Fraiberg 1969). She had to see me in order to hold an intrapsychic representation of me. She was not able to construct a solidly entrenched introject of an external object. She needed to hang onto external objects, however, because they acted as organizers that enabled her to feel a sense of identity.

Compensatory phenomena must be considerably more intense than ordinary self-esteeming object relationships. For a partially deaf person, auditory stimuli have to be louder than usual in order to be perceived. Similarly, my patient needed constant external objects in order to register a minimal intrapsychic representation.

The intensity of the relationship—which for my patient meant constant availability or presence—leads to similar heightened and exaggerated intrapsychic responses. In order to maintain a coherent self-representation and a definitive identity sense, my patient had to experience herself in an exalted, idealized fashion. A needy person idealizes a prospective caretaker or rescuer. Because they feel so deprived, they require an omnipotent relationship to fill their previously unmet needs. Inasmuch as these are insatiable, infantile needs, even an omnipotent caretaker will eventually disappoint them. My patient felt the same cosmic emptiness because of her amorphous self-representation. She overcompensated by constructing an exalted, celebrity-oriented self-representation.

Borderline patients are characterized by defects in the ego's executive system and difficulty in adapting to the external world

(Giovacchini 1979a, 1986). Although patients who suffer from character disorders have problems in all ego systems, different clinical entities reflect different disturbances in certain ego subsystems over and beyond general disturbances of ego organization. This patient's difficulties focused on the perceptual apparatus, which made self- and object-representations unstable (Jacobson 1964, Sandler and Rosenblatt 1962). This led to corresponding problems in the development of affects.

Some patients have difficulty in discriminating feelings. They report that they do not feel genuine emotions. My patient stated, later in treatment, that she did not believe she had ever felt real feelings. As an actress, she had learned the facial expressions and gestures that accompany the expression of emotions, but subjectively she felt nothing. She even had trouble describing what *nothing* meant. At most, she conveyed that there was a blunting of affect.

In fact, there was a blunting of all inner sensory perceptions. She apparently had a high threshold for pain; as an adolescent, she had nearly died of a ruptured appendix. At the time she was aware of some abdominal sensations, but they were neither localized nor painful. The surgeons were puzzled and could not make a diagnosis. The pathology was detected when they did an exploratory laparotomy.

As has been true with other patients suffering from structural psychopathology, this patient never had distinct inner sensations that would discriminate bodily needs, such as hunger, thirst, fecal and urinary pressure, and temperature regulation. She seldom felt cold or warm and was able to tolerate wide ranges of temperature. She viewed herself as an unfeeling person, but her psychic structure and superego development were sufficient to cause her not to like herself because of her lack of feeling. She had formed a rudimentary ego ideal, and her self-image fell far below its standards. Although she was generally unfeeling, she was able to feel miserable, but at times she doubted how sincere even this feeling was. Knowing something about psychiatric jargon, she frequently referred to herself as a sociopath.

Analysts focus on the patient's view of reality and refrain from imposing their reality onto the patient. This lack of imposition is the essence of the analytic nonjudgmental stance. Clinicians need to see the world through patient's eyes. When the patient's defects are perceptual, however, analysts may be momentarily or profoundly unable to establish an analytic ambience that allows them to make the patient's perceptions their own.

Paradoxically, to perceive as the patient does is not particularly difficult for many therapists when the perceptual distortion involves external perceptions. Patients may view the world in their own idiosyncratic fashion; in extreme cases, this includes the formation of delusions. The analyst can perceive the patient's reality even in the delusional world, as long as he does not participate or act in a way that prevents his getting back into his own world (Giovacchini 1979a). In order to retain this perspective, the analyst often must climb back onto the observational platform of the psychoanalytic setting. This may be difficult with some psychotic patients, but, as a rule, the analyst's inner organization is not particularly threatened by the externally directed delusion. The delusion is a distortion of a familiarly constructed external world.

It is when analysts become involved with the patient's inner world—the intrapsychic forces that compel the patient to replace the familiar world with their primitive orientations and parts of the self—that they are entering dangerous territory. This is a countertransference hazard that therapists face not only with psychotic patients; patients like the one I have just described can provoke similar disruptions.

My patient had to construct the outer world so that she could continue to receive infantile gratification—or, more precisely, narcissistic replenishment—in order to maintain a sense of self. But these experiences of intense admiration replenished an unstable, evanescent false self; they were not directed toward the creation of self-esteem and self-confidence. She had been used as a transitional object for her mother, and her mother's seeming ministrations were meant to enhance herself, not her daughter. These interactions represented false caretaking and specious nurturance and soothing, so they were not internalized and integrated into the general ego organization.

Like patients suffering from privation, this patient lacked an endopsychic representation of a satisfying nurturing matrix that could be expanded as constructive experiences were incorporated into its structure, leading to higher levels of developmental integration (Winnicott 1963a, 1963b). My patient did not suffer from privation to the same degree as did patients who can be described in terms of primitive mental states. Her organization, from a developmental point, was relatively primitive, but she received some amorphous gratification from the outer world, even though it was at the false-self level. Nevertheless, she found it difficult to constructively integrate helpful experiences and retain them as introjects that would be assimilated by both the perceptual and executive ego systems.

To enter the inner life of the psychotic patient can be at best painful and at worst devastating. In working with severely disturbed patients, therapists often have to partially regress with them so that they function as a resonance board that will help the analyst at some deep empathic level to comprehend primitive mental processes. This understanding can lead to interpretations that may be liberating for both patient and therapist (see Part III). Giving up our usual hold on reality and letting our primary process dominate can be disruptive and personally distressing as we open up areas of our personalities that we would rather let remain dormant (Lichtenberg 1986).

This type of disruption is an example of an idiosyncratic countertransference response that applies only to the content of our disturbance. The frequency of such disturbances, however, would place them in the category of homogeneous countertransference, but whatever we call them, they can reach the proportion of a countertransference catastrophe.

In such situations, analysts relinquish their hold on the world of reality. This relinquishment of logical thought can be considered analogous to the evenly suspended attention Freud (1913) recommended as a method of relating to patients. With psychotics, the suspension of reality is carried to an extreme; not only is logical thought set aside, but all the subtle supportive anchors that connect us with the external world must be, for the moment, given up.

To emotionally understand some primitive orientations may involve too great a sacrifice. In order to fully appreciate mental processes governed by distorted and defective ego states, we may have to suspend all hope and even relinquish our capacity to return to our own world. By way of analogy, I refer to the efforts of some anthropologists, sociologists, and novelists to appreciate what it is like to be a member of a lower economic class or a minority group. Some have worked in the fields or as dishwashers, and others have taken drugs to darken their skin so that they appear to be black. Although they may learn something about their difficult external circumstances, they still miss the essence of what it means to be poor or to be black. These investigators are on a temporary sojourn; they will return to their world and they know it. To fully appreciate poverty or racism, one has to give up hope of ever being anything but a field worker, a dishwasher, or a black person. There *is* no other world, and that is a position that is too dangerous to accept.

The external world is a universally cohesive force. Our milieu must support our adaptations. By demanding a replenishing environment to sustain themselves, patients who are unable to hold mental representations can subtly destroy the supportive elements of the therapist's milieu. By forcing their analysts into their inner world, they dehumanize them. Because they partially relinquish secondary-process thinking and, consequently, their rational environmental supports, these therapists may feel considerable internal disruption of their own. The disruptive countertransference can become very intense as patients impose upon and, at times, invade their analysts with their primitive orientations and mental processes.

Depending on the patient's psychopathology, a variety of circumstances can surround the tumultuous transference–countertransference interaction that frequently characterizes relationships with patients who cannot integrate nurturing experiences or hold mental representations and structuring affects. For example, the actress patient constructed a transference based on the reversal of roles, a fairly common situation in the treatment of patients suffering from ego defects. Her mother had basked in her daughter's limelight, but she related to her as if she were an inanimate, nonhuman (Searles 1960), transitional object. Although the mother doted on her daughter and seemed to be admiring and giving, she did not acknowledge her as a person in her own right. Consequently the child's development of feelings and needs and a true sense of being alive was thwarted. In turn, the patient now treated her admirers and her analyst as if they wer nonhuman transitional objects who existed to act as her handmaidens. This was not obvious, since she was not overtly arrogant or imperious as is so common among patients with overcompensatory narcissistic disorders. On the contrary, most of the time she was timorous and overtly anxious, but over many months of treatment it became apparent that she had no consideration whatsoever for my feelings. I felt as if I were a genie who had to be constantly present and that I had to subjugate all my needs to hers. She expected that I would not take any time off for trips or holidays unless she was away on a vacation at the same time. She would go into rages when I left, and she quit treatment on several occasions, but she always returned.

* * *

Another patient who had similar problems tried to dominate my world with hers, which was the product of unintegrated object representations and a transitional-object self-representation. She had been named after her mother's favorite doll. At the beginning of treatment, she wanted to know exactly when I would be out of town, and then she would fill her sessions with complaints about my upcoming trip. I tried to understand her needs and to remain tranquil during her onslaughts.

At the point when I was seeing her six times a week, it happened that I was suddenly and unexpectedly required to take a short trip. I was scheduled to leave after her session on Saturday and would return Sunday evening before her Monday morning session. I had decided not to tell her about this trip since it would not affect her schedule. Consequently, I was astonished when she walked into my office that Saturday morning and angrily asked me where I was going. I asked, with some embarrassment and hesitation, what made her think that I was going anywhere. She immediately replied that I was better dressed than usual and that I had not dressed that way for her, and furthermore, that I had the look of anticipation of someone who was going to do something outside of his usual routine. Upset and irritated at having been found out, I defensively asked her what difference it would make since my leaving would in no way affect the frequency or continuity of our sessions. She calmly replied that I simply did not understand, to which I retorted that she expected me to remain in one spot, twenty-four hours a day, seven days a week. In a soft voice she said, "Of course."

I finally appreciated the depth and intensity of her character disorder, but I also felt uneasy and I understood how rational her viewpoint seemed to her, and I realized that I would have to make her viewpoint my own if I were to maintain a therapeutic perspective. Still, it was not comfortable to travel in her autistic world of inanimate objects. Paradoxically, she could feel alive only if she dehumanized those around her, treating them as she had been treated in her infantile world. If I were to have therapeutic value, I had to allow her to use me as a transitional object and suspend my autonomy as well as deny my needs. I could not submerge myself completely, of course, and carried on as usual, but I had to be prepared to face her wrath without reacting to its content. At times, this was difficult to do.

Another factor that often leads to painful countertransference reactions is based on the patient's desperate need to be understood. In contrast to the tumultuous reactions evoked when patients want us to become involved with their external milieu, these responses are brought forth when patients attempt to draw us into their inner world. Because these patients have never been acknowledged or understood as persons in their own right, they attempt to get special attention from their therapists. Analysts sometimes become complacent about their patients, especially if they are not obstreperous and appear to be relatively comfortable. In these circumstances, the therapist may lose sight of how severely disturbed some patients are, preferring to believe that they have considerably more ego integration than they actually do. Often, the therapist's attitude is partially stimulated by the repetition compulsion; he unwittingly assumes the role of the indifferent, obtuse, uncaring parent.

Unable to tolerate this seemingly calm atmosphere indefinitely, the patient feels compelled to do something drastic to upset it. In a sense, these patients have to introject the therapist and then put parts of themselves into the therapist. This process could well be a variation of projective identification, but instead of projecting and then identifying, the patient begins by introjecting and then allowing—or in some cases forcing—the therapist to identify with him. This is not just a projective form of countertransference (Racker 1953). For a time, the patient feels that he carries the therapist inside of him, but as is the case with all internal object representations, the analytic introject is poorly formed and unstable.

The therapeutic environment may appear chaotic, tense, and seemingly destructive to both patient and therapist. From a psychic viewpoint, however, these patients are struggling to survive. By reversing roles, they are seeking mastery and trying to establish a sense of autonomy and aliveness. Making their analysts part of themselves serves a similar function. It is an attempt to construct an internal, representational world (Sandler and Rosenblatt 1962) that enhances ego integration and psychic structure and could eventually lead to a cohesive self-representation. In order for the patient to achieve this, he has to make an impact, and this often means that the analyst has to experience the primitive and painful elements of the patient's personality. Instead of seeing them as being better integrated than they actually are, these patients want their analysts to participate in and share their disorganization.

Analysts, in turn, reflexively resist being drawn into the maelstrom of chaos and agitation. My patient introduced her frame of reference, which included my constant presence; her world was at total variance with mine, and I was at first incredulous that she should have such expectations. To become part of her representational world would have been a painful and dehumanizing experience. I would have been deprived of my sense of autonomy and my ability to move freely in my familiar world.

* * *

Another patient became furious with his therapist when she decided to extend her vacation for three days. He was not experiencing a crisis at the time—in fact, his life was relatively serene—but he felt that his therapist was unfair and thoughtless. He resented the fact that all his life he had had to subjugate his feelings to the whims of others. When his analyst, according to him, arbitrarily decided to leave, she expected that he would be dutifully waiting for her to return.

He was always waiting for someone to return, as was the situation with his parents, who had frequently left him behind when they went on innumerable trips and vacations. He ranted and raved against psychoanalysis and psychoanalysts who remained uninvolved with their patients and who failed to appreciate the depths of their misery and isolation. His anger mounted to the degree that he issued an ultimatum. He had accepted with great reluctance that the therapist would go away over the holiday weekend, but she had to be back on the following Monday and not extend the vacation the extra days. He knew that the therapist was taking the extra days because her husband had to attend some meetings and he wanted his wife to accompany him, but this made no difference. In fact, it made matters worse, because his mother had rationalized her trips by stating that her husband needed her to go along with him.

On the surface, the patient's demands were unreasonable,

but, in view of his experiences of being abandoned and of being treated as a transitional object, they made sense. At least, they were understandable as a consequence of his infantile milieu. Nonetheless, it was difficult for his therapist not to react to the content of his protestations and not to feel some resentment. She did her best not to be irritated with him and tried to explain his attitudes on the basis of infantile experiences. This made no difference to the patient; he understood perfectly, perhaps better than the therapist, the antecedents and bases for his feelings, but it did not matter. He angrily terminated treatment.

He then sought another analyst who was professionally close to his therapist and whose treatment philosophy was similar. He asked for an appointment on the Friday after the holiday, which would have been part of a four-day weekend. The other therapist had planned to leave town for these four days, so he offered the patient an appointment for the following Monday. The patient could easily have arranged the time, but he rejected the offer. He had to be seen during the vacation weekend by the second analyst; nothing else would do. The second analyst did not give a second thought to the prospect of canceling his plans just to see the patient.

Some years later, with still another analyst, it was learned that he really had expected both therapists to give up their trips in order to meet his need to be seen. Moreover, his need was based on the fact that their plans would be drastically disrupted and that many persons would be disappointed. His expectation had the qualities of a psychotic transference. Another part of him recognized that despite his protestations, he was not going to have it his way, because he believed—accurately—that his therapists did not have a total investment in him. They felt it necessary to preserve their lives outside of treatment and to avoid being totally drawn into his inner world. This can be justified by analysts' needs to be comfortable in their own external milieu so that they can survive the vicissitudes of their patients' primitive needs.

This patient was able to create a dilemma that would inevitably frustrate him and that contributed to a view of the world as unreliable and untrustworthy. Inasmuch as he had some reality elements to support his contentiousness, he was not traditionally paranoid, nor was his transference based entirely on delusional distortions, as would be the situation with a typical psychotic transference.

In a sense, it is unfortunate for patients that we have a natural aversion to having our lives so completely controlled. The patient is acting out of desperation to create a world that will give him a feeling of substance. The tragedy resides in the fact that no one can abide by his conditions, and any analyst who could would have no substance. The patient would be unable to use him as a model for eventual introjection.

This patient is both similar and different from the patient who wanted to dictate the decor of the consultation room (see Chapter 4). Both patients needed to master the infantile environment by changing it. Both also made peremptory demands, but for the "interior decorator," as she could later humorously refer to herself, the need was not as encompassing. She had some capacity to form and hold mental representations as well as to structure feelings. Her demand was to change the setting and to have the analyst acknowledge her, but she did not insist that he completely change his orientation; she wanted him to accept hers but not necessarily to give up his own.

In contrast, the patient just discussed could not maintain internal object relations and was deficient in structuring affects. He could recognize only one frame of reference and expected his therapist to live within its confines. Understandably, such a demand can evoke painful countertransference feelings that can be a reaction to more than just limitations on autonomy. As the analyst is being coerced into giving up his usual sustaining adaptations, he is also being submerged by the misery inherent in the patient's psychopathology. This goes beyond the professional self-representation and mode of operation. It digs deep into the core of the therapist's sense of being.

* * *

In Chapter 2, I gave the example of the therapist who suffered an existential crisis as the patient projected feelings of emptiness into him. What I am about to describe refers to deeper primitive orientations, and the resultant countertransference reactions are much more disruptive. The patient's internal lack of structure follows a destructive and self-destructive path, and the analyst is engulfed by the patient's turmoil. The analyst is not assaulted by projections. Rather, he is engulfed by the patient, and he feels psychically crushed. What makes matters worse is that these analysts are usually not aware of what is happening. Instead of thinking beings, they have momentarily become a bundle of feelings and reactions.

As previously noted, therapists can lose sight of the severity of their patients' disturbance and tend to see strength and psychic structure that are not really there. The patient has to "teach" the analyst how to view and understand him as he really is by having the analyst, at least temporarily, suffer the same painfully constricting ego defects.

This patient is the same one who berated me for not telling her about a short trip because I did not want to subject myself to her attacks. For a while, I had been able to accept, at least intellectually, her insistence that I had to be in my office twenty-four hours a day, seven days a week. At the beginning of treatment, she had given me a wooden statuette. I liked it and grew fond of it. It had no arms and an amorphous, featureless face; it bore a slight resemblance to a Giacometti sculpture.

I accepted the statuette without hesitation because I strongly felt that I had to accept it if I wanted to treat her. The patient who wanted to change the decor of the consultation room was experienced by her therapist as intrusive. I had no such reactions about the statuette, although, as already illustrated, this patient could be infuriatingly intrusive. Rather, I was glad to have it and felt it was decorative in the alcove next to my chair, where I put it. To my mind, its presence did not disturb the harmony and balance of my surroundings. It was an unobtrusive addition, rather than a jarring alteration. Most of my other patients did not even notice it, and those who did either liked it or offered no comment.

As this went on, I regarded the statuette as part of my decor and I became attached to it. Whenever the patient got angry at me, usually because I had to cancel some sessions for a trip, she would seize the statuette and break it in half. The first time this happened, I was both outraged and shocked, but I soon learned that it was easy to glue the statuette back together. Its weakest spot was at the umbilicus and that is where it would break, making it easy to repair. I would be disturbed at seeing it broken, however, and would regain my composure after I had fixed it. As it was repeatedly broken, I became more complacent knowing I could easily put it back together again.

In Part III, I will discuss how my state of mind reflected the patient's ego defect, her inability to hold a mental representation. The statuette represented the patient, and I required to have it undamaged while it was in my view. To that extent I was similar to the patient; in a symbolic form, I had to have the patient within my sensory sphere if I were to continue to acknowledge her existence. As I became more comfortable within the treatment setting, I must have become too comfort-able and complacent from the patient's viewpoint.

I had not realized that the patient's anger toward me was mounting. I had been somewhat casual in telling her that I would be away for a few days in several weeks. During the session after I had told her about my trip, she angrily denounced me for having no consideration for her. She stated that I ignored her and had no interest in treating her. I demanded that my patients be at my beck and call; I expected that I would be able to leave whenever I wanted to and that my patients would be there when I returned. I was concerned only about my own feelings. The patient was gradually working herself into a rage, which reached its peak when she demanded that I cancel my trip. I could feel my own anger rising, but I said nothing. She interpreted my silence as a refusal to accede to her demands, which, in part, it was. She became so furious that she got off the couch, grabbed the statuette, and threw it into the fire that was burning in my fireplace. I reached my saturation point in response to her destructive action. I jumped up out of my chair and shouted, "Now you've done it!" as I extended my arm in a gesture for her to leave. She became very frightened at my unexpected outburst and ran out of the consultation room. I was angry, anxious, humiliated, and ashamed.

As my senses returned, I remembered that I had a gas fireplace, and all I had to do was flip a switch in order to turn it off. I quickly extinguished the flames and retrieved the statuette from the fireplace. Its base was slightly charred and, as expected, it was broken in two. I glued it back together and then composed myself in order to see my next patient.

The moment I finished seeing my last patient, the tele-phone rang. My patient was on the phone and she simply asked, "How are you?" I replied "I'm all right," to which she responded

"And how is the statuette?" I told her that I had repaired it. She concluded by cheerfully stating "That's fine. I'll see you tomorrow." I felt weary and somewhat depressed, but I was glad that the patient seemed to be doing well.

She was very pleased with herself during our session the next day. She explained that she could not stand my shutting her out and that she had to do something drastic to capture my attention and to keep me from drifting away from her. She accomplished this by evoking in me the same misery, disruption, and isolation that she always felt. I had to know what it was like to lose contact with sustaining internal and external objects, which, in this instance, were represented by the statuette.

In order to understand the patient, I apparently had to descend to the same primitive levels of the mental apparatus that determined her responses to the external world. In so doing, I lost control in the same way the patient often did, and reacted as if my psychic survival depended on the intactness of the statuette. This response was similar to the patient's need to keep external objects within her psychic sphere so that she could maintain some semblance of internal organization. My perceptual and integrative systems were, for the moment, disturbed and malfunctioning in the same fashion as the patient's.

When I emerged from my countertransference regression, I more fully understood her character structure and psychopathology and was thus better able to withstand her onslaughts. I still felt intruded upon and continued to resent some of her imperious demands, but I could also more easily switch into her frame of reference and understand her on her own terms and on the basis of her neediness, misery, and paralyzing anxiety. In the past I had been trying to refrain from reaching down with my psyche into the primitive recesses of the patient's mind. I must have sensed how painful it would be. It was easier for me to see her as a well-integrated, competent person and to relate to her at this structural level rather than give up my secondary-process organization and become involved with her inner chaos.

* * *

In this therapeutic interaction, a highly unorthodox, explosive outburst led to a deeper understanding of the patient and a better treatment relationship. It can be asked whether it was absolutely necessary to weather such a storm in order to establish an effective treatment setting and to conduct successful therapy. This question can be asked about all countertransference reactions that are accompanied by dramatic upheavals and lead to disruptive impasses. Could these painful moments have been avoided? It is possible that therapists who have had sufficient experience with these types of patients can appreciate the extent of their misery and their precarious psychic organization without having to experience it themselves. They might not have to construct defenses against potentially painful countertransference feelings.

These are difficult and, in my mind, still unanswerable questions. We may be navigating between the Scylla of shallow intellectual comprehension and the Charybdis of chaotic, destructive regression. It is conceivable that in some clinical encounters, the sequence of complacency and powerful countertransference feelings may be an intrinsic aspect of the therapeutic process as it re-creates the infantile environment in the context of the repetition compulsion. It may not have to be experienced with the painful intensity I have described, however. Most clinicians are aware that they have had comparatively little experience with these patients in a psychoanalytic framework and that each patient represents a new learning experience. It may be that we have to live through occasional countertransference catastrophes in order to perfect our understanding and develop techniques that will help us survive the treatment and maintain our equanimity. We have to examine both our professional and personal vulnerabilities as they are stimulated by the patient's overcompensatory adaptations.

Generally, these patients have created a false self to defend against and cope with infantile trauma. The surrounding world is modeled after the infantile world, a process I have called *externalization* (Giovacchini 1979a, 1986). Patients seek facets of the contemporary milieu that bear some resemblance to the world of childhood. If they are in treatment, they try to do something similar within the consultation room. The analyst may experience this as threatening because it upsets a personal orientation and presents a different view of reality. The patient introduces an alien frame of reference and expects the analyst to join him in a milieu that is chiefly derived from childhood. These expectations may produce adverse countertransference reactions.

THREATS TO THE THERAPIST'S PERSONAL ORIENTATION

This group of treatment interactions emphasizes conflicts that are related primarily to the construction of the therapeutic ambience. For the purpose of this discussion, the treatment setting must be further divided into several more components that are facets of familiar elements of the therapeutic process. The two components most often referred to by clinicians are the transference–countertransference axis and the holding environment. In the treatment of patients suffering from primitive mental states, many analysts believe the holding environment to be of primary importance in conducting effective treatment (Winnicott 1963).

Within the transference–countertransference context, the analyst's interpretations are similar in effect to the mother's nurturance of her child. Clinicians who treat patients suffering from character disorders—and most of the patients we see do—like to compare the therapeutic sequence with the course of emotional development, because the purpose of treatment is to enable the patient to achieve higher levels of ego organization and psychic structure. Treatment differs from ordinary development, however, in that in treatment, the effects of ego defects must be overcome before the developmental drive can once again be set in motion. Interpretations should be integrated and should lead to enhanced intrapsychic balance and harmony. This occurs within the context of a soothing, holding environment.

The comparison between the treatment relationship and the mother–infant interaction is strengthened as we focus on the interplay of nurturance and soothing on the one hand and interpretative activity and the holding environment on the other. Infants cannot be adequately nurtured if they are not properly held and soothed. They need a calm, loving environment if they are to derive maximum benefit from the nurturing experience. If there are problems in either the nurturing or the soothing components of the mother–infant relationship, the child will develop specific manifestations of psychopathology that will later be reflected in therapy. The countertransference problems in the treatment will reflect difficulties in supplying adequate interpretations or constructing an effective holding environment.

The construction of the holding environment has particular relevance to potential countertransference responses. The analyst's distinct personal style is an important facet of the construction of the holding environment. I believe this personal element is the reason that those analysts who advocate that only patients with good ego strength are suitable candidates for analysis and attribute the success of some analysts in treating patients with primitive mental states to their unique talents and virtuosity at best, or to their character peculiarities and psychopathology at worst. Consequently, the successful treatment of a severely disturbed patient is an idiosyncratic event and need not be pursued further in order to understand the therapeutic interaction. This cavalier dismissal is unfair to suffering patients.

Interpretation is an active process involving a number of psychic mechanisms, including introjection, assimilation, and, finally, integration. The holding environment cannot be so explicitly described. It is an ambience that analysts create to facilitate the integration of interpretations. The analyst's style largely determines the supportive elements of the analytic process. The therapist's nonjudgmental attitude, serenity in the face of disruption and anxiety, stability, and constancy are all responsible for preserving organization and structure in what might otherwise become an unmanageable regression.

Holding qualities become even more difficult to define when we focus on the analyst's capacity for empathy, intuition, and sensitivity to the patient's needs. The principle feature of a successful holding environment is its capacity to soothe the patient and to make inner disruption bearable enough so that it can be understood in an analytic context—that is, so that it can become a subject of interpretation. The therapists' perceptual sensitivity and integrative processes help to create an atmosphere that makes the intrapsychic approach feasible and comfortable for the patient. These activities cannot be concretely described because they are often the outcome of orientations that either are unconscious or are so automatized and integrated that the analyst is not particularly aware of them. In some instances, it is easy to understand how such attributes can be viewed as the special gifts of talented and charismatic therapists.

The analyst's background and character structure are responsible for this personal facet of the holding environment. They contribute to the production of a subtle interaction that introduces an element of reason and security to the treatment setting. It is similar to the mother's humming and rocking as she lovingly nourishes her infant in an atmosphere of calm security.

The supportive aspects of analysis are based primarily on its constant reliability, the focus on the intrapsychic, and the absence of blame and not taking sides with any part of the patient's ambivalence. These features are the essence of psychoanalytic therapy. They stimulate regression and the emergence of dependence. The couch, the frequency of appointments, and the analyst's exclusive attention as to how the patient's mind works provide security and are the intrinsic qualities of Winnicott's (1952) holding environment. According to Winnicott, the holding environment is a setting that can contain the patient's absolute dependence. It is an environment that stresses our faith in the mind's integrative capacities even when the patient is momentarily disrupted and disorganized. The better the integration of the analytic perspective and the analyst's personal orientation, the greater the patient's sense of security, and the better his ability to tolerate regression and to learn from it.

* * *

Winnicott, the analyst who first formalized the concept of the holding environment, seems to have been particularly adept at constructing it on the basis of his unique and creatively sensitive personality. His wife describes his early childhood as particularly gratifying and happy (Epstein and Feiner 1979). Those who have had the privilege of knowing him personally have been impressed by his charm and optimistic enthusiasm. A colleague who was analyzed by him emphasized a childlike, playful quality that Winnicott exuded and maintained even while discussing the grimmest of topics, a quality this colleague found reassuring. Winnicott was apparently able to take him seriously but, at the same time, to maintain a sanguine, hopeful outlook. His humor and wit is evident in his writings and is not at all at variance with the complex conceptual issues he discusses.

Winnicott was able to express salient ideas in a captivating, amusing fashion. For example, in response to a question about why he makes interpretations, Winnicott stated, "For two reasons. One is to let the patient know I am still alive and two is to let him know I can make mistakes." In a simple, witty, but, more important, nonthreatening fashion, he is stating that he has been able to survive the patient's hostility and that he is neither omnipotent nor omniscient. It is perhaps this ability to present serious thoughts in a casual manner that renders the inner life of the primitive mind less ominous and dangerous.

Another element of holding capacity is the therapist's ability to maintain a foothold in his own reality even while being drawn into the patient's inner world as the patient's needs dictate. Analysts can thus preserve their equanimity, and their countertransference reactions, rather than becoming disruptive, can be used for therapeutic exploration. Remaining anchored to reality helps make the journey into the primitive layers of the patient's mind less perilous. ideally, therapists can allow themselves to be absorbed in the patient's chaotic self-representation while, at another level, keeping a cohesive self-representation.

Previously I referred to the professional self-representation; now I am emphasizing the personal sense of identity that encompasses all aspects of the therapist's character structure. Once again I return to Winnicott to illustrate this point. Winnicott, in a clinical monograph, discusses the treatment of a patient who had been periodically depressed and whose behavior had been self-destructive and punctuated by failures (Giovacchini 1972). During a particular session the patient was in a much better mood than usual. He was elated about an achievement, a modicum of success he had enjoyed, and he was enthusiastically telling his analyst about it. After a while he stopped himself and admonished Winnicott for not responding with the intensity he had wished for. Although Winnicott was pleased with his patient's accomplishment, the patient had been hoping for a much more vigorous reaction. Winnicott replied that it was true that he did feel as elated as the patient did, but Winnicott pointed out that when the patient brought his feelings of misery and inadequacy into the consultation room, he also did not feel as depressed as the patient did.

It is curious that Winnicott introduced these statements by writing, "I made an interpretation" and then proceeds with his explanation and reply. I was struck by his introductory phrase because Winnicott is talking exclusively about his feelings and not the patient's. He is making observations not about the patient, but only about himself, or so it seems. Nonetheless, I believe that Winnicott was intuitively correct when he said "I made an interpretation." He was interpreting the limits and qualities of the analytic setting, which, in this instance, reflected his personal contribution to a facet of the holding environment. He was asserting that he had a spectrum of reactions beyond which he could not go, for both professional and personal reasons. He had a range between good feelings and bad, or perhaps, neutral feelings, and the patient could rely on a certain set of responses within that spectrum. This imbued the analytic setting with a high degree of constancy and predictability, which, for this patient, increased his security.

Winnicott could let his responses reflect the patient's needs, but the range of responses had definite boundaries. Anything that the patient brought in, whether a demand or expectation, that exceeded these boundaries could be viewed as transference phenomena. When such limits are set, the patient learns to understand excessive demands or expectations as the manifestations of infantile defenses and adaptations and, therefore, as a subject to be analyzed rather than directly responded to. Thus, the holding environment creates a setting that makes analysis possible.

Analysts have various spectrums of responses, but a range that is either too narrow or too wide can lead to countertransference complications. Too narrow a range can lead to a lack of response, often rationalized as analytic neutrality (see Chapter 6), or to a rigidity that works against the establishment of a holding environment. Especially with patients suffering from primitive mental states, the analyst will not form a bond as long as he does not permit himself, to some extent, to enter and respond to the patient's inner world.

On the other hand, an overly wide range can create such chaos and disorganization that it will eventually disrupt the treatment relationship and cause its collapse. What may begin as a benign countertransference reaction, such as a desire to form an emotionally nurturing bond with the patient, may break the therapeutic boundaries, breach the frame, and destroy the relationship. The therapist usually believes that trying to meet most of the patient's infantile needs is part of a technically ideal therapeutic endeavor. Usually, however, it is a countertransference reaction based on the therapist's personal orientation, an effort to fulfill certain infantile needs and defensive adaptations that are aimed at preserving the analyst's personal and psychic equilibrium rather than the patient's. On the surface, these therapists seem to be dominated by concern for their patients. This may be true in part, but there are other unconscious motivations that intensify their need to be helpful to the point that they eventually lose their professional identity as their personal needs become increasingly apparent. These therapists' heroic responses are not confined to a particular type of psycho-pathology, and in some instances they may be manageable and productive. In most instances, however, their outcome is tragic.

* * *

During a workshop, an analyst was presenting material from a patient who was displaying many obsessive-compulsive symptoms and character traits. Somewhere in the course of his presentation, that analyst casually mentioned that the patient had defecated on the couch. He did not pause at all when he gave us this information and proceeded as if it were a pedestrian occurrence. As the co-chairman of this workshop, I did a double take and interrupted the presenter to ask for more details about this patient's behavior. Since the other members of the group agreed with me that patients' defecating on our couches was not an ordinary occurrence, my further inquiry focused on the unique qualities of this treatment interaction.

The behavior seemed to be outside our spectrum of toler-able reactions and involvements with patients, but well within this therapist's range. In fact, he was somewhat surprised at our apparent lack of understanding and explained that he viewed the patient's excretory behavior as representing progress. Previ-ously, his patient had been extremely rigid and constricted. His body was tense and he was depicted as having tight sphincters. He had relaxed considerably and was able to communicate much more freely, both verbally and somatically. Although we could easily understand this analyst's rationale, none of us was inclined to expand our spectrum to include this type of somatic communication. We also learned, incidentally, that this was the last patient of the day and that the couch was covered with washable vinyl.

This analyst was able to tolerate aspects of his patient's behavior that other clinicians might find awkward and difficult to handle. Nonetheless, the workshop group was able to recognize the therapeutic relevance of this clinical interaction and accepted his psychodynamic conclusions. We wondered why the therapist went to such pains or permitted what we considered to be an assault on the treatment setting. He saw it in a different light and did not consider the decor of the consultation room to be so sacrosanct, especially since this was his last patient and he could clean up afterward. Questioning therapeutic motivation can become a delicate issue. This analyst was obviously highly motivated to treat his patient and, from all appearances, was doing excellent work. To probe his unconscious seemed unjustified and intrusive.

Still, analysts focus on the intrapsychic, and this includes their own, as I have stressed. Heretofore, the countertransference issues discussed have dealt with situations in which analysts have felt disrupted and, for one reason or another, their capacity to deal with patients has been hampered. The treatment issues I am now discussing concern analysts who are willing, perhaps eager, to treat patients who would cause most of us to be reluctant to become involved in or remain in a therapeutic relationship. All the clinical examples I have presented emphasize some aspect of the therapist's dilemma about the continuation of treatment. The following discussion stresses the opposite, but, far from being an ideal situation or a good therapeutic perspective, the therapist's seemingly constructive motivations eventually worked against the treatment process. Such countertransference attitudes usually appear benign and designed for therapeutic benefit, but actually—that is, at more unconscious levels—they are motivated by infantile constellations and conflicts and perhaps primitive defenses and anxieties. The unrealistic aspects of the therapist's treatment expectations will eventually surface and create serious obstacles to the preservation of treatment.

What appears to be a much wider spectrum than Winnicott's is often the outcome of the therapist's unrealistic need to rescue the patient and to assume the role of a savior. The therapist may want to repair damaged parts of himself as he projects them onto the patient, an aspect of psychopathology that M. Klein (1946) described many years ago. Many of these therapists are suffering from intense guilt feelings about having damaged some important person of the past. They react to the patient's abject helplessness by trying to cater to impossible demands. Their attempts are based on the need to make reparation as well as to expiate their fantasied sins by masochistic surrender. There is a reciprocal interplay between the patient's psychopathology and the therapist's, and the potential for countertransference responses is well developed.

Various character structures impel therapists to become involved in difficult and sometimes impossible treatment situations. These constellations are far from universal. Healthy motivations may, in some instances, outweigh psychopathologically induced obsessions to rescue patients and may cause therapists to widen the scope of psychoanalytic practice, as Stone (1963) proposed. These relationships are not always successful, but even when they flounder or fail, there are no dramatic, intense, or painful upheavals. Many patients cannot be treated by the psychoanalytic method, but this may not be possible to predict before treatment begins. The patient and analyst are conducting a therapeutic diagnostic procedure to determine whether analysis is possible—a trial analysis, as Freud (1912a) called it. These relationships are fairly free of disruptive or unrealistic countertransference influences.

It is often difficult to differentiate when analysts are being accommodating to patients because of the intensity of the patient's past deprivations and the severity of psychopathology, or are driven by their own infantile needs—that is, by primitive countertransference elements. This distinction becomes clearer as the treatment becomes stormy. Upheavals may take many forms, a common one being a relationship in which the patient becomes angry and upset despite the analyst's intense ministrations and constant devotion, which eventually causes the therapist to feel frustrated and mistreated. This vicious circle leads to mounting agitation and finally to the dissolution of a therapeutic relationship that may have been doomed from the beginning.

* * *

I supervised a therapist in his early 40s because he was having great difficulty in treating a young woman in her middle 20s. He found her to be a very interesting and intelligent patient and was obviously devoted to her analysis. Because of her erratic demands and sometimes violent behavior, however, he hardly considered the treatment analytic. He equated analysis with a certain degree of orderliness and calm, something that was totally lacking in this treatment relationship. The situation was particularly striking in that she was shy and meek and had found it almost impossible to ask for anything at the beginning of treatment. He had anticipated a "quiet" analysis and was unpleasantly surprised when it turned out to be otherwise.

At first, the analyst was aware of fatherly feelings toward the patient. He thought of her as an injured bird who had to be healed before she could fly once again. She seemed so helpless that it was difficult to understand how she managed to get through the day. Almost everything was a dilemma, and ordinary tasks could drive her to a state of panic. She was able to function at work, but, as she reported, she pursued her activities in a routine, automatonlike fashion. She worked in an environment where drugs were available, and her therapist became concerned when she reported taking dangerous combinations of drugs to calm herself. Her agitation continued to mount.

The analyst became sufficiently concerned that he insisted on hospitalization. This was financially impossible for the patient because her insurance did not cover psychiatric hospitalization. She would have to go to a state hospital, a prospect that neither patient nor therapist considered desirable.

She did not threaten suicide, but her analyst feared for her safety because she seemed to be on a self-destructive course. She was, on one occasion, rushed to the emergency room of a hospital because she had developed cardiac symptoms secondary to hypokalemia as a result of the unwarranted ingestion of diuretics. She also started roaming the streets at night, frequenting bars and having sexual relations with unsavory characters. The analyst viewed her as the self-destructive protagonist of the movie Looking for Mr. Goodbar.

Because he could not hospitalize her to protect her from the dangers she was creating for herself, he suggested that, in addition to her daily sessions, she should call him at a prearranged time every evening. This would reassure him that, at least for the moment, she was safe. He hoped that their telephone conversations would deter her from promiscuous acting out, and they often did, especially when the conversations first started. The patient derived some tranquility from this arrangement, but it did not last.

She again pervaded the consultation room and her daily life with a desperate sense of urgency, and she went back to the bars. She frequently got drunk and, sobbing and agitated, would call her therapist in the middle of the night. He might spend over an hour on the telephone trying to calm her and to persuade her to take a taxi back to her apartment. The frequency of these middle-of-the-night calls increased, sometimes to as many as four a week. Still, the therapist was not aware of being annoyed, although his wife was. He formulated that the patient was reaching a rock-bottom regression which they both had to survive, and he was doing everything he could to ensure that survival. He hung on to the optimistic belief that she had to regress to the most primitive levels so that she could start building up again but, this time, without the impediments created by her traumatically assaulted infantile world.

As much as possible he was emphasizing the adaptive value of this self-destructive, primitive behavior. If the patient could regress to a level that preceded infantile traumatic experiences, then the developmental drive might be stimulated in the direction of acquiring healthy psychic structure, a therapeutic course and objective postulated by Alexander (1927, 1956) many years ago. With this woman, however, it was difficult to ascertain when and if such a pretraumatic moment ever existed. The turbulence of her early world seemed to date back to her birth. Nonetheless, her analyst continued to be patient and even encouraged her to call him rather than acting out her inner turmoil and self-destructive helplessness. We later recognized that he was trying to assume the role of the all-accepting, giving mother who would unconditionally love and care for the patient. At this stage of treatment, I could characterize his countertransference as dominated by good feelings, in the sense that he had strong positive feelings toward the patient and did not feel threatened by her behavior. Instead, he was dealing with it as an intrinsic aspect of the therapeutic process. He had something to work with, but it had to be contained to some degree because her behavior was dangerous.

This could represent an optimal therapeutic perspective,

but most clinicians would immediately feel uncomfortable expending such efforts and making themselves so completely available to their patients. The therapist's benign countertransference must be scrutinized in terms of its defensive elements, which, despite constructive intentions, may eventually threaten and disrupt the therapeutic process. The disruption, in this instance, is based as much on the personal needs of the analyst as on the patient's psychopathology.

As the patient's behavior grew more frenetic, the therapist, who heretofore had had the patience of Job, could no longer maintain his therapeutic calm and equanimity. The telephone calls in the middle of the night had a deleterious effect on his domestic tranquility, and he and his wife also began to resent the prearranged calls. To make matters worse, the patient no longer waited until the appointed time. She started to call at all hours of the day and night, sometimes making as many as twenty to thirty calls a day. Obviously the situation was intolerable, and the analyst tried to put a stop to it. The patient was furious and did nothing to comply with the therapist's limits.

In self-defense, the analyst turned on his telephone answering machine. She filled his tapes with expressions of her rage. She felt betrayed and abandoned, and her demeanor was drastically different. She changed from a frightened, meek, vulnerable, timid lady to an angry, raving monster. She continued her nocturnal forays, getting drunk and, instead of becoming involved in promiscuous sex, getting into fights with the men she picked up. She was frequently badly beaten.

It seemed almost ludicrous to believe that her regressed behavior had a potential for therapeutic benefit as it reached an intensity that made it impossible to continue outpatient treatment. She did two things that were the final straws. As the end of a session approached, she decided that she was not going to leave. She was going to remain all day. Once she had intruded fifteen minutes into the next patient's session, the therapist picked her up and literally carried her out of the consultation room. The alternative would have been to call the police, and he did not want to make a public scene. He felt embarrassed and humiliated as he faced his next patient. The patient returned several hours later and wreaked havoc on the waiting room. She tore up magazines, knocked lamps off tables, and overturned chairs.

This was disturbing not only to her therapist, but also to the analyst who shared the suite and waiting room with him. The therapist reluctantly decided that he could no longer treat this woman, but before making an irrevocable decision, he sought consultation. He canceled all future sessions with his patient but promised her he would call back and further discuss the future of the treatment. She was frightened about his implicit threat to terminate therapy and agreed to abide by his wishes. She also asked for a consultation for herself, and he was glad to refer her to a colleague.

During the therapist's consultation and supervision with me, he provided many convincing reasons to justify his attempts to be available to the patient. Basically he was trying to undo the traumatic rejections of the past by salutary experiences in the present. He was not trying to furnish her with a corrective emotional experience, as Alexander (1961) postulated. He was not assigning a specific role to himself within the transference context. Rather, he was trying to construct a holding environment with specific qualities. The analytic ambience was designed to create a supportive framework that would compensate for, and later help repair, the patient's ego defects. He believed that the treatment relationship would lead to the acquisition of psychic structure by supplying the patient with a constant, reliable holding environment that would heal the traumatic effects of the infantile environment. One would supersede the other.

* * *

What the therapist failed to recognize was that even by acting differently, he was still operating in the frame of reference of the infantile world. If the patient had experienced extreme deprivation in the past, the therapist's attempts not to deprive are, nevertheless, responses to primitive ego states. Patients demanding mother's milk, in severely regressed ego states, may actually want breast milk, but since this is only part of their total character, it will not gratify. Furthermore, mothers mother infants, not adults; when they try to mother adults, difficulties are bound to arise. As has been discussed, therapists can become immersed in their patient's and their own primitive psychic processes, but when this optimally occurs, it is to improve understanding of the nature of psychopathology in order to facilitate the treatment process. The purpose is not to enter the infantile world and attempt to relive it in a reconstructive, nontraumatic fashion.

The purpose of treatment is to convert reality into fantasy, and this occurs in the transitional space (Giovacchini 1986). The patient's maladaptations and symptoms are the outcome of anachronistic emotional orientations and faulty ego functioning. These faulty reactions are remnants of the infantile world that have now become involved in interactions with current reality. Ordinarily, the past and its associated modes of relating become incorporated into the memory system, but, as they are recalled, they are not usually actualized. They are recalled as memories or become incorporated into fantasies. In adult life, these recollections of the past, when elaborated into fantasies, operate primarily as primary-process orientations.

With the neuroses and character disorders, many facets of the past cannot be directly recalled. They remain in the unconscious because they are either repressed or split off. What emerges are derivatives or defensive distortions of infantile traumatic elements that become incorporated into the ego's executive system rather than being playfully and pleasurably elaborated in creative fantasy that can be conceptualized as occurring in the transitional space.

Although many patients suffering from primitive mental states have been raised as if they were transitional objects (Giovacchini 1986), they are incapable of creating a transitional space of their own. There is usually a paucity of fantasy activity, and their approach to both their inner and outer world is markedly concrete. The infantile elements of their personalities do not become elaborated symbolically into combinations of primary- and secondary-process constructs that enhance the functioning of the ego's executive system. Rather, they are expressed either directly by anxiety and insecurity, or reactively, by demands that go beyond the bounds of mature reason. This is the familiar situation of reversal. These patients are unreasonable toward the therapist because the treatment they received was unreasonable. Beside converting passive to active (Freud 1920), they are trying to get what they never had.

Once the therapist directly addressed his attention to the needy parts of the patient, he was creating further obstacles to bringing infantile needs into the transitional space. That is, he was letting the infantile reality intrude into the current reality, and the intrusion eventually became unbearable. It must be emphasized, however, that the therapist unconsciously encouraged the patient to be aggressively demanding by suggesting a telephone appointment, a therapeutic interaction that occurred outside the confines of the consultation room and invaded the privacy of his home. The therapist saw it differently at first, until the patient's intrusive momentum reached catastrophic proportions. Having mixed up frames of reference by not confining the manifestations of the infantile world to the consultation room, the therapist was dealing with the patient's feelings as if they were concrete reality. He was allowing them to enter the contemporary milieu and bypass the transitional space.

The psyche, in the context of object relations, can be conceptualized as moving through three areas: the internal world, the transitional space, and the outer world. In treatment, we attempt to place the patient's material, as it emerges from the inner world or as it is derived from the outer world, usually by projection, into the transitional space. Both the holding environment and interpretative activity operate within this in-between state.

The analyst does not actually hold the patient, as would occur in reality. In the transitional space, psychic elements and relationships are expressed in symbolic form or in fantasies. Although the latter are make-believe, they can nevertheless be gratifying as they are playfully elaborated into pleasurable illusion, just as the child learns to enjoy illusions that later become the bases of play. These activities are not confined to the inner world, since both the child and the patient are engaged in situations outside the self, but they are not, as yet, directed to the outer world as adaptations. It is thus conceptually appropriate to view them as belonging to a transitional world in which feelings of security and invulnerability are prominent. Play eventually leads to a sense of mastery, which will cause the executive system to function effectively and with confidence as the child moves into an external world that extends far beyond the limits of the infantile milieu.

I believe that the analyst I supervised tried to create a holding environment in reality rather than one limited to the transitional space. It is often difficult to reach such a conclusion by examining surface phenomena. Benign and interested analysts can make themselves available to their patients and still not let them intrude into or disrupt their lives. Responding to telephone calls, for example, may be therapeutically beneficial. These interactions are then discussed in an analytic context— that is, in terms of transference projections—and the analysis maintains an even keel. The interactions and their analysis occurs in the context of a therapeutically useful holding environment in which the patient–therapist relationship is confined chiefly to the transitional space.

As the therapist discussed how he related to the patient, it became apparent that his emotional involvement went beyond the desire simply to be a good analyst to his patient. It must be remembered that he volunteered to talk to her each evening on the telephone for a period of time that approximated the length of regular sessions, and that he did not charge her. Perhaps a sensitive therapist might have intuitively perceived the patient's neediness and might have believed that his availability by telephone would prevent psychotic decompensation or an unmanageable regression. Nevertheless, most therapists probably would not suggest a daily call that would significantly cut into their leisure hours and time with their families. The therapist in this case was already seeing the patient daily. If she needed more care, then she should have been hospitalized so that she could be looked after twenty-four hours a day.

There was also a driven quality to the therapist's eagerness to be helpful to his patient. He confessed that he usually felt anxious about fifteen minutes before the scheduled call. He was afraid that she might not call, and then he would worry about what happened to her. It now became apparent that his countertransference reactions included many infantile elements from his own background. The analyst brought his infantile orientations and his past into the current reality. This did not create a holding environment, because the analyst was not exclusively devoted to the patient's problems inasmuch as he was also struggling with his own conflicts, and he had moved from the transitional space into the real world. He was not responding to fantasies; rather, he reacted to her needs as if they could be gratified in the current milieu. In so doing, he was trying to construct a holding environment outside the transitional space, and such an effort was bound to fail. Instead of the patient's needs becoming imbricated into a fantasy system, they were made real by his eagerness to accommodate himself to them.

The therapist's background helped us understand the bases of some of his motivations. His mother was a depressed woman who had committed suicide when he was 4 years old. He had felt considerable guilt because he had not been able to rescue her. He had turned to his needy patients to relive the maternal relationship: By rescuing them, he could finally succeed in what was initially perceived as a failure. Whether the final failure of the therapy was the direct outcome of his repetition compulsion cannot be stated with certainty. The therapy may have foundered because the patient's infantile world dominated the scene and prevented the formation of the transitional space, but the therapist's unconscious undoubtedly also contributed. Much more can be said about the therapist's psychodynamics but such a discussion would not amplify our understanding. Most important was that he was able to accept the contribution of his personal conflicts and needs to the disruption and chaos that forced him to call a halt to treatment.

Clinicians will inquire whether this patient would be treatable in an insight-oriented outpatient setting by even the most qualified and well-adjusted therapist—at least well adjusted to this patient's character orientation. Given that the therapist overextended himself because of unresolved personal conflicts, could the eventual collapse of the treatment have been prevented by another therapist with a different background? I am inclined to believe that it might have been possible to avoid the pitfalls that arose if the patient had been handled differently but, again, this cannot be dogmatically concluded.

The therapist was finally able to contact the patient. He told her that, in part, he felt responsible for the debacle that the treatment had become, but that she had to share some of the responsibility. Her consultant had also pointed out that a therapist has some rights and that patients have some obligations to them if they wish to remain in treatment. The analyst suggested that they declare a six-month moratorium. He frankly admitted that he needed that amount of time to recover from her assaults and to be reassured that her behavior would not get out of control. She, in the meantime, could think over whether she wanted to remain in treatment with him. She protested that she was desperate to remain in treatment, but agreed to wait six months.

The treatment has now been in progress for four years. There are still occasional telephone calls, but they are not scheduled. At times, all the patient needs is to hear the sound of the therapist's voice on the telephone answering machine.

* * *

Infantile needs to rescue or make reparation are not rare among psychotherapists. Because of their own analyses, psychoanalysts should have either worked such feelings through or refined them through secondary-process elaboration so that they could contribute to the formation of the professional self-representation. When these needs have not been sufficiently resolved, they may increase in intensity, because of interactions with patients, to the degree that the analyst loses control. The therapist is often transformed into a caricature of a therapist, and the holding environment that is constructed is, in actuality, a pseudoholding environment.

When pressing forward in an adult psyche, infantile needs are difficult, if not impossible, to gratify in the contemporary milieu. I have heard several patients aptly describe themselves as "bottomless pits": No matter how much they are given, it will never be enough. Infantile feelings are often characterized by their insatiability. It is sometimes inevitable that these needs will be forever unsatisfied, and they frequently lead to self-destructive behavior. This may be due to the impetus of the repetition compulsion and the primary-process qualities of such feelings.

The traumatic past determines the intensity and urgency of primitive demands. As children, many patients with character-ological problems have suffered severe deprivation and priva-tion. They lack a stable endopsychic registration of gratifying experiences. They suffer from an absence of a nurturing matrix, as I have discussed (see Chapter 4), and they feel a pervasive sense of devastating emptiness. Consequently, in a defensive fashion, they may demand that the world take care of them. They need omnipotent nurturance because they do not have the capacity to integrate satisfying experiences. This is similar to the inability of some patients to form and hold mental representa-tions. They make what to us are unreasonable demands in that they insist on our constant presence. Similarly, because of a cosmic sense of emptiness, these patients require an infinite amount of nurturance and even that will not be enough.

As previously noted, analysts are not creating a genuine holding environment when they respond to the content of the patient's demands. To some extent, the therapeutic process provides some nurturance. The exclusive attention given to patients places them in a position of prime importance and approximates omnipotent giving. These are intrinsic qualities of the treatment setting, however. When analysts go beyond the boundaries of this setting, they are running the risk of creating an impenetrable impasse. They are, in a sense, participating in a delusion; that is, they are implicitly promising the patient their unconditional, everlasting devotion, and when they cannot keep this promise, the patient may feel devastated. The inability to fulfill the promise of omnipotent salvation can have catastrophic consequences. The patient just discussed is an example of such an extreme reaction. Sometimes the therapist's efforts are referred to as heroic, and the consequences of such attempts are often tragic.

* * *

A therapist attempted to treat an adolescent patient who had an extremely depriving, assaultive background and whose behavior bordered on delinquency. For some reason, this therapist deliberately tried to undo the traumatic effects of the infantile environment by providing the patient with what he considered an optimum environment in the present. While continuing to see the youth in therapy, he set himself up as a foster parent by bringing the patient into his home. After one week, the therapist found that the patient had hanged himself on a rafter in his garage. This therapist went as far as one could go in providing a supportive environment, but it was not enough. If the patient has been given everything that can be given and he still feels miserable, then he may indeed feel that there is no hope and that suicide is a way out.

This therapist's behavior was obviously so extreme that it is easy to infer that some very powerful countertransference feel-

ings were creating his boundless therapeutic zeal. Yet I have
heard colleagues, after hearing about this event, remark that the
patient committed suicide *despite* the therapist's well-meaning
efforts. They did not consider that it might have been *because* of
the therapist's efforts that the patient had to kill himself. The act
of suicide was most likely an attack on the therapist—revenge on
him for not having kept the implicit promise that the patient
would feel better. Many transference–countertransference interactions include similar psychic currents, but the patient's and
therapist's feelings and attitudes are not so obviously displayed
and acted out.

In many instances it is indeed difficult to distinguish between benign concern and disruptive therapeutic zeal. There is
often a continuum between the two, and the point of no return
is difficult to determine. Nevertheless, it is important that
therapists examine their reactions and behavior. Their approach should be exploratory and noncritical. Otherwise, as
often happens, they become defensive and lose sight of the
various facets of the problems they are confronting and creating.
They may try to justify their responses by developing a conceptual system or model to support them; or, once they recognize
the patient's adverse responses, they may withdraw behind the
mask of analytic neutrality. Frequently, the therapist is retali-
ating because the patient has not been appreciative of his efforts.
This is a reaction to a narcissistic injury or to a dim awareness of
having stimulated a dangerous regression.

The therapist's narcissism has a prominent position in
many countertransference reactions that are reflections of a
personal orientation. These are idiosyncratic reactions in that
they are determined by the analyst's unique past and are indicative of special sensitivities and vulnerabilities. Still, there are
certain sensitivities and attitudes that are found in most therapists, a commonality that warrants further exploration. We are

not simply dealing with the manifestations of the therapist's psychopathology or particular characterological style. The problems I have described are found in many therapeutic relationships: They have assumed a homogeneous quality that goes beyond individual personality attributes. We are all products of our past, and, insofar as there are some similarities in analysts' backgrounds, there may be certain predictable reactions to patients that should be made explicit.

Falling asleep during a session is such a common occurrence among analysts that it can be considered an occupational hazard. This phenomenon cannot be attributed to a specific transference–countertransference interaction. A variety of situations will cause the therapist to defensively withdraw into sleep. Sleep can simply be one possible representation of extreme withdrawal. It is not necessarily directly proportional to the severity of the psychopathological interactions of the transference–countertransference hub. Analysts may fall asleep because of relatively mild provocations—at least seemingly mild. Most likely, these therapists have some especially sensitive areas of vulnerability.

COUNTERTRANSFERENCE AND NARCISSISTIC BALANCE

During a clinical seminar, an experienced analyst reported his difficulty in staying awake while seeing a middle-aged, relatively successful businessman. He was especially puzzled because he did not find the patient demanding or otherwise difficult. On the contrary, the patient was polite and mild-mannered, and hardly ever asked questions. He was apparently content to talk throughout the session and did not expect anything in return. The patient's verbal productions were neither remarkable nor

particularly interesting, but they were meaningful and understandable in a wide context. This patient was able to view his
behavior in terms of unconscious motivation and to explore the
world from a psychodynamic perspective. The analyst's somnolent reactions appeared strange in view of the patient's psychological mindedness. To help us see the clinical picture more
clearly, the therapist taped a session and let us share with him
the impact of his patient's verbal productions.

We all felt immediate sympathy with the analyst as we
listened to the endless, monotonous droning of the patient's
voice. It was an unpleasant, atonal, boring monologue, and it
was easy to understand how a therapist might want to defensively withdraw by falling asleep. The analyst might indeed have
found his own inner world more interesting than the outward
manifestations of the patient's psyche. This comparison of psyches represents a value judgment, however, and perhaps a
somewhat arrogant judgment, as we assume a superior position
relative to the patient. This would certainly be a peculiar
nonproductive attitude, a refutation of technical analytic principles, for clinicians to adopt, and it would doubtlessly lead to
therapeutic nihilism.

As we listened to the tape, we were struck by the inconsis-
tency that we should find psychologically meaningful material —
that is, associations that revealed their unconscious sources —
boring. Some of us were less bored than others, and two
members of the group were intensely interested in what the
patient revealed. We all agreed, however, that the mode of
presentation was tedious. We could understand how the therapist, who had chosen to see his patient four times a week, might
feel the brunt of his patient's communicative style much more
keenly than any of us. We also gradually realized that there were
no manifestations of transference in the material. Not once did
the patient make any direct reference to the analyst, nor could

we detect displacements or symbolic elaborations that might have transference implications. The patient was totally absorbed in his own observations and viewpoints; putting himself in the center of every situation and everything around him served merely to reflect some aspect of his personality. He did not recognize anything beyond his own ego boundaries, which extended widely into the external world. True, in analysis the patient's mind receives the spotlight, but this man was so narcissistically absorbed that nothing existed beyond his psychic sphere.

One of the members of the group had seen this patient at a crowded party, although he had not met him personally. The patient had been talking to another man in an excited, animated fashion with considerable facial expression and gesticulation – a sharp contrast to the droning monologue we heard on the tape. He was apparently discussing in great detail a trip from which he had just returned. As he paused in his narration, the other person began to talk about some similar experiences of his own. The seminar member noted a remarkable change in the patient at that point. He described the patient's transformation as resembling a deflated balloon. The patient remained in the same spot but, other than his physical presence, he was no longer there. Listless and lifeless, he paid no attention to his companion. He looked like a robot that had lost its energy supply. When he started talking about himself, he once again came to life.

We concluded that his therapist must have felt like the person at the party. He agreed that he did not feel any connection to the patient, who was completely invested in himself and did not cathect his therapist. The analyst understood the patient's need for self-absorption, but he nevertheless felt deflated. It was as if the therapist's narcissistic supplies had reached such a low level that he was decidedly uncomfortable as the patient vigorously concentrated on himself. Such an exclusive devotion to the self was experienced as boring, and the analyst would defensively fall asleep.

In Chapter 4, I discussed a patient who ignored my attempts to make an interpretation and caused me to experience an existential crisis. As discussed, this was the outcome of the projection of his inner sense of emptiness and his devalued self-representation. The situation I am now describing apparently did not involve this type of projection, nor did the analyst suffer an existential crisis. The patient apparently related to his analyst as he did to everybody. He used him as an audience to enhance his narcissism, and the analyst was very much aware of how bored he felt.

The therapist was quick to agree with our speculation that he felt shut out because the patient had no consideration for his feelings. Patients, of course, have no obligation to make their therapists happy or to avoid upsetting their narcissistic balance. Nevertheless, analysts are human, and they will react to certain situations regardless of their professional orientation. This analyst found it difficult to give his patient the attention that he should have had in a therapeutic setting. He felt guilty about falling asleep, which he considered to be a dereliction of his analytic obligations. He recognized that he was withdrawing from the patient in the same way that most of us will withdraw from narcissistically oriented but mediocre persons who attempt to convert us into admirers. He understood that he was also seeking revenge. He was thwarting the patient's need for narcissistic enhancement by reactively decathecting him as he slept. The patient was so preoccupied with himself, however, that he did not even notice that he was talking to an inattentive analyst.

The therapist continues to find his patient tedious and from time to time becomes somnolent. He tells us that he manages to stay awake and that he is usually comfortable as he learns more about how his patient is holding together a vulnerable, threatened self-representation by soliciting and demanding narcissistic supplies. The patient maintains a precarious stability through his tenuously sustained, grandiose false self. When he finds himself competing with his patient for narcissistic enhancement, the therapist feels sheepish. At most, he now tends to momentarily identify with his patient's neediness as a means to gain further understanding and make therapeutic progress.

* * *

Narcissism as a mode of relating—or more accurately, not relating—may be either centrifugal or centripetal; that is, it is chiefly characterized by pushing or pulling. The patient just described is an example of the pull type. He focused everything on himself and recognized no one else. If someone, such as the analyst, tried to draw attention to himself, he would immediately pull the spotlight back to himself. Sometimes the patient would completely ignore others when they spoke about themselves or volunteered their opinions. This tendency was especially apparent when his analyst made an interpretation. As happened with my patient (see Chapter 4), he ignored what had been said and continued to talk about himself. The fact that the analyst was also talking about him made no difference. Because the therapist was the person making the interpretation, it was not entirely directed toward the patient. The observations were not completely objective; they were, to some extent, the analyst's opinions, and the patient could not focus his attention on something or someone outside himself. He had to pull attention toward himself, which meant that anything that counted had to be inside and part of his psyche.

Perhaps it is reflective of a fundamental ambivalence that polarities in psychic life tend to be found together and in the same place. As the narcissist pulls attention—or, in terms of psychic energy, libido—toward himself, he is also simultaneously pushing. He is obliterating external objects in order to dominate the scene. It is not enough that he is at the center of the stage: He has to be the only performer, and he achieves this by pushing everyone else off.

Being pushed aside can be experienced as a narcissistic injury, which, in turn, can lead to defensive withdrawal into sleep. Another analyst felt sleepy and would fall into hypnogogic states as a reaction to his talkative patient's high-pitched, screechy voice. He was aware of how unpleasant she sounded, and he did not look forward to their sessions. He also found her to be a domineering, attention-starved woman, but she did nothing to warrant such an impression. He did not view her as intrusive. She was not manipulative and made no demands upon him. She welcomed his interpretations and generally found them useful. Nevertheless, he found the sound of her voice irritating and was frequently overcome by waves of sleepiness.

During a session when the patient was experienced as particularly oppressive, the analyst had a vivid hypnogogic reverie. He fell into a state of half sleep as he was looking at and listening to the patient as she lay on the couch. He then saw himself sitting in a tub of water. The patient's voice sounded like a droning hum rather than a sequence of distinct words, and he could see a stream of water gushing from her mouth and filling the bathtub. He felt himself being inundated as the water level increased, and his anxiety mounted as he feared that he would drown. He rather abruptly pulled himself out of this hypnogogic fantasy.

The therapist was sufficiently frightened that he considered his dream a nightmare. He had been in danger of drowning and he had an intense fear that he would die. His existence was about to be blotted out.

He concluded that his spells of somnolence were precipitated by the patient's pushing herself into the foreground and, thereby, obliterating his psyche. The hypnogogic experience was a concrete representation of a process in which his psyche was surrounded and inundated, and his individuality submerged and extinguished. The imagery of his reverie—submersion in a bathtub—depicted a regressed ego state. The therapist associated this scene with being forced back into the womb, with having never been born.

Again, this therapeutic relationship should be distinguished from the interaction described in Chapter 4, in which the patient was projecting his inner sense of emptiness and nonexistence into the therapist. The somnolent analyst felt bored most of the time, but he did not perceive parts of the patient's mind projected into his psyche. If such a projection had occurred, he probably would not have been bored; rather, he might have been angry, anxious, or disrupted and agitated. Although the patient was actively talking, he had no feeling that she was relating to him. In a sense, it was the lack of projection that bothered him: He could not feel a connection with the patient. She was not flagrantly ignoring his presence, as other patients have done when their analysts become bored and sleepy. Still, the analyst reacted as if she were not acknowledging his presence, which, in her own way, was what she was doing. The patient was the youngest of nine children who had been left to fend more or less for themselves. Her father was a quarrelsome, constantly complaining alcoholic, and her mother was an angry woman who was always shrieking at her children and husband. The parents also screamed at each other. The household was apparently noisy and chaotic, and it was difficult to make oneself heard. The person who shouted the loudest would gain the floor and receive minimal recognition.

The patient had identified with her shrieking mother and with her pushy mode of relating. By drowning others out, she managed to achieve some narcissistic equilibrium. Allowing another person to gain ascendency would cause her to feel submerged and depleted of narcissistic supplies.

This patient is different from the patient who retained his narcissistic stance by tuning himself out whenever someone else tried to express his individuality. She did not withdraw; she did not pull away as he did. Rather, she filled the room with her presence. Instead of pulling, she pushed, and the analyst reacted to her narcissistically sustaining mode of relating by feeling threatened as he unconsciously experienced a depletion of his narcissistic supplies. He consciously felt the patient's stifling dominance even though she overtly expressed only one aspect of it—that which she derived from identifying with her mother's shrieking posture.

* * *

The clinical experiences with these patients illustrate some general principles about countertransference phenomena. Many patients suffering from primitive mental states can be tedious at times, and those clinicians who choose to treat such patients run the occupational risk of being bored or of falling asleep. Some patients are so narcissistic that they are extremely difficult to tolerate, and clinicians seek relief by withdrawing (Hoyt and Farrell 1984–1985). Still, we need to ask why someone else's narcissism has such a strong unpleasant, and often threatening, impact. In a social situation, there is a tendency to fight back. The narcissist is viewed as an antagonist, an opponent, who has to be put in his place or defended against. The feelings that are characteristic of such interactions stem from primitive ego states and early developmental levels. Although projection is recognized as a defensive adaptation associated with such primitive levels, the therapeutic relationships just discussed do not primarily involve projection.

The countertransference responses I have described are also derived from primitive levels of the analyst's psyche. For example, the hypnogogic imagery of the bathtub and water are drawn from the very earliest psychic states and refer to symbolic representations of intrauterine existence and neonatal stages. The analyst was no doubt conjuring such images as part of his regression as he relaxed his hold on reality and retreated into hypnogogic state. He was not actually reliving the birth process in reverse; instead, he was having a fantasy of being unborn as a reaction to the patient's need to establish her sense of existence. This interaction need not involve projection. Undoubtedly there were some projective elements at work, but for the most part, the patient and the analyst were creating an ambience that permitted the patient to survive and caused the analyst to feel threatened. Therapeutic relationships in which the narcissistic balance of both patient and therapist are disturbed lead to countertransference reactions that are chiefly responses to an ambience created by the patient rather than to an intrusion into the analyst's psyche that hampers his mode of relating.

These clinical interactions are less structured situations than relationships in which feelings or parts of the self are projected onto the analyst or, in the case of the analyst, onto the patient. The psychic levels and the particular defenses that characterize these transference–countertransference relationships are important determinants of the treatment process that, if not dealt with, can lead to serious impasses. Withdrawing into a shell of sleep is a very primitive defense that removes the analyst from the setting. Obviously, if this persists for any period of time, there can be no treatment.

The severity of the consequences of countertransference

reactions is not necessarily directly correlated to the primitive-
ness of their origins. An analyst's feeling sleepy or actually falling
asleep does not always pose a serious threat to the analysis. In
some instances, both patient and therapist see some humor in
such occurrences. The analyst absenting himself from the treatment setting is not always a grim event. For instance, there is a
well known joke about the therapist not being there, but the
patient starting without him. There is also a joke expressing the
opposite—the analyst starting without the patient.

Nevertheless, the interplay of the narcissistic balance of
two persons has many subtle features that require further discussion in order to understand why they should lead to negative
countertransference reactions. Repeating the question of why
someone else's narcissistic orientation should be threatening
causes us to inquire as to whether there are situations in which
narcissistic display is not disturbing. Are there relationships in
which the patient's self-enhancement is felt as pleasurable rather
than disruptive? If so, how do they differ from what I have been
describing?

I have treated some highly creative scientists who seemingly
bragged about their accomplishments, and yet it did not have
the same effect as most exhibitionistic displays have (Giovacchini 1986). Rather, I often shared these patients' enthusiasm
about their achievements and enjoyed their creative forays. I
consider my reactions examples of positive countertransference
attitudes that, in these instances, were favorable to the treatment relationship. Although positive countertransference attitudes are not neccessarily productive and can cause complications, this was not the situation with my patients. I believe
that this was due to two factors; one is generally true and the
other was related to elements of my personal orientation—
an orientation, however, that is commonly encountered in
psychoanalysts.

First, the patient's narcissism and grandiosity were not experienced as bragging or as unwarranted enhancement. In fact, whatever the patient revealed about his accomplishments seemed almost humble. There was a casual, everyday quality to the way these scientists talked about their discoveries, although the extent of their activities, from just pure description, would have bordered on megalomania.

Take, for example, Archimedes's grandiose assertion that if you gave him a spot on which to stand, he could move the world. One reason that such a statement is not offensive is that it is true. Having discovered the laws of levers, Archimedes offers a proposition that is theoretically possible. One does not feel that he is overextending himself or indulging in fantastic hyperbole. True, what he is stating is part of a fantasy, because no such anchored spot exists; but if it did, then what he said is absolutely correct.

Similarly, my patients' assertions about their achievements were also based on facts, and although they derived considerable narcissistic gratification from their creative abilities, they were in no way arrogant or condescending. What they revealed was a benign megalomania and grandiosity. To express this in terms not associated with psychopathology or primitive ego states, it can be said that these patients were referring to their inner sense of security, trust, and self-confidence. They did not need to wrest narcissistic supplies from others. Their self-esteem did not depend primarily on supplies from the external world; their creative activity was a sufficient provider of healthy narcissism (Federn 1952) that helped them define themselves.

Under these circumstances, even if a patient were concentrating intensely on himself and his involvements, it would evoke only positive responses in the therapist. The therapist's positive attitudes can get out of hand, as discussed, and there must be limits to the spectrum of the analyst's reactions, as

Winnicott (Giovacchini 1972) illustrated. But because the patient's material is anchored in his creative reality, it does not lead to an escalation that substitutes the patient's infantile reality for the current external world. Rather than feeling left out, the therapist may share the patient's enthusiasm about himself and his work.

As seems to be true of relationships that attempt to regulate narcissistic balance, the patient and the therapist are creating and reacting to an ambience that is primarily constructed by the patient. When the analyst experiences negative reaction, such as being overwhelmed by an urge to sleep, it is usually because the patient has managed to upset the therapist's immediate world. These interactions are located in external reality, whether it is perceived in terms of the current milieu or the past infantile world.

The scientists I have treated were operating in a different space. Their descriptions and narratives were often poetic, and their attitudes about them were playful. Although they frequently discussed in considerable detail the events of their daily lives and for long periods of time never once referred to me or ostensibly recognized my presence, I never felt bored or excluded. Instead, I had a sense of involvement in a relationship. What they talked about was interesting to me, and, in part, I believed they were trying to capture my interests. My involvement went beyond mere admiration. It related to their ability to present a subject in an interesting fashion such that I had a feeling of having participated and of having experienced a relationship in which both of us were giving and receiving. I was supplying them with an appreciative audience, but, at the same time, they were given to me in that I could share their creative adventures and their pleasurable and playful expositions. These patients, in their own way, were relating to their analyst.

We were not competing for a position of dominance in our surrounding reality—that is, in the reality created in the consultation room. Instead, we were relating to each other in the transitional space. The patient's creative endeavors, which involved combinations of primary- and secondary-process activities, are best conceptualized as occurring in the transitional space. The interplay of fantasy and reality takes place in this in-between world in which reality is transformed into illusion and then becomes part of an expanded, modified external world. In the transitional space, individual personalities are transcended. When these patients presented their accomplishments to me, it was the creative product or process that dominated; the patient was an appendage to this process, and I did not feel demeaned by their failure to directly acknowledge me.

As persons, therapist and patient were secondary in importance to the playful creative activity that had become part of the patient's ego adaptation and that led to the maintenance of self-esteem. Our relationship to the external world, our personal ambience and our source of narcissistic supplies, also receded into the background. We both derived replenishment in the transitional area. The patient was the active, aggressive participant, but I did not feel forced into a position of passive submission, as occurs when the patient's narcissism forces him to possess the external world and to step on the therapist in order to keep himself from sinking into oblivion.

My descriptions of these creative scientists may cause the reader to wonder why they were in treatment. Their involvement in creative activity and their high levels of self-esteem, trust, and self-confidence would indicate that they had attained sufficient ego integration that they would not require therapy. This would have been true if there had not been a breakdown of their capacity to create. These scientists sought treatment because they were suffering from inhibited creativity. Some were able to continue to be creative, but not at their previous levels; emotional problems—and in one instance, psychosis—overwhelmed their egos.

The scientists whom I treated had serious emotional problem, but their egos were generally well integrated. They were capable of forming sustaining object relationships, and they had a well-developed capacity for intimacy. They may have had conflicts and anxiety about ultimate attachments, but they wanted and sought them. Their self-esteem levels were labile, but they had been able to achieve considerable security and self-confidence throughout the course of their work.

The second factor that made a positive countertransference attitude therapeutically productive in these cases relates to specific emotional constellations within the therapist. Rather than feeling narcissistically depleted or shut out, I identified with these patients' creativity. To the degree that analysts value creativity, their ego ideals are enhanced by such an identification. What the patient and therapist share in the transitional space is also very much a part of the analyst's value system. If the therapist did not esteem creative activity, he would not be sufficiently in tune with the patient's material, nor would he have the same positive reactions to it. The positive countertransference, in these circumstances, made it easier for me to help create a transitional space as the essential element of the therapeutic ambience. As previously noted, the basic psychic mechanism used to achieve a productive positive relationship is identification, but generally a healthy identification. Rather than being a defensive adaptation to protect against the impact of infantile trauma, it is derived from the higher levels of the therapist's personality, the ego ideal.

I have discussed two types of countertransference reactions

that involve an interplay of the narcissistic balances of patients and therapists. In one type, the treatment is disrupted because the analyst distances himself from the patient when he feels his narcissistic supplies draining as the patient focuses all available libido onto himself. In the other, the analyst feels enhanced by identifying with the patient's creative perspective.

6

Countertransference Reactions to Inchoate Psychic States

The countertransference responses discussed in preceding chapters involve certain general qualities of the treatment interaction as they impact various aspects of the analyst's personality. The patient's psychopathology serves as a stimulus, of course, but it was not highlighted in terms of its unique elements. I now wish to describe specific types of psychopathology that are particularly apt to cause disruptive countertransference reactions. I will begin by discussing clinical entities that represent the primitive end of the developmental spectrum. As would be expected, they lead to highly disturbing countertransference responses and corresponding defensive stances in the therapist.

In the next chapter, I will concentrate on the so-called highest level of emotional development in patients whose psychopathology involves, to some measure, character defects, in contrast to the intrapsychic conflicts of the psychoneuroses. This sequence should give us an overall view of a spectrum of structural psychopathology and countertransference responses. It will be interesting to discover that there are many variables involved in the production of countertransference responses that obscure their correlations to the stimuli that patients provide. Such stimuli are the manifestations and barometers of the severity of psychopathology.

Regardless of the nature of psychopathology, it is easier to respond to some elements of the psyche than others. Easier and more difficult are also not self-explanatory evaluations of countertransference reactions. Countertransference comprises a compendium of feelings, and their combinations are not invariant. Pleasure and excitement may occur together, but excitement can also be painful. Some responses are easier to bear than others, and many factors may contribute to the final feeling.

In order to categorize a patient's material, clinicians can concentrate on its organization, which can range from chaotic and inchoate to well structured and logical—states that correspond to Freud's (1900) concepts of primary and secondary process. Therapists will experience different feelings in the face of material organized by primary process versus that organized by secondary process. They are not predetermined, however, because one set of feelings is primitively organized, while the other set is logically organized. Some secondary-process material can be boring, whereas primary-process associations may be exciting because they are inspired and creative.

Although countertransference responses cannot be predetermined by the organization of the patient's material, intense primary process–dominated associations are apt to be disturbing to the therapist; if the therapist is bombarded by them for long periods of time, they can be exhausting. In these instances, the therapist may defensively counterattack.

In addition to the organization of the material, the sources of the patient's transference projections can also provoke a variety of countertransference responses. M. Klein (1948) stated that all facets of the personality may participate in the transference; patients may transfer feelings, instinctual impulses, or parts of the psychic apparatus—the self-representation as well as the superego. I believe that therapists tend to be less disrupted by being made the target of the projection of infantile feelings than by absorbing psychopathologically distorted or defective parts of the patient's psychic structure. Impulses and feelings are less upsetting because they can be viewed as extraneous products that can be measured alongside the therapist's own residual of corresponding impulses. For example, if the patient insists that the analyst hates him, the analyst can readily compare the patient's evaluation with what he actually feels about the patient. Unless there are some idiosyncratic contributions to the countertransference, it is usually not too difficult to get in touch with our subjective reactions to patients.

On the other hand, the patient's attempt to force a part of the self onto the therapist may become quite painful to the therapist. The interaction often proceeds at an unconscious level; neither the patient nor the therapist recognizes what is happening. To the degree that much of the patient's self consists of infantile introjects, he is casting the analyst in the role of an emotionally significant and usually traumatizing person of the past (Loewald 1986). The assumption of such a role is usually ego-dystonic for the therapist, but he may not recognize the nature of the patient's projections. Consequently, he reacts as if a foreign body has been pushed into his psyche, and the experience can be painful and disconcerting. Rather than being able to analyze the interaction, such therapists, because their vision is obscured by disruptive feelings, may construct defenses to regain their equilibrium. If the defense takes the form of attacking the patient, it can destroy the therapeutic setting.

In this chapter, I will concentrate on a group of patients whose primary developmental fixation is at what I have called the *prementational phase* (Giovacchini 1979a, 1986). I choose this group because, as I have stated, I want to cover a broad spectrum of characterological psychopathology. Furthermore, I believe that since what therapists are responding to is so amorphous, it is difficult, if not impossible, to articulate it in secondary-process terms.

Therapists also find something going on within themselves that is not understandable in the language of secondary process—the language with which we are familiar. It is as if an unformed psychic amoeba has invaded the therapist's psyche, and he cannot elevate it to a sufficiently structured constellation that it can be recognized for what it is. Instead, he reacts defensively, which may be fatal both to the treatment relationship and to the analyst's therapeutic functioning.

Before proceeding with a clinical exposition, the concept of the prementational phase must be briefly elaborated upon by including it within the context of psychic development. Many developmental theorists, including Brazelton (1980), Emde (1980), Klaus and Kennel (1982), and Stern (1985), agree that there is an early neonatal state in which there is very little, if any, mentation. As research and observation proceed, we are learning that the duration of this period becomes shorter and shorter. Still, regardless of its brevity, the way in which the phase has been experienced markedly affects the course of psychic development and contributes significantly to later mental operations and adaptations.

No one knows exactly what neonates feel, especially during the prementational phase. Presumably, there are very few, if any, organized feelings. Rather than focusing on such elemental feelings as pleasure and pain, we can think in terms of homeostasis and fluctuations in equilibrium that correspond to diurnal variations and circadian rhythms. The vulnerable newborn is susceptible to inner tension and external stimuli, but these stressors are apparently processed through tension-reducing physiological mechanisms. When these mechanisms fail, the infant becomes disrupted; otherwise, there is a state of homeostatic equilibrium which is manifested as calmness when viewed through adult eyes. The disruption these infants exhibit resembles the purposeless kicking and screaming that are caused by frustration and are characteristic of tantrums later in childhood. The mother's role, as Freud (1920) described, is to protect the child from inner and outer disruptive impingements. Part of the early mothering function at this prementational stage is to act as a stimulus barrier—a *Reizschutz*, as Freud stated (Esman 1983).

I have divided the nurturing or caretaking function into two components (Giovacchini 1979a, 1986, 1987). The first consists of nurturance itself—the substance, such as food, that nourishes and gratifies. This nutriment is the foreground of nurturance, but it must be given in a proper ambience. This ambience is the second component of the maternal interaction—specifically, a tranquil setting that enables the child to assimilate and easily integrate the caregiving ministrations. As previously noted, the treatment situation can be described similarly, in that the analyst gives nourishing interpretations in the context of a soothing holding environment.

The agitation that occurs during the prementational phase is soothed by the protecting mother, who forms a bond with her baby (Klaus and Kennel 1982). This bond has a strong physiological component for both infant and mother. Winnicott (1956) called the mother's attachment to her baby *primary maternal preoccupation*, which begins at conception.

As the neonate acquires the capacity to be soothed, psychic development progresses in the direction of increasingly complex mental patterns. Mentation is established, and needs and feelings become structured in distinct sensory responses and perceptions. The organism becomes, in a manner of speaking, psychologically oriented; affects are elaborated, and self and object differentiation occurs. Freud (1905, 1917a) worked out a developmental sequence in terms of increasingly sophisticated instinctual needs and object relations as he outlined the various psychosexual stages.

If there has been sufficient trauma during the prementational phase, however, the future patient will suffer from pervasive inner agitation that cannot be soothed. These patients present unique countertransference problems in that they often baffle their therapists, who develop characteristic defenses to cope with their inner disruption.

Many countertransference reactions are characterized by confusion, but the confusion to which I am now referring has a special impact in that it is not the outcome of specific inner conflicts or traumatic object relationships. In order to discuss the construction of the countertransference, I must first present clinical material to illustrate disturbances in the prementational phase. I will discuss a mother–daughter relationship.

* * *

The patient, a mother in her mid-40s, was referred to me by a colleague of mine, but a personal friend of the patient. He was concerned about her physical as well as her mental health. She drank enormous amounts of liquor on a daily basis, to the point that she became totally incapacitated. He told me that she got out of bed in the late morning, and as she dressed and prepared for the day, she would feel some agitation and anxiety that had no obvious precipitating stimulus. She would then manage to find a friend or two and go out to lunch. She ate at the same restaurant every day. Her party would sit there for several hours, drinking an uncountable number of martinis. Then she would somehow find her way home and continue drinking, this time scotch, until she passed out. Prior to her collapse, she might rant and verbally attack anyone in her presence, usually her husband or children.

She insisted on late-morning appointments because, as I had learned, she would be drinking and drunk the rest of the day. She presented herself, however, as a genteel, sober woman who had agreed to see a psychiatrist because she had some problems in the management of the household and with her children, particularly a 17-year-old daughter. She stated that she hardly ever drank, perhaps a decorous glass of sherry or a glass of wine with dinner. She maintained this stance of sobriety even after we saw each other one late afternoon when I happened to be driving past the restaurant as she was leaving, stumbling and obviously drunk. Despite her intoxication, she recognized me and waved.

Her only sober moments were a few hours in the morning; she was semistuporous for the remainder of the day. She was not agitated during sessions; she was quite calm, well at ease, and spoke in a modulated, well-bred fashion. Her reports of her activities were examples of a remarkable capacity for denial. She spoke a good deal about the evils of drinking and emphasized that she was, in essence, a nondrinker. She appeared amazingly sincere about her temperance.

It is a common phenomenon that a person who uses denial as a prominent defense focuses intensely on the topic that is central to their defensive status. The thief praises honesty, the sociopath concentrates on morality, and the alcoholic, in some instances, talks about sobriety. Nevertheless, as occurs with reaction formations, the attitudes, behavior, or feelings that are being denied are very much in the forefront.

I gradually formed the impression that my patient actually believed that she did not drink. This was similar to, or might actually have been, a delusion; but more to the point, drinking was so much a part of her life that she was unaware of her indulgence. It had become an automatized activity that occurred outside the realm of consciousness. Inasmuch as we breathe constantly, we are not aware of breathing. Alcohol was my patient's atmosphere, and drinking would become a notable experience only if she stopped drinking. Her perceptions were usually blurred, and she was not particularly adept at distinguishing between what was real and not real. She lived most of her life as if she were in a fog.

During the first year of treatment, she kept bolstering a self-image of an aristocratic, gracious socialite, which, in fact, she was, although the major part of her life was sordid and tawdry. She spoke with pride of her ancestors, whom she could trace back, if not to the Mayflower, to many generations. There was a touch of arrogance to her manner and a pretentiousness to her pontificating. She seemed poised, calm, and contented at one level, but there was at the same time an air of delicate vulnerability about the way in which she related to me. Some of her alcoholic haze must have clung to her the next morning, and she brought it into my office. There were many moments when she appeared to be in a fog, although she maintained coherence as she described her life as a member of the gentry.

She minimized any difficulties she might have had, but she admitted that her daughter was having some problems. Apparently she was an alcoholic and a drug abuser, and was probably promiscuous as well. She had frequently shown up at school drunk, and her behavior had often been disruptive. When the patient first started seeing me, her daughter had been suspended from school and the family was in the process of finding a private school that would accept her. It was clear that she was genuinely concerned about her daughter's plight, but she tried to minimize it. She had a need to present herself as living in an orderly and dignified manner, passing herself off as a model mother and wife. Outward appearances were of primary importance.

During one session, her thoughts drifted to the past, and she started telling me how she had fed her daughter. She was practically unaware of my presence as she started, in a trance-like fashion, to relive the experience. She described and mimicked how she picked up her baby, by the hips and without any neck support, swung her in a wide arc, and forcefully positioned her in her arms. I wondered, if she had really picked up her daughter in that fashion, how she could have avoided serious neck injuries or whiplash. Then she caressed her by poking her fingers into her abdomen and moving her up and down in her arms in violent, jerky movements. I was astonished that those movements were meant to be soothing. Their appearance had just the opposite effect on me. I felt agitated as I identified with her daughter.

* * *

Most of us intuitively recognize a soothing experience and react sensitively to nonsoothing interactions. I recall a mass reaction when a film was shown at a meeting of the Illinois Psychiatric Society, an audience consisting mainly of professionals in the behavioral sciences. The film was about a longitudinal study of various aspects of the maternal interaction. It depicted a mother in a room with her 3-month-old son, who was sleeping peacefully in a crib. The mother had been told that we were making a movie, but she was given no instructions as to what to do. She was simply told that she should feel free to do whatever she pleased.

Apparently the mother found it difficult to just sit quietly and let her son sleep comfortably. She felt she had to do something, especially if she was on camera. First she got up and walked around the room. Then she leaned over the crib and looked at her baby. Finally, unable to contain herself, she picked up her son in the same rough and clumsy fashion my patient had demonstrated. She startled him into wakefulness as she continued walking around the room, bouncing him up and down in her arms. Again like my patient, she began to poke her fingers, which she moved in a pinching motion, into his body. The child, as expected, began to cry, and she increased her efforts by poking and bouncing him harder. The child cried louder. To add to this escalating disruptive scene, the mother tried humming to her infant, presumably to calm him. Instead, she wailed, a cacophony that must have sounded like the keening of mourners at a funeral.

Although the audience was psychologically sophisticated and familiar with the manifestations of psychopathology, they could not stand looking at the film and hearing the sound at the same time. They insisted that the sound be turned off. Apparently the audience experienced it as a jarring sensory overload.

If an adult audience with all kinds of defenses and adaptations could not stand the impact of this mother's attempts to soothe—actually an onslaught—imagine the disruption this poor, defenseless infant must have felt. Intense sensitivity to such disruptive behavior is based on the fact that we are dealing with tensions that are typical of the prementational phase.

As previously noted, the sensations attached to the prementational phase are, by definition, not psychologically elaborated and not capable of mental representation without the contributions of higher developmental levels. The closer various ego states get to physiological modes of operation, the less the likelihood of developing defenses against the perception of such states. This is certainly obvious when we consider basic needs such as hunger. The need to eat has to be gratified; defenses cannot be constructed to assuage such a feeling, and it cannot be connected with higher psychic levels that can be dealt with by various psychic mechanisms and defenses. Sex, another basic need, can, by contrast, become attached to psychic elements and then bound into a defensive system.

The need for soothing of prementational tensions, like hunger, must receive a direct response. This type of tension cannot be displaced, split off, or repressed. It can be dispelled, however, by a calming interaction at best, or absorbed by a person or an environment. The audience watching this film seemed to be absorbing the disruptive tension that was building up in the infant. The mother's efforts were escalating as a result of her lack of success at calming her son. Still, she did not seem upset by her failure. In fact, there was a hint of rapture in her facial expression. She was uneasy and restless when her son was calmly sleeping. She seemed to be putting her agitation into her son, and the audience was absorbing it.

My patient could, at times, get me to absorb some of her prementational tension, but she was able to soothe herself by drinking herself into a stupor. Often, prior to passing out, she could become quite violent and would break furniture, but because she was so drunk, she was too weak to hurt anyone. She was easily subdued. I believe that these physical outbursts also represented attempts to discharge her inner prementational turmoil; by the time she saw me the next morning, she was relatively calm.

Clinicians might question whether the tension states I am describing do not have some mentational components. The contributions of later stages of development cannot be discounted when we are dealing with tension states and feelings, and I believe that such factors might have been involved in the incidents I have discussed. Still, it was difficult, when examining this and other patients' dreams and associations, to find intrapsychic elements attached to these ego states. They were associated with vulnerable egos, low self-esteem, and poorly established self-representations, but these characteristics were the consequence of being unable to be soothed or of faulty self-soothing mechanisms because of a traumatic maternal holding environment.

From a countertransference viewpoint, these patients often provoke the analyst into absorbing their disruption and this can lead to disruptive, treatment-destructive responses.

My patient's daughter had had some interesting experiences in treatment that led to its termination. She was able to stimulate countertransference reactions that caused her therapists considerable emotional turmoil. She had acted out a fantasy that helped her maintain her equilibrium but was disturbing to anyone else who tried to get close to her. This fantasy was rather simple and did not involve complex intrapsychic phenomena. She was just maintaining herself in a protected setting and shielding herself from the impingements of the outer world. In her fantasy, she drove her car into the parking lot of her high school. The lot was reserved for faculty, and since it was winter, it was covered with ice. Illegally parked on the ice, she was calmly smoking cigarettes as two irate policemen were beating on her windows, demanding that she open the door. She kept blowing smoke in the direction of their faces, obviously pleased with being on top of the situation.

In reality, she had been suspended from that school because her behavior in the classroom was not at all calm, as it was in her fantasy. She had many hysterical outbursts as both drugs and alcohol rendered her helpless and vulnerable.

While thinking about her fantasy, she achieved a calm and satisfaction that she seldom felt in her daily life. Drugs and alcohol could tranquilize her, but the aftermath was painful and disruptive, as it was for her mother. She sought soothing experiences in noisy discotheques filled with the smoke of countless cigarettes. Where most of us would feel irritated by the atmosphere and the noise, she was comfortable, although this state was difficult to maintain on a prolonged basis.

I conjectured that because the initial soothing that her mother had attempted to give her as an infant was really an assault rather than a comfortable holding environment, she could find solace only in disruptive situations. The patient was suffering from what I have referred to as primal confusion (Giovacchini 1979b); that is, her respones to tension-producing or tension-reducing situations were paradoxical. She could not tolerate quiet, relaxed settings but was in her element at noisy, crowded parties and nightclubs.

I attribute this paradox to her early nurturing experience, in which incoming stimuli must have been physiologically confusing to her as a neonate. If a need is not met with an appropriate response, homeostasis is disturbed and the need is eventually perceived as painful. In order to survive, the child must adapt to such adverse circumstances, and the adaptations are the outcome of the maldevelopment of the prementational phase.

The agitation these children and adult patients suffer does

not contain any psychological meaning or purpose as do the depressions that will be discussed in the next chapter. As later stages of development become involved, the agitation acquires meaning, but initially these tension states are the result of defective physiological soothing elements. My patient's daughter had been able to make an intrinsically agitating experience into a source of comfort. It seems that her sensory and integrative ego systems operated in an antithetical fashion to those that are ordinarily familiar. Her modes of relating seem bizarre because, to us, they are at variance with basic physiologic and reflex responses.

These orientations can be conceptualized as a reversal of stimulus–response sequences. Warmth, for example, is experienced as coldness, and cold is felt as warmth. To my patient's daughter, noise was a quiet, calming experience, and breathing smoke-polluted air was similar to inhaling refreshing clean air. Another young patient of mine frequently dreamed of finding peace and refuge living in a cave located on an iceberg.

Another patient had either a fantasy or a delusion of having given birth to a monster baby who did not have the psychic or physical equipment to be soothed or nurtured. Its face had no features; it was simply a sphere without ears, eyes, mouth, or nose. Because it did not have a mouth, feeding, and thus nurturance, was impossible. Whatever solace an infant might receive from visual or auditory sources was also unobtainable. This monster also had no arms; the curlicued cords attached to telephones served as arms, so the child could not hug. Furthermore, warmth was destructive because, as the patient explained, this monster had leprosy, so placing it in the sun would cause parts of its body to crumble and break off.

Returning to my patient's daughter, the reader may object to my dogmatic assertion that listening to music at discotheques is a cacophonous experience that is intrinsically disruptive.

Perhaps a universal statement is unfair, but the fact that such music is very loud is easy to establish, and it has on occasion caused hearing problems. In any case, many would agree with me that this is not a soothing experience. The fact that many adolescents are attracted to discotheque music could indicate that there have been certain qualities to their early soothing experiences that, to some extent, resemble those of my patient's daughter and the mother–infant interaction that was depicted in the film.

My patient became concerned about her daughter because they could not find a school that would accept her. In the past, she had talked about her daughter often; discussions of her daughter dominated some of our sessions, but her affect was flat. Her manner was matter-of-fact, and she did not seem to be at all upset about her daughter's upheaval, turmoil, and destructive and self-destructive acting out. At times, her daughter would have periods when she would scream, kick, and beat her fists against the wall; she would then withdraw to her room for hours. She was usually toxic from alcohol or drugs but, often enough, she had a clear sensorium when she started this hysterical behavior. My patient had related all this to me as if she were reporting something she had read in the newspapers. Now that the daughter could not be sent away to a boarding school, my patient was upset.

I referred the daughter to a young psychiatrist who saw her for seven months. He felt very frustrated by her because her main activity in therapy was to sit with her legs crossed and blow cigarette smoke in his face. At first he became angry and had a desire to hit her. Later he felt strong sexual urges that he just managed to control. Because of these countertransference feelings, he terminated the treatment. I then arranged for her to see another colleague, and the same sequence of events occurred. Meanwhile the patient managed to find a clerical position in a rural community some 150 miles from the city, and she moved to the country.

Clearly, the patient was enacting her fantasy in the consultation rooms of these two therapists. She remained calm in the face of their agitation. In fact, she most likely achieved a state of calm *because* her therapists were agitated. The therapists knew about her fantasy and understood that it was the manifestation of modes of relating to the external world in which the patient felt safe and protected, but they could not prevent themselves from having reactive feelings. These feelings began with a vague, indefinable sense of agitation, which then became recognizable as anger and later reached a peak as they were felt as a pressing need to rape the patient (Gorkin 1985).

The therapist's function for the patient was to soothe her by absorbing her agitation. Perhaps this interaction might be viewed like any transference projection in that the patient put her feelings into her therapist and the therapist found it painful, as Racker (1953, 1968) discussed when he described concordant countertransference. I prefer to think of the interaction as being based on the absorption of an ego state, a prementational state, rather than an introjection of circumscribed feelings or parts of the self. The latter have considerably more psychic organization and structural integrity than does the amorphous, physiological agitation associated with a primal disruptive soothing experience characteristic of a traumatic prementational phase. The theoretical distinction between introjection and absorption may be minor, but sometimes the differences are more than abstract. They often stress important characteristics of the treatment interaction and level of psychic development (Schafer 1968). In this instance, the term *absorption* has a certain graphic clarity.

* * *

To return to the example of the monster baby, my patient could not feed it in an ordinary fashion, because it had no mouth. It lacked the receptive apparatus required for feeding. This organism could not introject experiences, objects, or nutriment if we think of introjection as a basically oral mechanism. We do not usually think of ourselves as introjecting food, but later in development, we use oral terms for learning experiences that lead to the formation of psychic structure and the integration of introjects. We swallow, digest, eat up, ingest experiences, knowledge, and people. We become intimate with love objects by eating them up. Thus, introjective mechanisms are the products of the development of the oral phase.

Introjection is closely allied to projection. These two mechanisms can be considered polar modes of relating and establishing connections between the internal world of the psyche and the external world. The monster baby, because it could not progress through an oral phase, could not achieve the capacity to introject. Presumably it could never reach a level at which it could project either, and since it was such an amorphous entity, it would not contain anything structured enough to be projected.

My patient believed that the monster baby was fed by being placed in the refrigerator, where it received nourishment by absorbing food vapors through osmosis. This is a grotesque picture; the therapists' interactions with such primitive levels of their patients' minds are often experienced as similarly bizarre and grotesque.

Patients who have paradoxical soothing mechanisms may evoke in their therapists a relatively intense reaction in the face of what seems to be minimal provocation. The two young therapists who felt intensely agitated by my patient's daughter seem to be examples of overreactions. Although the patient was obviously provocative and would have been frustrating to any therapist, one can question the intensity and quality of their reactions.

I recall a mother of an adolescent patient whom I saw in

consultation because her son's therapist wanted to learn more about the aspects of the mother–son relationship that might have contributed to the young man's antisocial acting out. At first, I believed that my reactions toward this woman were exaggerated because she was not, at least overtly, a provocative person.

She spoke in a soft, modulated voice and politely answered my questions. She was neatly dressed and well composed and seemed fairly comfortable. Thus, I was surprised that after twenty minutes, I felt an intense antipathy toward her. First I was extremely uneasy and agitated, then I became irritated with her. There was no discernible reason for my reactions.

As I pondered these curious circumstances, I realized that even though she seemed to be answering my questions, I had actually learned nothing from her. She was responding with words and not with information, as she skillfully dodged my questions or digressed in such a fashion that I was initially unaware of her evasive tactics. I had the feeling that she was amused, as if she were playing with me and keeping me dangling. All I gathered was that she had a schizophrenic brother and that her parents were violent people. She had eight children and did not seem to have much of a relationship with any of them. She displayed very little affect toward anyone. As I reflected, I could begin to see some reasons for feeling irritated, but the intensity of my feelings was out of proportion to the stimulus of her presence; they were inappropriate for a clinician who has some familiarity with defensive patients.

I later learned from the son's therapist that life at home was utterly disorganized and chaotic. The family lived on a neat suburban street with attractive houses and well-kept lawns. The inside of their house belied its external appearance, however. It was disheveled and dirty. Half-filled cups of coffee could be found on the living room couch and chairs, and floor lamps might be overturned. The father, who had been seen by the son's therapist, also mentioned that they would occasionally find frozen rats in the refrigerator.

The mother remained calm in the midst of all this chaos. She never appeared to be ruffled, and this often infuriated her husband and some of their numerous children. She seemed particularly attached to the son who was in treatment, the third-born.

The patient stated that she felt close to this son and could not understand his behavior. She had told me about his being her favorite, but it was hard to conceive of her having any favorites, inasmuch as she did not seem to have any feelings whatsoever. Still, after she had been with this son for a period of time, he would often become furiously agitated. He might steal money from her purse and then stay out all night drinking beer. Sometimes he would provoke the police and end up in jail. On several occasions he lost control. He would grab an ax and chop down doors. The mother would just stand by, unperturbed, and have no inclination to stop him.

The parents had separated and a divorce was pending. When the son stayed at the father's apartment, he behaved well and was not given to violent outbursts. When he returned to his mother's house, he would often go on such rampages and would misbehave at school, frequently being truant. In fact, it was the school authorities who had pushed him into treatment.

Other than chopping down doors, this adolescent did nothing that was dangerously harmful. He did silly, childish things at school such as spilling ink on girls' hair or clothing. He would chatter in the classroom and make annoying noises. He was clearly trying to be irritating, but it also appeared that he was suffering from considerable tension that he was trying to discharge through his actions.

I recalled one bit of the sparse information that the mother had given me. She told me that both her parents had had poor impulse control and that her infantile environment had been filled with violence. She had learned to survive these adverse, traumatic surroundings. Her home, although neat on the outside, apparently looked like a ravaged battlefield on the inside. Similarly, the patient could remain calm when surrounded by people, especially her son, who lost control. She remained sane while everyone around her went mad. In a sense, she was similar to my patient's daughter, who found solace in noisy, smoky discotheques.

Noting my irritation and later antipathy toward her, I concluded that I had absorbed her prementational agitation. I was able to control my feelings by suppressing them, but her son could not. He sought relief in somewhat destructive acting out.

* * *

The type of agitation I am describing cannot achieve mental representation. Elsewhere, I have described a process that I call *externalization*, in which the patient attempts to superimpose the infantile world on current reality (Giovacchini 1979b, 1987). I give the example of the hypothetical master-sergeant who, as a child, lived in a violent household and, as an adult, is perfectly at ease in battles that would frighten many of us to the point of panic. This sergeant could not survive a peacetime environment, however, because his executive ego system was dominated by adaptations geared to the violence of childhood. In the army, he could reproduce the infantile environment and adapt to it well. He did not have the executive techniques that would help him cope with a relatively nonviolent world.

The mother I saw in consultation also appeared, to some extent, to have reproduced her infantile environment within the confines of her family. To the degree that she did, she was using the psychic mechanisms of externalization, but she could also survive the nonviolent surrounding world. Her children, especially the adolescent son, absorbed her agitation, and she was soothed by their interaction. She could then face the external milieu with equanimity. As she had managed to get me to feel her agitation during our consultation, she undoubtedly could use others for the same purpose.

The feelings that are absorbed and form the basis of the countertransference are very primitive. As such, they can be painful to bear. The two psychiatrists who saw my patient's daughter could not survive her treatment. If they had acted out in an attempt to soothe themselves, they would have been ruined professionally. Their pain was so intense that rather than doing anything rash and ultimately self-destructive, they terminated the treatment.

After working for six months in a rural town, my patient's daughter came to see me. She had told her mother that she wanted an appointment. The mother agreed that this was a good idea, and she asked me to see her daughter. I could hardly call my treatment with the mother analytic, so I consented to see her daughter.

I was somewhat surprised that when I went into my waiting room to bring her into my office, she was sitting in a chair sleeping. She quickly woke up and after she composed herself in the consultation room, she told me of her activities of the past year. She liked the bucolic country atmosphere, but in the last several weeks she had become aware of a gradually mounting sense of agitation. Because she had become interested in a young man, she did not want to embark on a course of destructive and self-destructive acting out. She wanted to see me because I was older than her previous two therapists, and because her mother had shown a decided improvement in that her daily drinking binge routine had been whittled down to once a month or less. I was both surprised and delighted to hear about her progress because my patient would never have told me of her improvement, since she never admitted to any behavior that could be subject to improvement.

The daughter chatted pleasantly with me. She felt that her behavior had taken a downhill course and she was approaching a state of deterioration similar to her mother's. Somehow, the countryside and her job had been able to establish internal harmony. She did not know why, but she believed that her mother's improvement was a significant factor. She reasoned that if her mother could sustain herself by not reducing herself to a comatose state, then she could do the same thing. At the moment, however, she was frightened because her urge to drink and use drugs was intensifying. She said she felt safe seeing me and would like to come back to see me from time to time. I agreed to see her occasionally.

She returned several months later and reported that after our session, she had had no desire for drugs or liquor. She felt very peaceful in my home office. She had become engaged to the man she mentioned during the first interview and planned to marry him in the near future.

She did marry and now has two children. I saw her two or three times a year for six years, when she felt she did not need to return. There was no question in her mind that being in my office and talking to me in an atmosphere of relaxation was a highly pleasurable, soothing experience. She now believed that she knew how to avoid situations that would agitate her, and her husband and children were a great source of comfort. She was not passing herself off as idyllically happy, and I suspect that, like her mother, she was fairly adept at using denial as a defense. Still, in view of the chaos she had experienced and produced, it was obvious that there had been internal changes that enabled her both to achieve a modicum of self-soothing and to make herself receptive to potentially supportive relationships.

I wondered what had occurred that had caused her to allow herself to be soothed by seeing me. The reasons she gave for seeing me—that is, that I was older and that her mother seemed to have benefitted—are revealing. She had been able to put her agitation into others, such as the policemen in the fantasy and the two psychiatrists she had seen. Although this momentarily calmed her, she was nevertheless in a dangerous situation. The policemen were furious, and if she had dared to carry the fantasy further, they might have succeeded in breaking into the automobile and killing her. The two psychiatrists turned their agitation into sexual feelings, and she was in danger of being raped (Gorkin 1985).

She had sought me out because I was safe. She gathered this impression, in part, from her mother; in addition, because of my age, I would not become sexually aroused, or not as much as a younger man might.

As stated, her agitation, because of defective soothing mechanisms, incorporated elements of higher developmental levels. The tension associated with the prementational phase lacks organization and structure. Higher affective states can bind amorphous agitation and permit movement in the direction of reestablishing psychic equilibrium. Sexual feelings are distinct and organized. The two psychiatrists who saw this adolescent used erotism to organize the inchoate disruption that they had absorbed from her. This is another instance, however, in which the defense itself became dangerous and disruptive.

The psychiatrists also had the desire to attack the patient physically, which, when combined with erotic feelings, constitutes rape. Their anger was not simply a reaction to the frustration they felt because she had shut them out, as she had the policemen in the fantasy. It had that element, but more was involved. It was a reaction to their pain, but mainly, in my opinion, it represented a defensive attempt to organize their psychic turmoil. Anger, within certain limits, is a structured affect that can organize unformed feelings. The adolescent's psychiatrists used both anger and sexual feelings to control themselves, but these feelings only brought them closer to a collapse of the professional self-representation. Perhaps it was the combination that nullified the affects' usefulness as organizers of primitive feelings.

The ultimate countertransference catastrophe is when the therapist loses all sense of his professional role, stepping out of the treatment setting and becoming personally involved with the patient. Sexual involvement between therapist and patient is invariably catastrophic. I have known of some instances in which the patient continued to see the therapist and continued to have sexual relations, sometimes during the scheduled session. This sexual liaison is often kept secret and, in some instances, it has been rationalized that having sex with the patient is part of the treatment. More often than not, patient and analyst are sharing a mutual delusion.

* * *

I once saw in consultation a young woman from another city who had been impregnated by her therapist. He also beat her up occasionally. The patient had done nothing to terminate the relationship, but because of the abortion she had had and the obvious bruises on her body, her aunt reported the analyst to the ethics committee of his society and forced her to leave treatment. The patient loudly protested; she wanted to continue seeing him. She felt soothed by being beaten by and having intercourse with her therapist.

When I saw her, she was trembling and perspiring, and kept dabbing her forehead with a handkerchief wrapped around ice cubes. She looked like a person in an acute withdrawal reaction. Indeed, she was addicted to her therapist because, in a paradoxical fashion, violence and assault reestablished her psychic equilibrium. She resented me at once, believing that I was going to make judgments against her analyst. She saw me as an authority who was going to take away someone she valued. She was desperately anxious, but she was not depressed or suicidal.

Her therapist was also interviewed by at least one member of the ethics committee. He was suspended from the society and moved away. While passing through Chicago, he came to see me once. I learned that after his patient returned from her consultation with me, he did not want to see her any longer. He now recognized the enormity of his behavior, and he became severely depressed. His patient was finally persuaded to see another therapist. The family did not take legal action against the analyst, mainly because he promised that he would give up his practice. His license to practice was later revoked.

He described to me his feelings toward his patient. The first time he saw her, he had had a premonition that there was trouble ahead. He found her utterly fascinating both physically and intellectually. She had a strong presence. I had also noted her presence, but I did not find her particularly attractive. My perceptions were perhaps unduly influenced by the enormous distress and agitation she was displaying. In any case, her therapist felt excited at the prospect of treating her. His reactions were so intense that he wondered whether he should accept her as a patient. Still, part of him wanted very badly to continue a relationship with her, and this overrode his wariness. He wanted to be circumspect, but he felt throughout that initial interview that he was throwing caution to the wind.

He saw her daily for the first six months of treatment and described himself as "a nervous wreck." I could see what he meant, because his state of agitation was just as intense as that of his patient when I saw her in consultation. He was visibly anxious and agitated, to the degree that he found the tension unbearable. He emphasized that he felt he would be close to a psychotic break if he could not get some relief from his inner turmoil. He felt like murdering her, and in fits of agitation he would shove her against the wall. He might then throw her on the couch and have intercourse with her. Afterward they both felt blissful and calm. Both he and the patient knew that this was a precarious and dangerous relationship, but they were powerless to do anything about it.

I asked him why he had wanted to see me, and he admitted that his reason for seeing me was bizarre. His patient, despite her initial anger, had felt somewhat better after our session. She was less agitated. He conjectured that if I could soothe her, then maybe I could do the same for him. He also wanted me to treat him, but after he had made this appointment with me, he decided to move to another city. I have not heard from him again.

He had felt fragmented, a reaction that was, according to him, provoked by the patient. She had done nothing identifiable to get him so upset. All he could refer to was her ethereal beauty and what came through to him as arrogant aloofness. He wanted to knock her off her pedestal, which he literally did. As his inner disruption mounted, he would become sexually aroused. Sexual feelings were mixed with murderous rage. He felt he was trying to pull himself together as his tension kept increasing. The sexual act represented a release of pent-up agitation and they both felt wonderfully peaceful afterward.

His reactions were similar to those of the two young psychiatrists who attempted to treat my patient's daughter. They contained their feelings, however, whereas this analyst did not. Sexualizing the inner disruption he had absorbed from the patient gave it sufficient organization so that it could be discharged in a discrete fashion—that is, through goal-directed violence and sexual activity.

Both the therapist and the patient were, for the moment, soothed by this acting out. After several months, however, the situation became unbearable for both of them. The patient was beginning to feel that she had to pay a high price for the minimal soothing she was getting. She probably would have done nothing on her own and she still felt attached to her analyst, but it later became clear when she was with another therapist that she was relieved. I received this information from a relative.

Anger can be an organizing affect without necessarily being accompanied by erotic feelings. At times, it is difficult to understand how anger can function in such a fashion because it is ordinarily the affective component of a hostile object relationship. Clinicians are not accustomed to viewing the generation of anger as an attempt at self-soothing. We are more likely to assume that it is a manifestation of the negative transference.

* * *

A supervisee had been treating an adolescent college student for two years. The patient had seen three other psychiatrists prior to the current treatment. His former therapists had taken the initiative in terminating the therapeutic relationship, presumably because he was so unpleasant.

At the beginning of treatment with his current therapist, the patient explained in considerable detail his mistreatment by his previous psychiatrists. He complained that they were judgmental and sarcastic. They had accused him of intellectualizing and criticized him for his heartless treatment of women. They finally dismissed him because they believed he was not serious about treatment. He admitted that he was not a very pleasant person to have around, but he had hoped that by getting professional help, he could overcome whatever defects he had that caused people to shun him. He had expected tolerance and forbearance from psychiatrists. Having been forewarned, the current therapist tried to be as receptive as possible. The patient noted that he had chosen a female therapist this time, in the hope that a woman might be more understanding.

After several months, the patient began to criticize the therapist. He disagreed with her interpretations and felt that she was inattentive and stupid. He constantly complained that her mind was elsewhere, probably on some sexual escapade. The therapist believed that the patient was projecting his self-hatred onto her, but he did not accept this interpretation. He continued to berate her for being insensitive, unempathic, and uninterested in him as a patient. Perhaps she was a fine therapist for other patients or maybe she had done good work in the past, but now and with him, she no longer cared about treatment. This litany continued without any relief or lightening of his mood.

The therapist did her best to maintain an even keel. She did not defend herself or counterattack. She did not even make reference to how the three former treatment relationships had ended badly, probably because of his relentless attacks and persistent anger. The patient did not consider stopping the treatment, however, which would have been a logical decision if he believed the therapist to be incompetent. She often thought of posing this question to him, but she suppressed this inclination because she was aware, like his previous therapists, that part of her wanted him to terminate treatment. Still, after two years, she suggested a consultation. She made it clear that she wanted another opinion to help her understand him. It was odd that the patient saw no reason for a consultation, but he reluctantly agreed to go along with her proposal. He warned her that whoever saw him would not have a very high opinion of her as a therapist. He would hurt her reputation.

When I saw the patient, he spoke quite freely about his background and his work at school. He seemed somewhat pleased with himself and had been enjoying both his academic pursuits and his social life. He was generally satisfied and appeared relatively happy. I had received an entirely different picture of him from his therapist. I had envisioned an angry young man, not a friendly, cheerful youth who seemed to be enjoying life. I wondered if this were the same patient or if this youth had an immense capacity to use splitting mechanisms.

I finally asked what he thought about his treatment, because his feelings about it were the reason for this consultation. He replied that he was ready for that question; he had rehearsed his answer. He stated that he wanted to say all kinds of negative things about his therapist, but "good thoughts" kept intruding. He could not abolish them. He kept thinking of how gentle and understanding she was, how patient she was with him, and of how she never criticized him or defended herself against his anger. He was grateful to her for allowing him to be angry. At the close of the session, I asked him whether I could discuss his positive feelings toward his therapist. He chuckled and said that she deserved to know that he was really quite fond of her.

This young man used anger as a synthesizing force. Although he had never told his therapist, he always felt better after each session. He could not let her know that at the time, because anger would then have been an inappropriate affect.

He recognized that he needed to feel angry and to have a setting in which he could express it. Having a nonretaliatory target caused him to focus his feelings. What had been inchoate and dispersed in all directions could now be channeled toward a specific person. His feelings were elevated to the level of an object relationship, and this gave them form and structure. Previously he had suffered from constant tension and agitation. Now he enjoyed the vitality and vigor of his feelings.

Somewhat amused by the turn of events, he returned to treatment. It became difficult to sustain anger, having recognized how he was using this affect. He continues to feel anxious, but, on the whole, he is able to contain his feelings in the consultation room. He is still in therapy. My supervisee reports that it is a stormy and difficult treatment, but, unlike his previous experiences, he feels reasonably comfortable with this therapist. It seems that his anger has been replaced by anxiety.

Anxiety is an affect that can also be used to bind prementational agitation. At first this sounds like a contradiction because anxiety, in itself, is a disruptive feeling that has to be defended against. On the surface it appears to be the opposite of tranquility. One would not think of such an affect as having a soothing potential.

* * *

As I will discuss further in the next chapter, there are different types of anxiety that appear to be phenomenologically the same. The intensity of the affect also determines its function. For example, Freud (1926) postulated that anxiety functions as a signal to mobilize defenses as a response to inner danger. He also described anxiety as being associated with primitive ego states in which the psyche feels overwhelmed by feelings it cannot control. In some instances the latter is a state of regressive disintegration, the outcome of a breakdown of signal anxiety. Well-modulated apprehensiveness degenerates into panic. This indicates that an affect such as anxiety can be conceptualized in terms of a hierarchical sequence.

Postulating a continuum in which anxiety progresses from a primitive organization to a sophisticated warning signal reconciles Freud's first and second anxiety theories. Thus, anxiety can be studied in terms of functions other than that of mobilizing specific defenses that institute repression. It can also soothe and organize prementational agitation, much as anger and sexual feelings do. Its binding function can also lead to some cohesion of the self-representation.

I have seen several patients whose chief complaint is that they experience constant anxiety. In some instances the symptom of anxiety is the manifestation of prementational agitation; on other occasions it is a synthesizing affect that maintains psychic equlibrium. In the latter instance, even though it has a specific function of binding disruption, anxiety has become, in itself, disruptive.

Difficulties in the prementational phase can be manifested in various ways, especially as they impinge on later developmental stages. Lack of soothing is perceived as agitation, although I have described intrinsically disruptive external stimuli that paradoxically cause patients to feel comfortable. Anxiety is a self-generated stimulus that can have a similar purpose. It can lead to stability at the prementational level by giving the psyche a sense of aliveness. The other pole of prementational agitation is prementational deadness.

Some patients who suffer from primitive mental states have suffered primarily from traumas of omission. That is, they have had very little stimulation or object contact during the neonatal period. Spitz (1941) described an orphanage in which the children were almost completely isolated from human contact. They were kept in cribs that were placed in individual cubicles. The walls of these cubicles were sufficiently high that the children could not see beyond them. They were fed and their bodily needs were met, but there was no interpersonal contact. Most of the children died before they reached the age of 1 year.

The patients to whom I am referring were not agitated in

the sense that they had to be soothed. Most of the time they felt that they had no feelings. Their main emotional state was a sense of deadness. There was very little agitation, but the emptiness they felt could create intense panic. They felt submerged by feelings of annihilation, an existential nihilism and void. They suffered from deep identity disturbances.

These patients had been traumatized since birth. As was true of the children Spitz described, these patients had been emotionally abandoned as neonates. They received very little input, but obviously more than the orphans had, because they grew to adulthood and could function, if marginally. The emptiness of the prementational phase was reflected at all levels of psychic structure, particularly the self-representation. They have sufficient psychic structure, however, that they can generate anxiety. This specific type of anxiety serves as a defensive adaptation against existential nihilism. Inasmuch as it is an unusual type of anxiety, its significance is frequently misunderstood, and treatment and countertransference complications may result.

I was puzzled by a woman in her mid-20s whose chief complaint was constant anxiety ever since she could consciously remember. I tried to elicit precipitating causes and to explore circumstances that might ameliorate her anxiety. I was thinking in terms of an anxiety neurosis and conceptualizing the affect she complained about as signal anxiety.

Certainly what she presented seemed to be a description of a classic anxiety state. She had the subjective feeling of dread, the physical signs of accelerated breathing, tachycardia, and tremor, as well as vasomotor accompaniments. She looked anxious and her voice was tremulous. I found it difficult to understand how she could constantly sustain such a state of tension as I was trying to formulate her symptoms in terms of the psychodynamic hypothesis. The patient constantly admonished me for trying to find meaning when none was there. According to the patient, I was interpreting upward.

Finally, she admitted that she was not always anxious, but insisted that it was still futile to look for precipitants. She told me that she was the cause of her anxiety, that she could make it appear or disappear at will. She could turn it on and off as one would a faucet. Then, to my astonishment, she demonstrated what she meant. She said she would turn it off, and her anxiety promptly disappeared. She stood very still, hardly breathing and lacking any facial expression. I had the eerie feeling that I was looking at a corpse.

She must have sensed the impact she was having on me, so she decided to "turn on" the anxiety. Her face assumed an anxious expression and she developed a slight tremor of both hands. She showed me that her arms had developed goose bumps and there were trickles of perspiration on her forehead. I am certain that she also had tachycardia and possibly an elevated blood pressure. She then composed herself, relatively speaking, in that she still had an anxious expression, but her goose bumps and perspiration disappeared.

She went on to explain that the anxiety was painful and that was why she was seeing me. On the other hand, not to feel anxious was a terrifying experience. She described the mental state that was covered up by the anxiety as a state of "apathetic terror." These are exactly the same words Federn (1952) used to describe the subjective aspects of existential annihilation, but my patient had never heard of Federn.

I learned that she was an identical twin, her sister being ten minutes older than she was. The sister had been sick throughout childhood, and the family's attention and concern were focused on her. She had been hospitalized several times, and much money and time were spent for her treatment. My patient was healthy, and, as she stated, she grew up on her own. Because she was physically well, no one paid any attention to her. From an emotional viewpoint, she was sad, withdrawn, isolated, and constantly anxious, but she did not call attention to herself, so she went through childhood unnoticed.

Her sister apparently recovered her health during adolescence, but my patient continued to feel desolate and anxious; again, however, she was left alone. She was uncomfortable but not too uncomfortable, and she somehow managed to plod through high school.

In college she met a schizoid young man whom she married during her sophomore year. I conjectured that he was schizoid from her description of him, and he later had an obvious psychotic break, which tended to confirm her observations. Actually, she was a keen observer and could give clear and detailed descriptions.

She stopped going to school after she married, but her sister continued until she graduated, when she married a young medical student. Several years later, the patient sought treatment because she felt that her anxiety was becoming unmanageable, to the point that she finally succeeded in getting her parents, husband, and sister to show some concern for her. Her family had arranged for her to see me. Her seeking therapy was related to the sister's better economic and social position. It was clear that her brother-in-law was going to be a very successful, well-paid surgeon. The sister was displaying her affluence with expensive clothing, a large house, and foreign cars. The patient's husband earned a meager income when compared with his brother-in-law. The sister had always been in the limelight, and once again my patient felt eclipsed. These connections were worked out after a year and a half of treatment.

During the first year of treatment, she stressed how miserable she felt, but misery meant emptiness. She experienced herself as empty, as being nothing, which in some ways was worse than being dead. If she created pain for herself in the form of anxiety, then she could capture some sense of aliveness and existence. She compared her situation to a person's pinching himself to determine whether he was awake or dreaming, or, in her terms, whether he existed or not.

I have had other patients who have complained of constant anxiety and, after a while, I would feel irritated by the changeless status of their symptom. I did not have that kind of counter-transference reaction to this patient. At times I could absorb her underlying feelings of emptiness, but mainly I felt a sense of urgency, a need to establish a secure identity for her that did not have to be energized by anxiety. I was reacting to the threat of psychic dissolution.

I have presented this patient in extensive detail elsewhere (Giovacchini 1979a, 1986). I refer to her now because I wish to illustrate how another affect, in this instance anxiety, has a binding, synthesizing function. Rather than soothing premen-tational agitation, anxiety served as a defense against the disrup-tion of existential annihilation. This type of disruption is asso-ciated with the prementational phase and, as a basic feeling of dread or apathetic terror, it cannot be mentally represented. Like the patients discussed in previous chapters, my patient lacked the capacity to form and hold mental representations.

Needs that have mental representations stem from earlier physiologically oriented needs that originate during the premen-tational stage. Insofar as all levels of development are preserved in the adult psyche, physiological imbalances will affect higher stages of organization and the perception of basic needs. The participation of these earlier stages, as has been discussed, stimulate specific countertransference responses. I will discuss further how the traumas of the prementational stage contribute to countertransference impasses. More precisely, I will again refer to the way in which a primitive defense that is a reaction to early traumas becomes involved in the treatment interaction.

* * *

The patient, a woman in her 20s, was depressed and was so thin that she could be classified as anorexic. She sought treatment from a colleague (Flarsheim 1975) because life had no meaning to her, and she wished she were dead.

She had been a "fussy" infant. She had been quite agitated, cried constantly, and had frequent temper tantrums. The family hired a nurse who had a reputation for handling fussy babies. Her technique was simple. Whenever the baby needed something, the nurse immediately responded, but not to the need. If the child was hungry, she would change her diaper; if she soiled, she would feed her. She also put gloves on the baby's hands so that she would not be able to suck her thumbs. In several months, the child was no longer fussy; she became quiet, probably in a state of apathetic torpor. She created no further disturbance, and the family was pleased.

As an adult, she was lifeless. She suffered from anhedonia and was anorexic because, as with everything else, she had no interest in food. In fact, she seemed to be without feelings, and she avoided any situation that might be stimulating. Unlike my patient's daughter, she could not stand hearing music. Even ordinary sounds were disturbing. She could not tolerate either inner or outer stimuli.

Her therapist conjectured that life for this patient was painful. Initially, the feeling of aliveness is based on the perception of needs that are first felt physiologically in the prementational phase. Because of this patient's experience with the nurse, she was forced to feel basic needs with great intensity because they were not met. The intensity of her needs was augmented by the fact that they were frustrated in the context of a caregiving relationship. As a baby, the patient was being taken care of, but her tension continued to increase. There was no relief. Therefore, life-sustaining needs were dangerous and excruciatingly painful.

If everything associated with living was unbearable, then the patient had to construct an elemental defense that would enable her to survive and would allow life processes to run their course at the lowest possible energy level: she had to deaden her feelings. Her basic defense, deadness, paradoxically kept her alive. She operated on the basis of the fundamental oxymoron that to be alive is to be dead.

To therapists whose orientation separates life from death and views them as polarities, it is difficult to empathize with what, for the patient, is a life-sustaining adaptation. They are bewildered because of the confusion of pain and pleasure and the substitution of one for the other. If they absorb the patient's prementational state, they will also feel a need to deaden what are otherwise pleasurable feelings. The therapist's resistance to accepting the patient's paradoxical adaptation will create an uncomfortable distance between the therapist and the patient. In order to progress in treatment, these patients usually go through a phase of therapy in which they need to fuse with their analysts. These analyses often reach an impasse when therapists actively prevent patients from fusing with them. This is the primitive counterpart of Racker's (1968) discussion of concordant countertransference, in which the analyst finds it painful to accept the patient's projections and thus refuses to do so.

A common technical error stimulated by the therapist's fear of fusion is to encourage the patient to give up the sense of deadness. These analysts believe, or perhaps rationalize, that their patients are withdrawing from them. They mistakenly interpret their deadness as part of a depression or as a schizoid phenomenon that leads them to shut themselves off from the world. Thus, these analysts attempt to bring the patient into the world, but they are actually defending themselves against a potential fusion (Ehrenberg 1985). There is a degree of projection operating on the part of these therapists in that they are accusing the patients of withdrawing when, in fact, it is they themselves who are withdrawing.

Inasmuch as the therapists of "dead" patients intuitively sense that these patients want to put painful feelings into them, they try to get their patients to change their reactions to or get rid of the terror that they have toward feelings that ordinarily create a sense of aliveness. They encourage them to seek and participate in pleasurable activities. What they fail to recognize is that these activities are pleasurable for them but not for their patients. They feel that if fusion is to occur, both patient and analyst must have the same orientation toward pleasure and pain, and aliveness and deadness. Thus the patient must change as a precondition for therapy, rather than change being the outcome of a therapy that has led to developmental progression, and in which the patient has been able to form an endopsychic registration of the pleasurable satisfaction of the need for nurturance—what I have called a nurturing matrix (Giovacchini 1979b, 1986, 1987).

These patients usually feel misunderstood because their analysts believe that they are giving them emotional support by encouraging them to develop trust, which will enable them to seek pleasurable relationships and experiences. In a sense, the therapist's approach falls in line with the repetition compulsion. With the previously described patient, such supportive behavior by the analyst would be reminiscent of that of the nurse who responded immediately to a need other than that of the moment. Similarly, the analyst is extremely attentive to a needy patient, but his response is inappropriate to this patient's needs. The patient needs to feel dead in order to remain alive. The analyst, if successful in eliminating the feeling of deadness, would cause painful needs to emerge, just as the nurse had succeeded in creating such needs by responding to nonexistent needs. Fortunately, this patient's analyst did not try to eliminate the feeling of deadness by being "supportive."

Occasionally, patients similar to the young woman described will encounter an ananlyst who has a similar character orientation. In these instances, patient and analyst may fuse, but it is a unique type of fusion. I treated a middle-aged housewife who had seen another analyst for several years. She sought treatment with me because her former analyst had died. At the beginning of treatment she produced many dreams and associations that indicated how thoroughly they had fused with each other, but it was a fusion based on a mutual feeling of deadness.

She brought me some cartoons she had drawn about her treatment. She and her analyst were drawn as stick figures, but they were remarkably accurate representations of both of them. The first picture shows the patient walking through the door of the office as the analyst is standing beside his chair. In the next caption, she is about to lie on the couch and the analyst is about to sit in his chair. Both their necks are elongated. In the next picture, she is lying down and he is in his chair; both their necks are drawn as long, wavy lines. Their heads look like balloons and their necks are the strings fastened to them. The drawings continue with the patient lying on the couch and the analyst sitting in his chair, but the balloon heads and string necks become detached from their respective bodies and float away from them. They each float to the other body and attach to it. The analyst and patient exchange heads, such that one becomes the other. The cartoons generate a sense of utter lack of movement and feelings. They are sitting there lifeless, simply exchanging heads.

The patient is the analyst and the analyst is the patient. This is an interesting type of fusion in that one person does not dominate or submerge the other. There are different types of fusion, determined by the degree of involvement of the pair and the extent to which individuality is sacrificed. Many combinations are possible, ranging from one partner's completely obliterating the other to a well-balanced intermeshing and sharing of psyches in a truly intimate relationship. In the patient's cartoons, which reflect her fantasies, it seemed that the similarities of patient and analyst were being stressed in that their roles were easily interchangeable.

A shared fantasy between analyst and patient emphasized that they were two components of a single entity called psychoanalysis. The analyst ruefully commented that psychoanalysis was dead. Perhaps he could ensure its survival by having himself stuffed, put behind a display window in a museum, and labeled "psychoanalyst." The patient protested that there is no such thing as a psychoanalyst without a patient, so she would also have to be stuffed and put on a couch next to him in the museum. Then the display could properly be called psychoanalysis. Psychoanalysis may be dead or extinct, but it would survive forever in a museum.

* * *

This fantasy is a graphic description of how deadness can be an adaptive defense to preserve a sense of aliveness. It is not a vital or, in a manner of speaking, very alive sense of aliveness, but at the most basic level, the organism is preserved.

This last clinical example illustrates an extreme situation in which the therapist's psychopathology played a prominent role. He initiated the production of a somewhat macabre fantasy that can be easily understood in the terms that I have discussed. I believe, however, that treatment situations in which analysts are locked in with their patients through deadness are not uncommon. They may not be as obvious as the one just described, but then we usually do not have access to information that would help us understand the minute details of the transference–countertransference interaction.

The scope of analysis continues to widen (Stone 1963) as we understand more about the nuances of the transference–countertransference axis. In this chapter, I have explored that part of the interaction between patient and analyst that can be traced back to the earliest stage of development, the prementational stage. In these instances our responses are not the outcome of complex psychological processes such as reactions to the patient's dependent needs or infantile sexual impulses. Rather, our countertransference is based on the absorption of the patient's unsoothable agitation and our reactions to the defensive adaptations constructed to handle this prementational disruption. Affects, in these instances, have a binding function that at times appears incomprehensible.

As we learn more about the primitive end of the developmental spectrum, some puzzling symptomatic pictures become understandable. Both anxiety and hostile feelings are viewed in a perspective other than the traditional one and lead to further understanding of our countertransference reactions. Affects serve many more functions than we have previously recognized. They have adaptive significance in addition to their function as warning signals and sensory perceptions associated with specific instinctual impulses. In the next chapter, I will explore the affect of depression, an affect that is very much involved in a commonly encountered form of psychopathology.

7

Countertransference

and

Affective Disorders

In the previous chapter, I explored the therapist's reactions to particular types of structural defects. Patients suffering from affective disorders also have defects in psychic structure, and to the extent that they do, they will evoke similar countertransference reactions.

Because of the depressed patient's intense self-preoccupation, the analyst may feel depleted in the same way as he would by a narcissistic patient. In a sense, depressed patients suffer from a type of narcissistic disorder, but there are other aspects to their character that warrant separating them as a group.

Depressed patients are considered to be on a higher level than other character disorders (Giovacchini 1979, Klein 1935, 1946). Consequently, the countertransference reactions they provoke and the therapeutic complications they create have unique qualities that deserve examination. These are commonly encountered patients who, despite having attained higher levels of psychic structure, or perhaps because of it, cause particular problems and engender hopeless feelings in their therapists.

In discussing affective disorders, I will focus on depressions. Manic patients are difficult to contain in ordinary outpatient therapy. The management problems created by their symptoms often make these patients inaccessible to an analytic approach.

Depressed patients frequently prove refractory to treatment. Many depressed patients improve spontaneously, but others present a fixed, rigid clinical picture of melancholia. Their symptoms do not vary; they always get worse, never better. Anhedonia and hopelessness dominate their lives, and they pervade the consultation room with these feelings.

The treatment of depressed patients is in some ways similar to that of the overtly narcissistic patient. Perhaps there is less of a tendency to feel sleepy with such patients, but analysts often find themselves wanting to escape; they often feel a heavy sense of oppression and share the patient's hopelessness. The treatment experience may be quite unpleasant.

As Freud (1917b) postulated, patients who suffer from depression withdraw their libido from the external world and turn it onto themselves. Rather than feeling enhanced, they experience pain, because the feelings that are directed inward are highly ambivalent and a good deal of rage and hatred is introjected. Regardless of the quality of introjected libido, depressed patients are very narcissistic, as evidenced by their intense self-preoccupation. Although they are not overtly or covertly wrenching libido away from their therapists, it is easy to develop negative countertransference feelings when treating melancholic patients. And although these patients are constantly attacking and deprecating themselves, the effect on the therapist is often the same as that engendered by the boasting, arrogant, pretentious narcissistic character disorder. In a sense, depressed patients suffer from a type of narcissistic disorder, the difference being that they introject the negative aspect of their ambivalence. They immerse themselves in self-hatred rather than self-love, or more precisely, self-aggrandizement.

Many of these patients relate only minimally, if at all, to their therapists. They are almost completely absorbed with themselves. This preoccupation may be expressed as concern over physical symptoms, relentless hypochondriasis, and bitter attacks on their integrity, self-worth, and other character traits. For therapists, these self-recriminations are painful to observe, but they may be inclined to join the patient in the attack. What may have initially been sympathy and compassion can turn into a negative reaction toward the patient, similar to the feelings that these patients harbor toward themselves.

The discomfort that many clinicians experience with depressed patients stems from a lack of relatedness. As is the case with the more flamboyant narcissistic character disorders, libido flows only toward the patient, and the analyst feels narcissistically depleted. There is an added difficulty with narcissistic regulation, however. The patient will not let the analyst get through to him. The therapist will try to give something helpful to the patient, but the depressed patient, in general, will not accept or cannot use what is being offered. They fend off the analyst's ministrations, and this is felt as a narcissistic blow by the therapist. To have been able to help the patient would have given the analyst some narcissistic gratification of his own, but the patient denies him this satisfaction. These patients often will not let their libido flow beyond their somatic boundaries, so the clinician is again faced with a situation that causes him to feel narcissistically deprived.

These patients attempt to structure the therapeutic relationship along the lines of the medical model. Although they emphasize their misery and unworthiness, they take no responsibility for their condition from an intrapsychic perspective. Their self-condemnation does not indicate that they understand that their feelings and behavior stem from intrapsychic sources or that they have much understanding of psychic determinism. No matter how depressed these patients appear to be, they tend to be quite demanding and to put the burden of relieving them of their symptoms exclusively on the therapist's shoulders. They seek magical rescuing, often through the use of antidepressant medications (Brown 1985).

Therapists are forced into a delicate situation. They suffer all the countertransference reactions that are characteristic of relationships in which they feel narcissistically shut out. These patients cast their therapists in the role of omnipotent saviors, but usually without the idealization that is often associated with an exalted position. They make enormous demands of their analysts, but they do not elevate them or endow them with any significance. Consequently, whatever narcissistic gratification is involved in being idealized is also denied to the depressed patient's therapist. Granted, this kind of gratification would relate to primitive, conflictful, or immature elements of the analyst's personality, but its absence in the context of the patient's demandingness only makes the therapeutic task more difficult. Not that idealization would not create its own catastrophes, as has been discussed, but depressed patients create an atmosphere that is especially difficult for therapists, who want to maintain an intrapsychic perspective, to tolerate. Many analysts who are medically trained might, under these circumstances, welcome the introduction of the medical model.

I believe that much of the impetus toward attributing a biological etiology to depression is the outcome of subtle countertransference attitudes that are commonly evoked by depressed patients. This is not to say that none of the depressive syndromes have a biological factor operating in their production. Indeed, considerable data seem to indicate that a biological variable is instrumental in the etiology of some depressions. However, the psychiatrist's attitude, in embracing a neurochemical substrata and ignoring intrapsychic and characterological elements may, in part, be due to qualities of the patient–therapist interaction that are very much related to intrapsychic factors in both therapist and patient.

Being of no importance to the patient as a person has, as discussed, a disruptive effect on therapists. Depressed patients are capable of idealizing, but they have a need, intrinsic to their psychopathology, to demean those who set themselves up as potential caretakers. This need may not be obvious or overtly expressed, but it is a pervasively hostile, deprecatory attitude that has deleterious effects.

One aspect of the therapeutic interaction is not ignored and can be idealized by the patient. The therapist's knowledge of and capacity to prescribe drugs is exalted. The drug, not the person, is related to and idealized. Some therapists, in order to gain acknowledgment, orient their professional self-representation around the dispensing of drugs. They can maintain their narcissistic equilibrium as they identify with the powerful, potentially magical, curative effect of antidepressant drugs.

I am not suggesting that all therapists who treat patients from a psychopharmacologic rather than a psychodynamic viewpoint are struggling with the internal regulation of narcissistic supplies and are promising a magical cure in order to feel that they are being acknowledged. Many motivations, conscious and unconscious, determine a clinician's treatment approach. In my opinion, however, the factors I have just outlined are frequently involved in countertransference attitudes and may incline some analysts to think in terms of organic rather than intrapsychic components. I point to analysts in particular, rather than to psychiatrists in general, because analysts would have shifted from psychodynamic to neurochemical explanations, whereas psychiatrists are more likely to have been treating their patients from a pharmacologic perspective in the first place.

* * *

A man in his early 50s was referred to me because he had been having recurrent episodes of depression for the previous fifteen years. He had been given medication that had been fairly effective, but his most recent episode had not responded to the antidepressant he had been taking. He was referred to me by his friend, a surgeon, who had heard of me from a colleague whom I had analyzed some years ago for a moderately crippling depression.

It quickly became apparent that he had no idea that he was seeing a psychoanalyst. I rather doubt that he even knew what a psychoanalyst was. He approached me with a respectful, even reverential, attitude. He believed that I was a medical authority on depression. He gave me an orderly, well-structured, sequential history, going into great detail about every drug he had ever used, including dosages, frequency of administration, side effects, and effectiveness. As far as I could ascertain, he had tried every drug known with the exception of the antipsychotic neuroleptics, for the treatment of affective disorders.

From force of habit, I tried to direct his attention to intrapsychic factors, to a discussion of feelings and relationships. The patient reacted as if I were displaying some eccentricity, but because of his misguided surgeon friend's apparently strong recommendations and faith in my knowledge of the biological nature of depression, he must have decided to briefly indulge me. He told me that his first bout of depression had been temporally related to a fight with his brother that had led to the dissolution of both their business and social relationships, but he saw no connection between that event and his serious depressive "illness." It was as if a patient with a metastatic carcinoma were being questioned about his mastery of chess.

He finally revealed that he had been told that I was involved in important research on depression and that I was almost ready to publish my results. Apparently I had discovered some new drugs, and he was offering himself as a subject. I was, of course, quite astonished. I told him that there had been some misunderstanding. It was true that I had done some writing on depression and had been on a panel with a pioneer in the psychopharmacology of depression, but I emphasized that I had represented the psychoanalytic viewpoint. I was quick to add that the two were not incompatible and wondered whether, inasmuch as he seemed to have tried just about every drug on the market, he might be interested in looking within himself, to see what his feelings and attitudes contributed to the formation of his depressive symptoms.

The patient's change of demeanor was striking. He remained friendly and pleasant, but instead of being a revered authority, I had been relegated to the position of a lackey. He now called me "Doc" instead of "Professor" and spoke to me as if

I had no particular knowledge about his condition. He gave me his opinions on sports, politics, and the weather, but he was not in the least concerned about any of my thoughts or judgments. His transformation was sudden and complete, emphasizing a complete detachment from me as a professional. In fact, from his viewpoint, this was no longer a professional setting; he had completely shut me out, at least as an authority figure with a particular expertise that he might find useful.

The sequence from idealization to deidealization and narcissistic withdrawal was clear. He was not able to deal with me in an interpersonal context or as a positive transference object. He could idealize impersonal drugs, and inasmuch as I was linked with the drug, I could, to some extent, be included in his positive feelings. Once he realized that I could not be used as an extension of the magical qualities he attached to drug treatment, he cast me aside as an object of no importance. I knew that he did not want analysis or psychotherapy and did not offer him another appointment. He insisted on paying his bill immediately and in cash. He seemed glad when our time was up and he could leave.

I was immensely relieved when the interview was concluded and the patient left. After I had revealed to him that I had no particular expertise in the psychopharmacologic treatment of affective disorders, I had decided as he was talking that under no circumstances did I want to treat this patient. I felt that there was very little possibility of establishing a therapeutically useful tranference. Perhaps some other therapist might have had a different opinion and might have made more of an effort to engage him in a relationship, but I must have found the process of being cast aside too unpleasant. To be idealized can also be painful if one keeps in mind the consequences and often inevitable fate of idealization—that is, the patient's catastrophic disappointment and feeling of being outrageously betrayed. To be idealized for an attribute that is not at all connected to oneself can be quite disturbing.

* * *

This patient illustrates how concretely oriented some depressed patients can be (Brown 1985). I am still somewhat mystified about why he was referred to me or how the surgeon could have believed that I would be an appropriate referral. There are depressed patients who have a similar concreteness and somatic orientation who, nevertheless, have some psychological mindedness and can relate to the therapist. In spite of such capacities, these patients may also provoke disruptive countertransference attitudes that are not just reactions to feelings of narcissistic depletion.

Depressed patients, although intensely self-preoccupied, often use their therapists as targets for their anger. They are not completely narcissistically bound, as were some of the patients I have discussed. Their inwardly directed destructive feelings cause them to feel miserable and lead to self-deprecatory and self-destructive behavior. This behavior is also a mode of relating. At the same time, it represents a narcissistic withdrawal and an attack on the therapist. It is a seemingly passive way of expressing rage and a need for revenge. The impact on the analyst is experienced as aggressive and assaultive.

The treatment of depressed patients is frequently accompanied by what, on the surface, must seem like a paradoxical countertransference reaction. This reaction reflects some of the paradoxes inherent in their psychopathology. The therapist feels both narcissistically abandoned and intensely related to, but in a destructive, assaultive fashion. To a large measure, this is what depressed patients feel about themselves, and the situation that they create for their analysts can be explored in the domain of the transference–countertransference axis. It is an interesting phenomenon in that the outward flow of libido (destructive in this instance) by projection is also indicative of the patient's narcissistic withdrawl. This often causes considerable confusion and anxiety in the analyst.

As discussed, some analysts seek refuge in the medical model. Others may defend themselves against their patients' hostility by identifying with them. This is the now-familiar defense known as identifying with the aggressor, first described by A. Freud (1937). She emphasized aggression in terms of an overtly sadistic quality. Most depressed patients are not overtly sadistic, but their attacks on themselves, which can be defined as masochistic, are definitely experienced by the therapist as sadistic.

The therapist often identifies with the negative elements of the patient's reactions, his misery and hopelessness. Under these circumstances, analysts lose faith in the analytic method as they incorporate the patient's helplessness and hopelessness. They also feel vulnerable and inadequate to the therapeutic task, or, because they feel that these patients are so oppressive, they are unwilling to treat them in a relationship that revolves around the transference–countertransference axis.

I recall a colleague's telling me of how he felt enveloped by a depressed patient's sadness. He felt that there was a veil that completely surrounded him, beyond which was an atmosphere composed of hopelessness rather than oxygen. The patient's depression had totally pervaded the ambience, and the analyst, not the patient, was at the center of it. A description in a lighter vein comes from a *New Yorker* cartoon. The proverbial patient is lying on the couch, and the analyst is sitting behind him with the traditional notebook in his lap. He is leaning forward and saying, "Yes, I could treat you for your depression, but, as you say, what's the use — it's all so hopeless."

My colleague was stressing the patient's powerful influence on the ambience, whereas the cartoon was emphasizing the thoroughness with which the analyst had introjected the patient's conflictful, ambivalent feelings. These are further examples of how a therapist can respond, often simultaneously, from two different levels—that is, in a reaction to an oppressive ambience and by receiving the patient's projections. The ambience, of course, affects intrapsychic elements. My colleague's ambience of hopelessness created a tight envelope of sadness that must have permeated his psychic pores. He felt sad because the patient had succeeded in creating a hopeless atmosphere. The specific ambience that depressed patients construct and the intrapsychic changes that occur within the therapist because of both transference projections and the influence of the ambience lead to negative countertransference reactions that influence the therapist to give up or to avoid initiating psychoanalytic treatment.

The therapeutic ambience has several effects. As noted, it can affect narcissistic equilibrium and produce painful affects such as sadness. It can also be coercive, causing the therapist to feel that the sword of Damocles is constantly hanging over his head. With many patients who suffer from affective disorders, the threat of suicide is constantly present. The profound effect of having a patient who is on the brink of suicide spills into various areas of the analyst's world. It goes beyond a mere technical problem; more than just the analytic ambience is involved.

Earlier in this book I discussed how certain patients intrude into the treatment setting, upsetting therapists' professional self-representations and interfering with their modus operandi. Depressed patients can create similar problems, although they are not always so obviously intrusive. Those who are withdrawn and retarded would appear to exhibit the antithesis of intrusiveness; nevertheless they are very often experienced as impinging upon the therapist's space, sometimes as much as do agitated depressed patients who vociferously inundate their therapists with outrageous demands. Intrusive patients also attempt to persuade the therapist to leave the analytic setting and enter their contemporary world. Patients who suffer from affective disorders have similar strivings, but their unique subtleties add specific qualities to countertransference reactions, and these once again involve an interplay between the treatment and the outside world that is stimulated by the constant threat of suicide.

There are suicidal persons who might not be classified as depressed, but the suicidal characteristics of depressed patients are the most familiar to clinicians. Among the many devastating effects of patients' killing themselves is the fear of the opprobrium of the outside world, including the critical and condemnatory appraisal of colleagues. Suicide also has moral and pragmatic overtones in our litigious society. The sword of Damocles has two types of steel: one alloyed to the humanistic need to have a live patient, and the other alloyed to the threat of a malpractice suit—two disparate but powerful factors that can have disastrous effects on the therapeutic setting.

Thus far, I have stressed several characteristic countertransference responses to depressed patients, including the pain of feeling narcissistically shut out, anxiety stemming from concern for the patient's life, and the fear of being legally attacked. Anxiety is also caused by attacks from the superego. Another countertransference element is manifested by confusion that may be sufficiently intense to cause the therapist to be functionally paralyzed.

The essence of psychoanalytic treatment is an exclusive devotion to the inner world of the mind. Although analysts may, to some degree, become involved in some aspects of the patient's external world, their chief interest is in intrapsychic processes. Depressed patients, especially because of their propensity for suicide, force the analyst's attention elsewhere. Instead of dealing with the patient's suicidal orientations and threats as analytic material, they tend to deal with suicide as a realistic possibility, which it often is. If clinicians dwell on these threats, they become linked more and more to external reality, and the patient's material is no longer viewed in terms of intrapsychic phenomena. Being pushed from one frame of reference to another—that is, from exploring intrapsychic phenomena to protecting patients from themselves—is both uncomfortable and confusing.

It has been recommended that, ideally, the analyst's orientations should not stray from an intrapsychic focus and that the threat of suicide should not evoke any more response than any other clinical material. I know of some situations in which such a firm adherence to the analytic method has been lifesaving, but this is a very difficult position to maintain when facing a genuinely self-destructive patient. Some analysts believe that they cannot continue to function as analysts if they believe that suicide is imminent. They relinquish their analytic perspective and institute measures to protect the patient, usually by hospitalization. Unfortunately, the relinquishing of the analytic role can sometimes precipitate a suicide attempt. The patient—accurately—interprets the therapist's behavior as representing a loss of hope and faith in the analytic method.

The patient's self-destructive reaction to the analyst's loss of faith in the analytic method implies that such a depressed patient might have had some expectation that psychoanalytic treatment would be helpful. The descriptions I have given of them and the countertransference attitudes they evoke would seem to indicate otherwise, but there are other facets to their characters that make them, to some extent, capable of entering into a psychoanalytic interaction. Paradoxically, the fact that depressed patients are often very skillful in thwarting their therapists might indicate that they have some understanding of some of the principles of psychoanalytic treatment and that, because of this understanding, it might be possible to engage them in an analytic relationship.

The recognition that the patient might be potentially analyzable can have favorable countertransference consequences which may, in turn, stimulate a positive feedback sequence, enabling the patient to become increasingly involved in the treatment process. The psychopathology involved in affective disorders often has certain unique features that facilitate a gradual immersion in a treatment relationship despite bitter initial resistance and intense disruptive regression that would seem to make the prospect of psychotherapy ludicrous. If the therapist can obtain a glimpse of a hidden therapeutic potential, however, then he might be able to persevere in the face of a seemingly impossible situation. He might be able to survive the countertransference vicissitudes that are characteristic responses to patients who suffer from affective disorders.

* * *

The husband of a middle-aged woman suffering from an agitated depression called me to make an appointment for his wife. She was in her mid-50s and had been unable to work for about five years. She had been a highly efficient, competent office manager and was very much valued by her employer. Her behavior had deteriorated to the degree that she was unable to do anything for herself. That is why her husband made the telephone call for her.

I can still vividly remember that first telephone call. It was difficult to hear him because of the background noise. The patient was wailing and screaming at her husband, berating him in an incomprehensible and eerie fashion. I heard a low moan, which gradually increased to a wail, and then abruptly erupted into a high-pitched scream. It was occasionally possible to make out a word or phrase, such as "miserable," "terrible," and especially "help," and "I can't stand it any longer." She would then shout about how desperate she felt and would break down sobbing, babbling incoherently.

Her symptoms had begun after her new employer gave a party in her honor because he recognized the value of her services. Her previous employer had taken her for granted. She was known as an energetic, witty woman who was very skilled at restoring calm and finding optimal solutions for thorny situations.

After the party, she had become depressed and agitated to the degree that she could no longer function. Her psychiatrist tried to control her symptoms with drugs, supportive psychotherapy, and group therapy. She had been hospitalized four times during the previous five years as her condition worsened. She had tried most of the tricyclic antidepressants as well as a monoamine oxidase inhibitor. She was also put on lithium, but it did not help. Finally, she was given twelve electric shock treatments, which resulted in a transient but frightening memory loss. I gathered this information from her internist, who referred her to me.

I must confess that I had no great urge to see her and even less of a desire to accept her as a patient in view of her history and her behavior during the telephone call. My countertransference reactions were decidedly negative. I anticipated a disruptive, unmanageable patient who would upset the reflective tranquility that analysts equate with an optimal therapeutic setting. I envisioned her as demanding, intrusive, and incapable of viewing her situation from an intrapsychic perspective. I felt a degree of hopelessness even before I saw her. I was confused as to what my role would be because I had not visualized myself as her analyst. I doubted that I could establish a relationship with her.

On the other hand, her internist was very fond of her and had considerable respect for her past creativity. He wanted her to receive psychoanalytically oriented treatment. He did not believe that drugs or somatic therapies were the answer, as experience had proven. He caused me to ponder about the possibility of treatment, and I reluctantly agreed to see her in consultation. There was an element of grandiosity in my accepting the referral. True, I did not want to disappoint her internist, but I envisioned the remote possibility that perhaps I might succeed where everyone else had failed. This element of grandiosity sustained me through my predominantly negative countertransference feelings.

I am describing in terms of countertransference what is inherent in the psychopathology of depressed patients—that is, the capacity to sustain opposites, to maintain polarities. This is a manifestation of a fundamental ambivalence. In fact, opposites in depressives support each other, and this was clearly evident in my countertransference responses.

My grandiosity was based, not on the possibility of success, but on the inevitability of failure. After all, everyone and everything else had failed. Her condition had only worsened throughout the years. Therefore, it would not be so horrendous if I also failed. From the viewpoint of my narcissism, I had nothing to lose. There would be no expectations of success, and the worst criticism I might incur would be that I was foolish to have accepted her as a patient. I had buttressed myself against onslaughts on my professional ego ideal, which is, of course, dependent on maintaining an adequate narcissistic balance. I tried to adopt an attitude of contained, moderate grandiosity in order to survive what I anticipated would be a very difficult patient. I also had very little hope that I would be able to engage and keep her in a therapeutic relationship. Perhaps, to some measure, I was hoping that I would not be able to treat her or, more accurately, that she would not let me.

I expected the worst, but my preestablished countertransference helped me maintain equanimity. I emphasized to myself that she had once been competent and creative and that she had been able to engage the concern of her internist, whom I respected. It was with these polarized attitudes—defensive and pessimistic as well as somewhat hopeful as I reflected on her previous ego integration—that I greeted her on our first appointment.

Our first session was dramatic and chaotic, but she demonstrated an understanding of the psychoanalytic process. This conclusion, added to the tenuous positive elements of my countertransference, enhanced my professional narcissism. We were on thin ice, however, and I had to silently accentuate the minimal positive evidence that she might be treatable.

When I first saw her, she was truly a spectacle. She was agitatedly pacing back and forth in my waiting room while her husband sat calmly on a small couch. She was quiet until the moment she saw me. She had apparently been able to distinguish me from my previous patient because as soon as he left through the waiting room door, she faced me and began to moan. She seemed powerful and massive, although she was actually less than 5 feet tall and of slight build. Her eyes had a wild, frenzied look, a penetrating stare that pierced right through me. She made immediate eye contact and never relinquished it.

Without looking away, she grasped her husband's hand and, still moaning, started pulling him into my office. Almost reflexively, I positioned myself at the threshold of my door, letting her through but blocking his path. I told him that it would be best if I saw his wife alone. Not at all perturbed, he quietly sat down again. He seemed relieved. As soon as he let go of his wife's hand, she began to scream loud objections and started moving toward him to once again lead him into the consultation room. She demanded that he come in with her, but by this time I had shut the door and stood there for a moment, barring the way. I motioned her to a chair and she reluctantly walked toward it as I sat in my usual chair.

She remained standing and started again to scream that she would not be able to tolerate the interview, that she would not be able to tell me anything unless her husband was beside her. She begged me to let him into the room, insisting that he would tell me everything I wanted to know. I told her that she had already told me a good deal about herself. She screamed even louder, protesting that she was too disorganized, miserable, and crazy to say anything useful, that nothing good could come out of her. I would have to listen to her husband. I replied that I wanted to listen to her mind. If I let her husband in, I would have to listen to his mind, and it was difficult enough to listen to one mind and impossible to listen to two. As I might have anticipated, she shouted, "Mind! What mind? I have no mind!"

Despite her bizarre and agitated behavior, I felt fairly at ease with her. I surmised from her immediate contact and from the fact that she was making a demand of me that she was relating to me. In spite of her tremendous self-preoccupation, she had a capacity for object relating. The axis of our relationship may have been destructive and self-destructive, but I saw a potential for the development of transference. What I feared, perhaps, was a precipitous, overwhelming, unmanageable transference. Nevertheless, her extreme regression and possibly bombastic transference did not indicate to me that she was going to experience an unanalyzable psychotic transference. It was the strength of her infantile impulses that I thought could disrupt the beginning and establishment of a treatment relationship. I felt that we were relating to each other; I was not narcissistically being shut out. I envisioned our relationship as if we were pulling in different directions, and this tug-of-war feeling became very familiar as the treatment continued. At that moment, I felt as if I were trying to pull her into analysis and she was pulling in the opposite direction. However, I had the impression that she knew, at least unconsciously, what each direction meant. It was this thought that gave me an inkling of hope, which contributed to a weakly positive countertransference.

Her denial that she had a mind indicated, as I saw it, that she felt that there would be nothing to analyze. I thought of resistance when she started toward the door, presumably to let her husband in. I remained seated and quietly said that if she insisted, she could summon her husband, but that once he crossed the threshold, the door would be closed and she could not return to the room. I regretted the situation, but it was her choice. I was surprised at the strength of my feeling, and I later concluded that this was a crucial test of the feasibility of conducting treatment. If she could not contain whatever she was acting out by having her husband beside her, then she had no capacity to separate the infantile from the current world, and therapy would thus be impossible. We would not be able to construct a transitional space of fantasy if she brought the external world, to which she was regressively bound, into the consultation room.

She stopped dead in her tracks. She became hypotonic and looked like a deflated balloon. Her arms, instead of swinging wildly, hung loosely at her sides. Her facial muscles sagged, and she became hunched over. Gradually she straightened up, and as her muscle tone increased, she began shuffling her feet. There was a rhythmic quality to her movements, as though she were practicing some dance step, and the upper part of her body swayed in synchrony with her legs. She would occasionally stop this shuffle and stand in one spot, crossing and uncrossing her legs as a young child might who has to go to the toilet. She did not again mention her husband; instead, she abruptly shouted, "Give me drugs, for God's sake! Give me drugs!"

This patient had been referred to me for analysis, out of desperation, because nothing else had helped. She had been explicitly told that I did not prescribe drugs, although I would not object to anyone else's doing so. I was aware that this information had been given to her when she was referred to me. Keeping this in mind, I did not feel any compunction to consider her request, even in terms of refusing. I was able to hear it simply as material that did not require any response at the content level.

So instead of answering her question, I asked if she was taking any drugs now. She enumerated all the drugs she had taken since the onset of her depression. Since there were so many, I noted to myself with some amusement that she had, at least in one respect, a phenomenal memory—that she did, indeed, have a mind. I then asked if any of these drugs had helped, and as I anticipated, she shouted "No!" Clearly drugs had not helped, and now she was asking me to prescribe them for her. I pointed out that drugs had failed, and that by asking me to prescribe drugs for her, she was expecting and wanting me to fail. She stopped her shuffling dance step and slumped in the chair. Then, in a plaintive and exhausted voice, she gasped that no one could help her. I motioned her toward the couch and, without protest, she lay down. Without prompting, she began to talk about her background in a calm and organized fashion, a miraculous contrast to her initial chaos and agitation.

She was not exactly free-associating, but she was revealing many interesting and relevant aspects of her background. From what she was telling me I was able to make some tentative formulations about her psychopathology. I directed and asked very little. Only at rare moments when my curiosity was aroused did I ask her a question or ask her to amplify something she had said. Otherwise, she organized her recitation and supplied me with considerable data. She had calmed down considerably and behaved quite rationally.

Naturally, I welcomed the change of scene. I was quite impressed by the tremendous range of her ego states. I began to develop the feeling that perhaps I could analyze her. It seemed as if she were trying to help me to understand her, that she was trying to communicate useful information. For the moment, I felt as if we were actively engaged with each other.

Apparently she could not endure for long a situation in which someone was having good feelings. Upon finishing her narrative, she remained silent for about five minutes. Then she exploded. She looked as if she were having a convulsion. She was writhing on the couch, twisting her neck in agonizing positions, and her arms and legs were flailing in all directions. She protested that she could not continue to lie on the couch and abruptly sat up. She then stood up and started her peculiar dance shuffle, all the while screaming and sobbing. In loud, harsh, but muffled tones, she begged me to help her, give her drugs, and let her husband in.

She fell to her knees like a supplicant, wrapping her arms around my legs and pleading for help and for drugs. I quickly disengaged myself and motioned her to the couch once again. She responded with a powerful flow of obscenities that were not directly addressed to me or to anyone, but she went back to the couch and sat on it. She looked pathetic as she sat there with her head bowed, sobbing.

Although she was genuinely tormented and suffering intense anguish, there seemed to be a ritualized, repetitive pattern to her behavior. She seemed to be following a predetermined sequence (Thorner 1985). Furthermore, there was a comic element to her actions, somewhat of a paradox in the midst of her tragic life and painful misery.

The end of the hour was approaching and since, at that moment, she was relatively quiet, I decided to summarize my conclusions and recommendations. I explained my requirements as an analyst in terms of fees, frequency of appointments, and limitations, the boundaries I had to preserve. She already knew that I would not prescribe drugs, and I added that I would not become involved in the management of her life. If she were to require hospitalization, a colleague would look after her, although we would try to arrange to keep our appointments.

She screamed and protested that she did not know why I was suggesting analysis, that there was nothing to analyze because she was a "rotten, empty shell." Proceeding as though I had not been interrupted, I stated that analysis was all I could offer her. I could see nothing else that could be done for her since everything else had been tried and failed. There was a strong possibility that analysis would also fail, but I also knew that part of her wanted it to fail. She would try to defeat me as she had everyone else. I emphasized that she had a need to put others in a position where they felt powerless and confused, perhaps to make them feel what she felt. In a most unexpected reflective fashion, she said, "I never thought of that." Then she looked momentarily stunned and quickly resumed moaning and wailing.

My countertransference reactions during the end of this first session ran in many directions. Her behavior had been so outrageously out of control that I wondered what I was doing pressing analysis the way I did. Her begging for help indicated that her orientation was toward the outer world and that the only mode of relating she would permit would occur in the surrounding external world rather than in the inner space of her mind. In fact, she had denied having a mind. A good deal of her behavior seemed to represent a resistance to getting inside her mind.

In view of her disruptiveness, I felt a degree of hopelessness, which I now recognize was, in addition to an identification with her similar feelings, a response to my injured narcissism. She refused to remain in an intrapsychic frame, which meant that she did not value what I had to offer – but then she did not value anything, especially herself. On the other hand, there were moments when I was hopeful that she could be introspective and could relate to me at the level of a recognizable transference. I was experiencing that peculiar countertransference ambivalence of feeling shut out at one level and mildly grandiose and hopeful at another.

The patient's moaning and wailing intensified, however, and it seemed then that my short narrative had gone completely beyond her, as if I had been speaking in a foreign language. Nevertheless, she did not want to leave. I pointed out that our time was up, but she kept screaming at me to help her. I walked to the door, opened it, and motioned for her to leave. She walked over and stood in front of me. She suddenly clutched her bosom and with an anguished expression screamed, "I have a pain here!"

I replied, "It must be the pain of parting."

Again her mood quickly and drastically changed as she calmly responded, "No, I have it all the time."

I chuckled, "See, you are already trying to defeat me." She then saw her husband and began once again to wail and to do her shuffling dance step.

He ignored her as he approached me and asked for a report of his wife's condition. I told him that his wife would be able to tell him everything he needed to know. The patient loudly protested. She howled that she could not tell him anything. She was too upset and disoriented to do anything and reviled herself for being a worthless amoeba. She wanted to curl up and die and spend the rest of the day in my office. She actually walked toward the consultation room door, but I stood in front of it and barred the way. Her husband intervened, telling her that she could not stay and would have to leave with him. Again she regained her composure and told him that I wanted to see her four times a week and that she would have to lie down on the couch. She then named my fee and said that I had told her that she was trying to confuse others and drive them insane. Although I had said nothing about driving other people insane, I felt this would have been a plausible interpretation. I had the distinct impression that her husband agreed with these conclusions.

After she left, I pondered further my ambivalence about being her therapist. Regardless of what was perhaps an underlying capacity for integration and coherence, as exhibited in the list of my conclusions she had given her husband, did I want to get involved with such a disruptive patient? This was an important question, especially for an analyst who is accustomed to working in a relatively serene atmosphere. True, I have worked, and continue to work, with patients suffering from severe psychopathology, in most instances more severe than hers, but these patients usually keep the volume within a fairly comfortable range. Most patients do not exhibit the pressing desperation that this woman did—at least not to the same degree. I also wondered about telephone calls, crises, and the emergency situations she might create.

I let my associations roam, and soon I had an image of a giant woman in front of me. She was wearing a bulky, ugly coat, made of rags and ripped in many places. Despite her inauspicious appearance, there was a certain grace and delicacy about her. I wondered what she would be like if she discarded this bulky garment. What would her real self look like? This image represented the positive side of my ambivalence, emphasizing that there might be an integrated core within her with a potential for growth once we got through the ugly, chaotic outer mantle of the false self (Winnicott 1960).

I discussed the situation with a colleague who does a fair amount of hospital work. He agreed that if hospitalization were necessary, he would be in charge of all aspects of management. He would talk to her husband if need be and otherwise handle details related to her daily adjustment. This was designed to help me avoid becoming involved in environmental manipulation or rescue operations so that I could maintain the analytic setting.

* * *

I have published the details of this patient's history elsewhere (Giovacchini 1979a, pp. 296–298). A complete presentation here is not particularly pertinent to the discussion of countertransference. The psychodynamics of this patient's depression can be understood by examining the transference–countertransference interaction, and historical factors can be discussed in such a context.

A detailed description of some aspects of her treatment, particularly the interaction between the patient and me, is of interest here. This will give us a view of the unfolding and shifting of the countertransference as well as the transference. The countertransference can be observed microscopically and from its origin. As we simultaneously emphasize the transference, we will be able to better understand the treatment process and the nuances of this depressed patient's psychopathology.

This patient demonstrates many features that are the essence of depression. The intensity of her symptoms is both detrimental and helpful for our understanding of psychopathological processes. As they are intrinsically disruptive, they can upset the therapeutic setting to the degree that treatment becomes chaotic. The fact that the symptoms are uncontainable would naturally hamper both understanding and resolution. The patient's intense manifestations of psychopathology stand out in bold relief. This patient, at times, seemed to be a caricature of a depression; and like all caricatures, certain features are so exaggerated that they become conspicuous. This patient, because of her caricature-like qualities, illustrated transference feelings and the inner aspects of her psychic life more clearly than do patients who are less noisy but whose defenses are much more subtle and effective.

The therapist will tend to react to the patient's feelings with a resonance that is quantitatively similar to the intensity of the patient's reactions. As the patient expresses herself directly, without much secondary-process mediation, the therapist will respond with feelings at a level of organization that approximates the patient's. These patients bring their analysts closer to their primary process but allow them to maintain some restraint. Nevertheless, as I reflect on my first interview with this patient, I am somewhat surprised by my outspokenness. I was comfortable with it, but I am certain that with a patient with greater psychic integration, I would not have had such feelings, and if I had, I would not have felt free to express them.

The treatment of patients suffering from primitive mental states produces various paradoxical features in countertransference relations; this is especially true of some depressed patients, who may not be quite as primitive as patients suffering from other character disorders. With my patient, I felt a certain freedom of response, which did, in fact, have the effect of making her somewhat receptive to the intrapsychic viewpoint.

I speak of paradoxes because I really was not trying, at least consciously, to encourage her to engage in treatment. Before she reached my office, I had had very little anticipation that she would remain in treatment. I had been thinking in terms of a single consultation and perhaps of setting up a supportive situation with a general psychiatrist who could try some of the latest antidepressant drugs. Anticipating not having her as a patient made me feel relaxed in the face of agitation and disruption. Consequently, I was a more effective therapist in the first interview than I would have been if I had been actively and consciously trying to encourage her to accept a psychoanalytic approach.

This situation was similar to those that some of my colleagues and I have experienced when talking to prospective patients on the telephone. In these instances, therapists are referring patients to colleagues because, for some reason, they are not able to treat them themselves. I have often found myself talking to such patients in a relaxed, pleasant, and, I believe, sensitive manner. Sometimes the patient does not want to accept a referral; because the conversation has made the patient feel soothed and understood, he wants that specific therapist. We can be particularly effective under these circumstances because we do not feel any responsibility for the patient other than to make an appropriate referral. We know that we will not have the burden of dealing with the primitive, unreasonable parts of the patient's psyche and with the defensive demandingness of their psychopathology. On a casual contact, we can relate to the patients' better-integrated aspect, which shapes the positive side of their ambivalence about seeking therapy.

My patient was confused about and frightened of treatment, but she presented, especially during that first interview, a sequence of reactions that could be considered a caricature of the analytic process as well as of the psychopathology of depression. The feeling of freedom stemming from my intention to refer her elsewhere created a positive countertransference attitude in spite of all her turmoil, and made me especially inclined to view her disruptive behavior from a psychoanalytic perspective. Instead of seeing a hopelessly disturbed patient, I heard a series of associations and witnessed behavior that could be conceptualized in terms of resistances and manipulative-defensive adaptations, as well as of primitive id impulses expressing themselves in a transference context.

If I had been anxious about keeping her in treatment, I doubt that I would have been able to separate myself from the content of her material and thus maintain a psychoanalytic perspective. I would have viewed her as a helpless, agitated woman who had to be taken care of. As much as I might consider myself as operating on a different plane, I would still feel some responsibility and considerable concern about her welfare and about the possibility of suicide. Whenever clinicians commit themselves to the treatment of patients, they feel some responsibility for what happens to them outside the therapy sessions. Depressed patients, because they are overwhelmed by self-destructive feelings, intensify the therapist's sense of responsibility and pull it beyond the intrapsychic.

After the first session, when I began to believe that perhaps the patient would remain in treatment, I was not as relaxed as I had been during our first interview. My initial analytic focus had helped in getting her started, however, and although there were disruptive, stormy moments that made inroads into my relaxed, positive stance, we were both able to survive her assaultive agitation, although there were times when the likelihood of continuing treatment seemed very remote.

I was able to sustain some of my positive countertransference feelings after I had made the aforementioned arrangements with my psychiatrist colleague. He represented a refuge for the patient in the external world that would remove the pressure from me to respond directly to her infantile demands and would thus help me to preserve the intrapsychic focus.

I will now report some selected sessions in detail in order to highlight the countertransference as it related to the treatment process. Some of the difficulties ordinarily encountered with patients were magnified to an inordinate degree, but other problems that I had anticipated turned out not to be particularly troublesome.

* * *

For example, one of the obstacles to treatment that this patient presented was her insistence that she would be unable to keep her appointments because she was incapable of getting to my office. She lamented that her husband could not take so much time away from his business, because then he would become bankrupt. She could not take a taxi alone because she would be stricken with panic if she did not have someone she knew to accompany her. Despite all this, she never missed a session. Either her husband or a neighbor transported her, and finally she came by herself.

She entered the office for the second session in her previous explosive fashion, but she did not try to bring her husband into the room with her. She repeatedly wailed, "Doctor, you must help me. I feel so terrible. I don't know what to do," and then tearfully, "Please help me; tell me what to do." She was doing the same peculiar shuffle dance step that had characterized her posture during the first interview.

She continued her litany and ritual for several minutes, and I found it distinctly unpleasant. I did not believe that her pleas were object-directed, that she was sincerely asking me for help. As mentioned, they seem organized around a ritual, a form of automatized behavior that did not have the potential for object-related communication. I noted that after their initial bombastic quality, her pleas gradually lost volume and decelerated so that they became a slow, monotonous drone. They reminded me of the artificial voices of robots and computers. Furthermore, there was no substance to them. She was presenting an impossible situation because, in order to be able to respond to her needs, the therapist would have to know about the needs themselves, something she could not articulate. Not only would I not have known how to respond, but I did not even know what she wanted.

This time I found it difficult to maintain an analytic perspective as she continued dancing and droning in front of me. I had made a commitment to treat her, and I must have felt some diminution of the freedom and positive countertransference feelings I had felt in the first session. Her motor behavior seemed to drag me further into her world, and I felt that my function as an analyst was being overlooked. I was experiencing a subtle form of narcissistic depletion. I simply motioned her to the couch, and she meekly and timidly dragged herself to it.

She was still sitting on the couch as she looked out the window. It was a beautiful, sunny day. As she recognized this, she shouted in an anguished and frightened voice, "It's a beautiful day!" I was surprised by the discrepancy between the stimulus and the content of her response and her anxiety and feeling of being threatened. There seemed to be no connection between stimulus and response.

Later in the session, her responses to unpleasant stimuli were qualitatively appropriate, although, characteristically, they were considerably exaggerated. She reacted intensely to a harsh siren and to a spider that enjoyed spinning a web outside my window. She spent the greater part of the session lying on the couch crying and in a weak, quavering voice telling me how miserably incapable she was of coping with even the simplest exigencies of daily life. She lay quietly except for her legs, which jerked in a convulsive movement accompanied by a peculiar flexing of the thighs followed by a sudden extension and adduction, the legs noisily slapping each other.

She continued in this dismal self-condemnatory fashion for many months, but compared with the first session, she was relatively quiet. I was grateful for that, but analytically, I felt that there was nothing I could grasp. She presented a paradox; her reactions to certain stimuli seemed to be outside the context of human responses. Pleasant stimuli, such as sunny days and receiving praise, as she had been in connection with her work, evoked anxiety and horror. Her whole life was punctuated with anxiety and misery. I was frustrated by her peculiarities because I did not know what to do with them.

At the moment, she was asking for nothing, but I felt that she was fending me off for reasons I could not yet understand. As discussed, her fending me off made me feel as if I were being narcissistically shut out, a feeling that was reinforced by her withdrawal and intense self-preoccupation. My self-esteem was deflated by my belief that I could not help her with integrating interpretations. Keeping these countertransference responses in mind, I finally told her that she found it very important to present her helpless side to me. I added that in so doing, she could prevent me from seeing other sides of herself that she was reluctant to reveal to me and perhaps to herself. The relatively serene atmosphere abruptly vanished. Sitting up, she screamed that she was, indeed, helpless and that there was nothing to reveal. In fact, she was nothing. She then demanded that I save her from herself and made a tremendous commotion when the session was over. It took at least five minutes to get her to leave.

After she left that session, I had positive feelings about the therapy. At first this seemed odd, a paradox among the many encountered in the treatment of depressed patients. She was once again becoming agitated and might possibly disrupt the treatment. Perhaps the holding environment was not sufficiently established to contain her infantile feelings, but she was having a very distinct reaction to my interpretation. I had been able to touch something inside her; I broke through her protective barrier, had made an impact. Instead of withdrawing, she was reacting, although the extent of her reaction threatened to become overwhelming. Nevertheless, at the moment I believed that my interpretation had been effective in that she had reacted to its content. I felt that I had engaged her in a treatment encounter and that we were relating to each other.

Her remarks had been directed toward herself but they were also directed at me, as had happened in our initial session when I first had positive but guarded feelings about the prospects of treatment. Although her involvement with me consisted of making impossible and incomprehensible demands, I viewed it as a psychic investment in me as a person. From this perspective, she was exhibiting a transference, although the feelings invoked were extremely infantile and primitive (Gill 1983).

Her behavior continued to be bizarre and from time to time escalated to chaotic proportions. Instead of lying on the couch, she would stand in front of me, very close to my chair, and reach toward me, begging for help. I might remark that she was confirming my interpretation about her need to be helpless. This would cause her to become incensed, and her agitation would mount. She might let loose a series of invectives, usually anal, but she never directly attacked me verbally or actually touched me. When I motioned her to the couch, she would scream that she could not lie down, often as she was about to do so. Once on the couch, she would suddenly jump off it and abruptly sit up.

In spite of the intensity of her misery and the pitiable nature of her supplications, I could not help feeling that there was something comical in her demeanor. I became especially aware of the lighter side of her actions—at least, those that I found amusing. For instance, once she suddenly sat up on the couch, looked at me with a peculiar stare, and in an exhausted voice said, "I am just a vegetable." Turning her forlorn gaze toward the floor, she remained motionless for about thirty seconds. Then she rolled her head in a circular motion and, looking toward the ceiling, said, "Not even a good vegetable." I found this funny, but I did not say anything about it at the time. This comic relief helped make the treatment bearable and was like a ray of sunshine in the atmosphere of gloom, hopelessness, and neediness that she was so skillful in creating.

I found myself almost anticipating her sessions rather than dreading them. Her capacity for creating humorous situations was more than just entertaining. If her behavior and attitudes could evoke positive feelings in me, I reasoned that there must be something remaining inside her that had potential for being valued. My reasoning might have been specious, and I may have been giving meaning to material that had no meaning except to enable her to further revile herself. Nevertheless, I believe that many of her comic actions, which began as a manifestation of low self-esteem, later acquired a creative meaning and had an integrative effect.

In any case, the comic aspect of her behavior, in the midst of such turmoil and misery, seemed to lighten my burden. My reaction must be distinguished from what in some instances amounts to hostile depreciation and ridicule of the patient. It must be admitted that clinicians, in order to defend themselves against their patients' attacks and the crushing atmosphere they construct, sometimes depreciate their patients by making fun of them. I have noted this in many clinical seminars in which the presenter, rather than viewing the patient's psychopathology in a clinical context, dwells on its bizarre manifestations in a joking but depreciatory fashion. These therapists are often not particularly aware of their negative countertransference, which can intensify to the point of contemptuousness and loathing. If they were aware of such feelings, they would find it difficult to justify their belief that they were functioning in a benign therapeutic context. These attitudes eventually increase the patient's sense of inadequacy and often provoke rage. Many of these patients angrily leave treatment, carrying their hatred of the therapist with them.

Apparently my patient must have sensed something about my reaction to her, because she began thanking me for my interest in her. If I was interested in seeing her, there must be hope. Her demeanor again changed drastically: She became considerably calmer. She spoke with pride of her achievements, but this only accentuated her depression; remembering times when things had seemingly gone well only made the bleak present worse. I shared her sadness as I listened to her bitter-sweet memories. It was not exactly a painful experience for me, but I could incorporate some of her sorrow.

From time to time, she hinted that she occasionally had dreams, but she never told me anything about them. During a session when she was commenting about previous successes, she again hinted that she had had a dream. I asked why she never told me her dreams. Apparently she had a need to withhold and conceal them from me. Nonetheless, I asked her to tell me about this specific dream. She hesitated and clearly did not want to do so. She insisted that it was a rather banal dream and had no value in helping us learn what was going on in her unconscious.

Despite her wish to withhold material, my positive countertransference feelings soared: She was now acknowledging that we were involved in a treatment relationship. She spoke of *our learning* about what was going on in her unconscious. She was making judgments as to what might be valuable, an obvious resistance to free association that Freud wrote about in his first psychoanalytic monograph (Breuer and Freud 1895), but she was operating in a psychoanalytic frame of reference.

I suspected that her reluctance was based on the fear that the dream would reveal too much rather than too little. My curiosity was stimulated, especially because she was so calm and reasonable. Although I did not want to intrude, my curiosity prevailed, so I once again urged her to tell me her dream. This time she complied.

She was walking down the main corridor that led to the lobby of my building. She was especially aware of how energetic and healthy she felt. People were looking at her and smiling. Their friendliness made her feel beautiful. Then she saw a shadowy figure, a man who was swiftly approaching her. She was afraid she would go mad, but she smiled feebly, hoping he would go away. She awakened at that moment, feeling some mild anxiety that rather quickly changed to a good feeling. The positive feeling rapidly vanished and she felt depressed once again.

I remarked that I was surprised that she did not want to tell me a dream that for the most part dealt with good feelings. Her mood shifted again and she screamed that she had no good feelings. Toward the end of the session, however, she admitted that all her dreams involved something positive and referred to her beauty and intelligence.

Remembering her paradoxical reactions to positive views of herself, I let my mind roam to the circumstances associated with the onset of her depression. I believed that the transference element in her dream was found in the shadowy figure, who I conjectured was me, and that she was either afraid of my seeing others admire her or that it was dangerous to let me see the good parts of herself. Her reluctance to disclose the dream would support the possibility that it was dangerous to reveal anything positive. This hypothesis was further confirmed in the course of the therapy.

* * *

There was a marked change in her demeanor beginning with the next session. She underwent a profound regression that lasted for approximately six months. It is superfluous to state that no analysis proceeds in an orderly, sequential, circumscribed fashion, and certainly this patient demonstrated many discontinuities and upheavals during the course of her therapy. For the sake of exposition, however, I am pulling together the dominant themes that persisted for certain periods of time. Within these blocks of time, certain sessions are particularly illustrative of the course of the analytic process and the unfolding of the transference, and the parallel shifts in my countertransference responses.

This latest regression did not exactly reproduce the ego states that had characterized her previous chaotic episodes. I knew very little of how she was getting along in the external world during her calm periods, but now she again complained about her inability to function. She was intensely demanding, but her attitude was not always one of frenzied hopelessness and agitation. For example, at the end of one session, she clutched my hand as she was leaving the office and looked at me gratefully. She thanked me for my faith in her ability to recover. She presented a peculiar mixture of fierce self-condemnation and absolute helplessness, but she also felt that perhaps there was some possibility that she would recover from her crushing depression. This picture of abject misery and tenuous hope was especially poignant.

I questioned then, and still question, what factors were chiefly responsible for my ability to sustain a somewhat optimistic attitude toward the patient's therapeutic potential. The most difficult moments in the treatment were when I had to bolster the grandiose components of my countertransference perspective. In a way, I was countering her pessimism by being reactively optimistic. I have discussed how grandiosity in itself, if controlled, can lead to progressive changes in the treatment setting. In these instances it becomes an adaptation designed to enable the therapist to survive the doom and gloom that depressed patients so pervasively spread, the miasma that could suffocate all therapeutic efforts. Furthermore, this reactive optimism is supported by the assumption that there are positive elements and valuable parts of the patient's self that are also stifled and submerged by the intrapsychic forces that are the essence of the psychopathology of depression.

I was, in fact, beginning to believe that I was seeing various facets of her self-representation, rather than just the miserable, hopeless parts. I also knew that she was exerting a tremendous effort just to hold herself together. She was fighting against succumbing to an ego regression that might have led to a diffusion of the identity sense (Erikson 1959) and to ego dissolution. The effort required tremendous energy, and the patient felt chronically exhausted. Still, I felt that she occasionally revealed positive parts of herself, as regularly occurred in her dreams. She could reveal certain things at night that she could not face in the daytime.

During one session, she was speaking in a relatively relaxed, calm fashion. She was talking about the events of the previous day and was commenting about a cousin's inability to take proper care of her ill son. Apparently this cousin was making a crisis out of a fairly simple situation. She added that anyone in their right mind would know instinctively what to do, and then she told me exactly how she would have handled this child's illness. She seemed confident and competent.

I thought of our first stormy session, when, after I had told her that I was interested in how her mind worked, she screamed that she had no mind. I called attention to her phrase "anyone in their right mind," from which I could infer that, at some level, she felt that she had a mind, and that it could function efficiently and competently. In an obvious attempt on my part to introduce the transference element, I added that she was showing me valuable and valued parts of herself.

She vigorously resisted my confronting her with what she had said about "anyone in their right mind" and with the inferences I was drawing from it. As often happened with her, I felt as if I were pulling a rope in a tug-of-war; in this case, the rope was the phrase "anyone in their right mind." I envisioned her trying to pull it back inside herself where she could hide it, and I was pulling in the opposite direction, trying to get it out in the open, to expose it to the light of day.

I had begun my confrontation by asking her to expand on what she had meant when she referred to someone being in their right mind. She angrily retorted that she never said anything of the kind. I insisted that I had distinctly heard what she said, repeated it in the context in which she had said it, and then referred to her reaction during her first session when I had spoken about wanting to know how her mind works. I then went on to disclose my inferences from this exchange about her showing me valuable parts of herself. She became increasingly upset and continued to deny that she had ever made such a statement, on which I had based all my assumptions. Therefore, everything I had said was wrong. There was nothing of value within her.

I had a peculiar feeling about this interaction, a mixed

countertransference response. Although she was pulling away from me, the two of us were relating intensely to each other. She was resisting what I was saying, but she was not shutting me out. We were locked in with each other and she was very much aware of my presence, if for no other reason than that she had to protect herself from exposing herself to me. However, her persistent denial of what she had said represented a very difficult resistance; its self-protective intent was to render me useless. My feeling of uselessness, of course, was the negative aspect of my countertransference and caused me to feel irritated.

In retrospect, I believe that I must have revealed a note of irritation when I said that I had distinctly heard what she had said, that I was not hallucinating or otherwise misperceiving what she was telling me. She had become somewhat timorous in response, and in a feeble tone replied that maybe she had said something about right minds, but that I could not possibly have heard her because she was inaudible. I was mildly amused by her reply. She had been speaking in low but audible tones. I persisted, but now I reassured her that she had, regardless of her quiet way of speaking, succeeded in communicating something important to me. Then I again commented that she found it threatening to let me see the good side of herself. Instead of the denial I had expected, she burst into tears and lamented, "Yes, I once was competent, but look at me now." She sobbed for the remainder of the hour. She left the session on the final note that she knew that I was trying to help her but that she could turn anything into a disservice.

She continued to sob during sessions for many months, and her agitation continued to mount as she became increasingly helpless. She constantly reviled herself and begged me, as she had in the past, to help her. Once, as she was flailing her arms in all directions, she knocked a lamp off the end table near my couch. Her scream was the loudest I had ever heard from her, and she wailed about her horrible, destructive behavior. She crawled on her hands and knees toward the lamp, tearfully contrite and repentant for the damage she had done. Actually she had done no damage, and I placed the lamp back in its usual place. Noting aloud that she was particularly sensitive about destroying good things, whether they came from within her or from me, I motioned her back to the couch.

I saw another dimension to her reactions to my interpretations. It was easy to understand why she would resist accepting their content, but I had noted on many occasions that she had not even acknowledged that I had made interpretations. She often ignored them, and it was particularly disturbing to me, in the face of her repeated pleas for help, that when I offered an interpretation, it did not count as a vehicle of help. At those times, her rendering me useless evoked a slight narcissistic injury. I saw this as an act of self-defense on her part. I now viewed her resistance as having another meaning. In her way, she was protecting me. If she allowed herself to be open with me, she would destroy me as she felt she had the lamp. Just as she was afraid of destroying her own good parts, she was also fearful of damaging the valued parts of me (Klein 1935).

Her anxious reactions to pleasant situations became more understandable. Good things caused anxiety because she was afraid that she would destroy them. They acted as a stimulus that further threatened her tenuous control over her rage. In a pleasant environment, her anger became even more difficult to contain. Furthermore, her inability to integrate such an environment with her inner world was experienced as painful. This feeling is similar to depressed patients' intensified feelings of loneliness when they are in a crowd or among people who are having fun.

* * *

From this point on, by this time in her second year of treatment, she was occasionally able to refer to past accomplishments and rudiments of skills that persisted in the present. Still, the greater parts of her sessions focused on her showing me how helpless she was. Her expressions of vulnerability intensified after she revealed that she possessed other qualities beside misery and worthlessness.

In treatment, she developed a remarkable manner of speaking that reflected different orientations and ego states. I have noted this propensity in other patients suffering from primitive mental states. When she was speaking of positive aspects of herself, for example, her voice was low, calm, and well modulated. We referred to this mode of communication as her adult or sane voice. When dealing with her hated vulnerable self, she screamed, howled, or moaned, usually loudly, and we referred to this as her crazy or baby voice, depending on whether she was being just chaotic or pleading, demanding, and frustrated. She was particularly adept at switching back and forth between these two voices. It was a handy barometer by which I could measure the depth of her regression. Through her voice, she revealed her dominant ego state and specific facets of her self-representation. On the rare occasions when she told me about a dream, she used her sane voice, but as the anxiety of her dreams began to mount, she gradually introduced her baby voice.

Again my reactions were mixed, which I believe once more were a reflection of the ambivalence inherent in the depressed patient's inner turmoil. This ambivalence is manifested in both patient's and therapist's orientations toward treatment. This patient dramatically illustrated a sequence of being introspective and inwardly directed and, alternately, chaotically clinging to the external world in a concrete, infantile fashion, abandoning all attempts at self-observation. I was pleased that the patient could reveal her current status in such a visible fashion as the tone and quality of her voice. On the other hand, when she used her baby voice, I had some trepidations about the all-encompassing nature of her regression.

Her baby voice was heard more frequently when her dreams contained elements that threatened her sense of well-being. In a dream, she was accompanied by her family while driving a car. She became terrified when she saw the funnel cloud of a tornado on the horizon. On another occasion, she was going to a party for both family and business friends when a fire broke out and destroyed her home as it became increasingly uncontrollable. For quite some time, she dreamed about threatening, impersonal forces. I viewed these dreams as expressions of her inner turmoil, of raging inner forces in which the destructive aspects of the self-representation threatened to devour the more limited parts of the self, which she had, to some extent, been able to value.

I wondered about the transference implications of these dreams. The danger was always an act of nature or some other kind of threat that did not, at least phenomenologically, involve a person. This made me think in terms of primitive parts of herself. Still, the shadowy figure of the first dream was a person, although she could not determine whether it was a man or a woman. I felt as Freud (1900) did, that doubt about dream elements is, in itself, part of the manifest dream content, and that the inability to tell whether the shadowy figure was a man or a woman meant that it was both, indicating that it incorporated qualities of the self-representation and an object representation, the latter indicating the transference element.

Her anxiety continued to mount and her disruptive feelings

dominated to the extent that she was no longer capable of exploring her mind. She was experiencing increasing anxiety about the emergence of good parts of the self, as she had little faith in her capacity to keep good and bad parts separate so that she would not destroy them.

Returning to her regressive patterns, she wanted me to rescue her from her inner destructiveness. At the same time, she was fearful that I despised her because she was such a mess. She believed that I secretly wanted to kill her, but that I was restraining myself. In one series of associations, she commented that a volcano must be raging inside me and that I was putting a lid on it so that it would not erupt. According to her, this was a precarious and dangerous situation. She was thus faced with the paradox of needing to be rescued from her inner destructiveness by a person who hated and wanted to kill her. Her associations seemed to indicate that the catastrophic forces in her dream were impersonal but rageful representations of me, and she filled me through projections with the primitive parts of herself.

I pondered whether there was any objective reality to what she said. I certainly did not feel any desire to kill her, nor was I aware of even feeling angry at her. True, her outlandish behavior could cause me to feel irritated and annoyed, but not intensely so. As she continued in her chaotic fashion, however, I was beginning to experience some feelings similar to the ones she had attributed to me. I wondered whether I was absorbing her projections or whether she was stimulating some hostile and destructive impulses that were lying latent within my mind. Analysts tend to stress that there is a core of truth to the patient's belief in their projections and that the receptacle they choose must, in some way, be appropriate.

I concluded that, for the most part, I was reacting to her projections, that she was pushing the bad parts of herself into me as she was also letting them invade the ambience of the consultation room. The latter was usually manifested by immense guilt, as indicated by her exaggerated reaction to the knocking over of my lamp.

During this period of treatment, she spoke exclusively in her baby voice. I again commented on how she had to let the infantile, helpless side of herself dominate the conversation. She became angry and made some sarcastic remarks about my use of the word *conversation*. She had seldom, if ever, revealed anger. Helplessness and misery were her prominent feelings, but anger as a destructive affect was hardly ever directly expressed. Even when she hurled obscenities, it was difficult to determine their target.

Now I could feel her sarcasm as an attack. She bitterly shouted that we were not having a conversation. I was simply letting her rave and rant. How could I care for such a miserable person? On the other hand, why did I not do something to help her? She knew that I was contemptuous of her, but no matter how much she deserved it, I could at least try to pay some attention to her. Throughout several months of sessions, she continued in this vein, becoming increasingly bitter and vehement. She did not stop attacking herself as she attacked me. In fact, she intensified her self-depreciations, but this time they lacked the comic qualities I had noted previously, and the atmosphere she created was lugubrious and oppressive.

I felt myself gradually becoming immersed in her gloom, and on occasion I told her that she had a need to show me only her depressed side, that she was trying to put her depression and anger into me. I tried to state this in positive terms, stressing that she had succeeded in putting these feelings into me. Predictably, this seemed to have little effect on her. I believe that, in part, I was trying to calm her because her attacks on me were becoming tedious.

On the one hand, she was very much relating to me. She

made me into a transference figure of her withholding past, when she was forced to fend for herself and take care of her siblings instead of being taken care of. Thus, I was witnessing the repetition compulsion, and I should have viewed this as a therapeutic accomplishment. On the other hand, I felt frustrated because she insisted on revealing only the negative aspects of her character. I knew that she was deliberately, although unconsciously, withholding the revelation of the valuable parts of herself. To some degree, I continued to feel shut out, although, as I have stated, she was intensely relating to me. Still, she was relating only in terms of her internal bad object representations, and I felt as if I were a part object.

She was minimally involved in the analytic process by bringing in the repetition compulsion, but in hiding all the good internal object representations she was not dealing with it from an observational frame (Thorner 1985). Furthermore, I felt partially narcissistically shut out inasmuch as she introduced me only to her damaged, bad parts.

Her demeanor changed once again. Perhaps I had been able to calm her somewhat. In any case, she became relatively quiet in contrast to the screaming and moaning that had characterized her earlier sessions. Now she would lie quietly during the entire session. If she started to speak, she would abruptly stop herself and refuse to talk for the remainder of the session. If I questioned her or otherwise encouraged her to talk, she would not respond. I increasingly felt that she was both pushing me away and withdrawing from me.

A patient's silence ordinarily does not disturb me. There is usually some adaptive motive behind it. The patient may need to withdraw, defy, or merge. With this patient, however, I initially reacted with some discomfort to her silence and had a definite need to get her to continue talking. I surmised that she wanted me to pursue her. Again I envisioned myself as being involved in a tug-of-war. I also believed that she was censoring and suppressing her associations, and I told her so. She remained silent, neither confirming nor denying my suspicion.

* * *

After about a month of silent hours, she admitted that she was suppressing thoughts about me. She viewed me as pursuing her, and she had to escape. At first she said that she was afraid that I would rob her, but, as generally occurs with parapraxes, she quickly corrected herself by saying that I would murder her. I noted her deep preoccupation with being robbed, and that being killed was easier for her to face than robbery, but at the moment, I did not feel inclined to pursue this. My feeling was that both being robbed and being murdered were pertinent.

The silence was broken. She vacillated between periods of quiet sobbing and noisy agitation, as had been the situation at the beginning of treatment. She also presented some dreams that had many similarities to previous dreams, but also significant differences. As in previous dreams, she found herself in a situation in which she was being admired for her competence. Then something destructive would happen, and the appealing and tranquil setting would be totally disrupted. Some madman might rush into the room, for instance, and overturn furniture, knock people down, and otherwise destroy the pleasant atmosphere that had characterized the beginning of the dream. She usually awakened in a state of terror.

Her anxiety intensified within the context of depression and self-depreciation. She literally trembled during some sessions, and during others she presented herself as totally nonfunctional. Paradoxically, her behavior in the external world, according to her reports, was much improved. For the first time in years, she was able to manage her affairs fairly well. She had, at that time, no problems in getting to my office on her own, and she was able to cook meals and take care of the house. She was apparently not as reluctant to reveal good qualities and competence outside the analysis. To function well in my presence, on the other hand, posed an overwhelming threat.

In the context of the dream, I pointed out that she had to appear helpless in front of me because I would destroy her good aspects if she dared expose them to me. I had steeled myself for the deluge of protestations that there were no good parts of her, only miserable ones; but she remained calm. Then she blurted out that if I really knew her, I would be envious and afraid of her. Again she quickly covered this slip by insisting that everything she had said was gibberish. Since I thought I detected a forced quality to her self-depreciations, I decided not to pursue this material further. I wanted to avoid another tug-of-war in which I would be cast in the role of pulling everything she valued about herself toward me. I conjectured that this would only serve to strengthen her resistance, which contained the resolve to protect these parts of herself from my envy.

Still, the die was cast. She was no longer able to immerse herself completely in her self-depreciation. She began to acknowledge that she had some potential, but as she acknowledged that there might be some hope for her, she became overwhelmed with fright. Her anxiety reached a peak in a session during which I surmised that she might be afraid of destroying me with her newly available powers. I had recalled the time when she let it slip out that I would be either envious or afraid of her if I really knew her. I believed that she was referring to the hidden parts of herself—not the surface misery and depression she flamboyantly exhibited. The patient switched the emphasis to my envy, which would cause me to be overwhelmed with a desire to kill her. She screamed that she did not care about destroying me. She was petrified with the fear that I would devour her, and she expressed this exclusively in oral terms. She felt that I would tear her apart with my teeth as I bit into her abdomen. I would then chew her and swallow her up. Her material bordered on psychosis as she turned to look at me with an expression of horror. Then she cried fearfully for the last few minutes of the session. When I indicated that our time was up, she literally ran out of my office.

She called me on the telephone that evening, something she had not done in eighteen months. She shouted that she could not stand it any longer and that she was "falling apart." She kept screaming that she was "eating herself up" with unbearable anxiety. As she had at the beginning of the treatment, she begged me to give her drugs. I did not want to respond to the content of her demands and misery because (1) I did not know how and (2) I wanted to remain in an analytic frame of reference. In view of her disorganization and emotional pain, however, the latter seemed to be a ridiculous approach.

I finally replied that if she could not maintain herself between sessions, she could be hospitalized by the colleague who had consented to take over her management if her regression became overwhelming. She was not at all pleased with my meager offering. I added that another possibility would be to increase our contact to daily sessions, but this was also an unwelcome suggestion.

Early the next morning her husband called and left a message to cancel all sessions and to send a final bill. Later that day I called back, and her husband answered the telephone. I asked to speak to his wife, but she refused to talk to me. I could hear her moaning in the background. The husband added that she was adamant about not speaking to me, and that she did not want to see me anymore. I then inquired as to what they were going to do. They had contacted a neuropsychiatrist who would hospitalize her and try to stabilize her with drugs. After that he did not particularly know what they would do. Perhaps they would seek some treatment similar to mine.

I sensed that I was facing an impossible situation, and that she was not going to return to therapy at that time. They were still seeking magical solutions, although I could understand her desperate need for relief. I simply stated that I regretted the necessity for their decision. When and if she desired to return to see me, I would be glad to continue her analysis.

My reactions were mixed. Despite her mounting agitation, I was surprised at the abruptness of the termination. I was also aware of some anger at being summarily dismissed and at her refusal to talk to me on the telephone. They sought their own psychiatrist, ignoring the fact that I had already made arrangements with a colleague should such a situation occur. Furthermore, if she were to seek psychotherapy in the future, he made no mention of her returning to me. I concluded that their actions were based on anger toward me because I had not been able to magically rescue her.

I felt that I was being demeaned and treated as if I were incompetent. I no longer counted and was of no importance in her life. I had been fired, just as an incompetent maid might be summarily dismissed. I suppose my countertransference could be characterized as dominated by, if not narcissistic rage, at least a degree of narcissistic anger. I had firmly believed that I understood what was happening in the context of the transference–countertransference interaction and her refusal to accept or use my insights. She had attacked me personally, and psychoanalysis in general, by reverting to drugs as a final answer. I was aware, of course, that many of my feelings were the outcome of projections of the way she viewed herself, but I regretted that she had to respond by acting out—that is, by withdrawing from her analysis and seeking some omnipotent solution.

I also realized that the emergence of valuable parts of the

self evoked tremendous anxiety in an ego that had lost some of its defenses. Nevertheless, I had to keep asking myself what I might have contributed to her becoming unable to sustain a therapeutic relationship or to the formation of such a severe regression that she could not function anywhere, in or out of treatment. She had returned to her pretreatment state.

It has been my experience that whenever patients regress to such a self-destructive degree, the therapist's negative or disruptive countertransference has been the precipitating factor. With my patient, it could be rationalized that her disturbed state represented her initial psychopathology, which she continued to manifest at the time she withdrew from treatment. It was not a regression from her pretreatment ego state. Still, there were many moments in treatment when she had been better integrated and more able to maintain an intrapsychic focus. From this perspective, her behavior represented an unmistakable regression.

I surmised that my countertransference orientation acted as a partial stimulus for her disruptive, agitated regression. I reasoned that I was demanding too much of her. I was expecting her to make therapeutic strides and to change her behavior because of the insights I was offering her. This would have satisfied my professional ego ideal, and she would be grateful for such tangible help. This was a defensive countertransference that I believe is fairly frequently encountered and somewhat specific to depressed patients, although it occurs with other types of psychopathology as well. It may, however, be a response to the depressive component that is frequently found in character disorders.

Depression is characterized by rigidity. These patients tenaciously cling to their symptoms and resist efforts designed to free them from the tyranny of a sadistic superego (Abraham 1927). Clinicians are familiar with countless unchanging sessions in which these patients engage in a continuous litany of self-recrimination, self-hatred, and complaints about their misery, pain, and inability to function. Implicitly or explicitly, they blame the therapist for their suffering and hopelessness. If there is even a glimmer of change or improvement, the therapist may want to pounce on it in order to bolster his sagging self-esteem. The desire to hold on to something positive is designed to strengthen the aspect of the holding environment that supports the therapist. The analyst's expectation that the patient will continue to change is a defense against the stubborn, almost automatized repetition of painful, depressive complaints. Furthermore, these expectations enable the analyst to feel useful. Such a feeling both helps to dispel the gloom and oppression characteristic of depressive symptomatology, and serves as a defense against feeling blamed and attacked.

My countertransference attitudes would cause the patient to believe that she is forbidden to experience the manifestations of her psychopathology and to give up defenses that, although painful, still have some adaptive significance. In the past she had been unable to hold herself together. Now the same type of psychic disintegration occurred, but she could make me the cause of it. If I tried to change this equilibrium, maladaptive though it was, she would regress even further and, as happened, treatment on an outpatient basis would no longer be possible.

* * *

The treatment of severely disturbed patients always requires that they get in touch with primitive, disruptive parts of the self. Both patients and therapists must survive these agitated states. Patients have to live through these regressions for as long as is necessary so that they can begin to integrate and develop higher levels of psychic structure. The amount of time required cannot be predetermined.

The therapeutic environment has to be constructed so that it can accommodate and noncritically accept regressed states. Freud (1913) expressed this well when he stated that the optimal treatment attitude is one whereby the analyst has no therapeutic ambition or preconceived notions. He should allow the patient to express himself without being critical and be surprised by every turn in the material. With depressed patients, however, because of what seems to be an interminable duration of painful, miserable psychic states, the analyst's acceptance is sometimes strained to the breaking point. Consequently, countertransference expectations that patients prematurely give up the expression of the manifestations of their psychopathology may cause further regression that can destroy the treatment setting and disrupt the transference–countertransference interaction.

I had many reactions to this patient's leaving treatment. To some extent I was relieved. She had been a noisy, vociferous patient who commanded my full attention. She did not permit me—or, at least, she made it difficult for me—to relax and to listen with the free, hovering attention that is so vital for the analytic interaction. The level of involvement that she demanded was tiresome and, at times, exhausting. On the other hand, I had lost a very interesting patient who, on occasion, had shown some capacity for analysis despite the seemingly impossible picture she often presented. She was suffering intensely, and I had hoped that the acquisition of insight would have given her some relief. Until the time she started treatment, nothing had helped. Still, after approximately three years of analysis, she seemed to be, if not worse off, at least as disturbed and emotionally paralyzed as ever.

I consoled myself with the thought that analysis is not for everybody. When I had decided to try it with this patient, it was as a last resort. I had tried and failed, but I concluded that she was unanalyzable. This, I believe, is a frequent rationalization among clinicians. I reasoned that it had taken me three years to acknowledge the failure of treatment, but I again consoled myself by asking what else could have been done in the meantime. There were many months when she had functioned quite well in the outside world.

My ruminations were interrupted two months later, when she called me to ask whether I would give her an appointment, or whether I despised her so much that I did not want to have anything to do with her. I commented that maybe it was important to her that I despise her, that she had a need to believe that I hated her, and that was a good reason to give her an appointment. She quietly replied with an anal expletive.

I learned that she had been hospitalized and placed on a regimen of antidepressants. After three weeks of no improvement, she was also put on lithium. Later she was given thioridazine (Mellaril) and various sedatives and antianxiety agents. Despite participation in group and individual supportive psychotherapy, her symptoms remained unabated. She continued to suffer from constant anxiety, bordering on panic. Finally, the attending psychiatrist recommended electroconvulsive therapy, but she refused it and called me.

We resumed treatment, and I was particularly impressed that we continued as if there had been no interruption. She reacted as if the last session had occurred the previous day.

She continued her efforts to hide the valued parts of herself from me. Two themes that had only been suspected before now clearly emerged. She was afraid that some omnipotent power would get out of control, and this was manifested in the transference by her fear of destroying me. She was also afraid that I would attack and devour her. These fears were the outcome of the greed and envy she had projected into me. As a defense, she tried to keep her inadequate, depressed self in the foregound so as to avoid exciting my envy and greed (Klein 1935).

I decided to focus on her attitudes about my potential feelings of envy and greed, her fear that I would devour the attractive aspects of her self. I believed that such feelings were the dominant transference theme, and my countertransference reaction accentuated this belief. I still felt as if we were involved in a tug-of-war struggle. I did not want to devour her valued self, but I did want to bring it out into the open in order to demonstrate that she need not be afraid to reveal it and that she did not have to hide it under the cloak of misery and depression. This would also emphasize that her fearful attitudes were the outcome of projection.

I believed that the patient would be better able to accept a transference interpretation that referred to feelings that had been projected into me. The fear of the loss of control of omnipotent power was also part of the transference, but projection was not primarily involved. She was afraid that she would destroy me, and she defended herself, although not particularly successfully, against losing control of her destructiveness. She had brought these feelings and defenses into the treatment setting, but she had to deal with them in the external world as well. They were not exclusively directed toward me, and in that sense the transference was diluted and only minimal projection was involved.

I believed that she would vigorously resist recognizing the transference element of her attempts to control her inner rage because she was faced with the danger of her hostility every day. She had been forced to conceal her anger as a child, and this concealment had become adaptive in her current world as well. I conjectured that hiding feelings had become ego syntonic, and that it would be difficult to convince her that it was an unwarranted carryover from the past, a reaction to the traumas she had had to master in the infantile environment. It is much more difficult to analyze the transference of ego-syntonic adaptations than to analyze the patient's projections.

My wanting to destroy her because of my envy of her megalomanic orientation clearly involved projection. She had projected feelings as well as internal object representations. Her competent self was contaminated and threatened by her rageful self. In order to protect the former from the latter, she projected both into me, and this helped explain her tremendous ambivalence about treatment. A paranoid patient, by contrast, would project only the bad parts and keep the good parts internalized in the core of their megalomania. The therapist is then perceived as a persecutory object. My patient sometimes behaved as if I would rob and exploit her. When she was in this mood, she felt that I was cold and ruthless, interested in her only for scientific purposes. On the other hand, she could thank me for my care, interest, kindness, and desire to help her.

Later, I learned that she believed that I was better able to keep anger and good parts separated than she was. Consequently, I was being used as a safety deposit box for her valuable parts, which I could protect from the destructive elements she had projected into me.

She had another reason for not wanting to reveal the competent side of her personality to me. While still a child, she had been forced into the role of caretaker for her many siblings. Because she was capable and competent, she had been coerced into a precocious maturity. If she displayed her competence to me, she was unconsciously fearful that I would take her for granted and ignore her infantile needs. If she were strong and self-sufficient, I would abandon her. She believed that I would surmise that she did not really need me or that other patients needed me more, so I would turn my attention and concern toward them. Consequently, it was safe to keep showing me her weakness and helplessness.

I continued to interpret that she was projecting hateful feelings and parts of the self that she felt were trying to rob her and destroy the valued parts of the self. She gradually accepted my interpretations and confirmed them by describing in detail what she felt about me. She elaborated that she had the distinct feeling that I had absolutely no interest in her as a person. My interest was only in enhancing myself and using her in whatever manner suited me best.

She was nevertheless able to understand that her need to view me as selfish and envious was the outcome of her psychopathology. Despite such understanding, she might revile me throughout the entire session and not even consider the possibility that her attitudes were based on transference projections. If I said nothing, it would be easy to believe that she really hated me and had no insight whatever. During other sessions, if I interpreted the projection, she would immediately calm down and rationally discuss her feelings as phenomena worthy of analytic scrutiny. Interpretations seemed to have a significant effect, as evidenced by the immediate and profound mood changes that followed them. Later, either during the next session or even in the course of the same one, she would continue to revile me as if she had not at all understood the psychic processes we had been discussing.

Her demeanor was considerably different than it had been at the beginning of treatment. She lay quietly on the couch and spoke in a calm, well-articulated fashion. She was, however, distinctly angry, but she was able to express it eloquently and sanely. I believe that because she now behaved rationally, her anger had much more impact on me than it would have had if it were voiced in the frenzied, chaotic manner that had characterized her entry into treatment.

For a time, my belief that I was ineffective made me feel impatient. It had been easy to view this attitude about my professional competency as a countertransference reaction when she was acting in an almost psychotic fashion. When it emerged in the midst of the chaos she created, the feeling of being useless had not really threatened my analytic ego ideal. It would have been difficult for anyone to feel useful in the face of the intensity of her agitation. Now I felt impelled to give more credence to the substance of her feelings toward me. I wondered about the accuracy of my interpretations that stressed projection and about whether there might be a reality basis to her complaints.

As is well known, there is a core of truth to substantiate patients' transference projections, which helps them maintain a sense of conviction about their feelings. During this period of treatment, my patient did not argue with me nor otherwise resist my interpretations. She freely acknowledged that I was correct, and for a short period of time her hostile feelings would vanish — but not for long. She did not fundamentally change her behavior, and as far as I could tell, she continued to complain to her husband about the cost of analysis and its meager results.

* * *

As repeatedly described in this book, the feeling of uselessness is a painful countertransference experience. Because the patient's behavior had drastically changed—to the extent that the treatment setting had acquired a civilized ambience—I felt impatient and expected that she would reflect these changes in her relationships in the outer world and with me. I did reinforce the impression that my interpretations were correct however—a conviction that she intellectually supported for the most part, despite my therapeutic ambition, which she claimed was designed for my personal and narcissistic enhancement.

I slowly realized that it was necessary for her to experience me as she did. She needed to react to her projections, and I could not predict how long this phase would take. Meanwhile, I concluded that other factors might be causing her to cling to her hatred. This investigatory attitude helped me to regain analytic equanimity. I also noted that when she had been at the height of her agitation in the past, attempts to understand her behavior in terms of infantile trauma, projections, and the repetition compulsion introduced some calm, at least in my outlook. I felt that the reason my interpretations of the transference did not modify her outlook was that other aspects of her infantile world were as yet unrecognized but were nevertheless active and contributed to her angry denunciations.

She had often spoken of her large family and many siblings. She had emphasized how inadequate and incompetent her parents were, especially her helpless, useless mother. She was reliving these archaic relationships in the transference and was trying to disengage herself from them. I had recognized early in the treatment the projection of the helpless and vulnerable aspects of her self-representation. Now I noted that she was dealing with archaic objects that made up part of the transference projections. As Freud (1923) stated, the ego is a precipitate of past object cathexes—or, in this instance, the self-representation embodies early object relationships—and as it is projected, it will carry these infantile relationships along with it. The transference had proceeded to a point at which early introjects were discernible.

I was cast in the role of the inadequate, useless mother. Her negative descriptions of me, as they became more and more detailed, were strikingly similar to her descriptions of her mother. I had the distinct impression that she was trying to mourn and free herself from a primitive constrictive imago through projection and then abandon the tie to this introject.

I had hardly needed to point out to her how her perception of me was the same as her view of mother. She spontaneously understood the resemblance, but her attitudes and behavior only intensified.

She continued to emphasize a wish to disengage herself from treatment. At times she was able to acknowledge that she had been helped by therapy, but she insisted that the gains were minimal. I reminded myself that the aim of mourning is to decathect the lost love object and that that could mean, in the treatment setting, a need to diminish the importance of my influence on her life. She found it more difficult to keep appointments and protested that they were useless. She was now proud of her resolve not to accept a rescheduled session if either of us had to cancel a session.

At first I felt manipulated by her canceling sessions and thereby upsetting my schedule. She was acquainted with my flexible rule about missed appointments. I ordinarily do not charge if the patient gives me twenty-four hours notice of cancellation. This patient developed the habit of calling right on the deadline—at 2:09 P.M., for example, on the day before a 2:10 P.M. appointment. I found myself resenting her cancellations and contemplated telling her that this rule no longer applied to her; she would have to pay for all missed appointments regardless of when she canceled them. On several occasions she had failed to notify me that she was not going to keep her session. This behavior was in marked contrast to her previous punctual, and usually early, arrivals to sessions.

My countertransference became more negative. I now detected more than a projection of her feelings and of hated parts of herself. In her efforts to disrupt my schedule, she was acting out as well. I was ambivalent about changing the "rule," however. The fact that I would be doing it as a reaction to my annoyance at her caused me to hesitate. I wanted to understand her motivations before taking action. I could see that my reactions were quite personal. Both the inconvenience and the financial loss angered me and most likely intensified my sensitivity to her attacks on my professional competence. I had been able to resolve my feelings about her attacks on me as I further understood the substance of her projections. Her acting out by canceling appointments hindered my attempts to resolve my sensitivity by understanding the nature of the therapeutic interaction. Nevertheless, I did nothing, having decided to wait and see both how long she would persist in her behavior and in what direction the transference would take us.

I was, in a sense, declaring a moratorium by not acting out my negative countertransference feelings. I had begun to believe that my wish to change the rules in midstream was partially motivated by retaliatory and punitive impulses. With this frame of mind, I was better able to tolerate her behavior. I consoled myself further by recalling her bizarre, disruptive behavior; her current behavior was, by comparison, a relatively mild attempt to be troublesome. I also tried to view her actions in terms of their defensive or adaptive potential.

I stopped thinking in terms of resistance and defiance. I tried to recognize the positive, adaptive aspects of her behavior, and I began to conclude that she was simply trying to assert herself, that she was protecting a newly discovered sense of autonomy. I could now view the range of her reactions in a broader spectrum. Although unpleasant, her behavior was essential to the treatment process. She seemed to be saying that she was not going to be a passive reflection of my wishes or arrange her life to suit my convenience. She was acknowledging that she had a valuable life of her own. She was going to do things in a way that satisfied her, and although she would regret it if I were discommoded or neglected, her interests had to come first. I knew that there were other factors involved, such as defiance, murderous rage, and other destructive elements, but at that moment, I chose to emphasize autonomous strivings.

I shared my thoughts about seeking autonomy with her. My comments released a flood of material. She experienced intense rage, some of it still directed toward me, but most of it associated with memories of early and late childhood, when she had felt deprived and exploited. She was furious with her parents and felt that everything that might have worked to her advantage had been taken away from her. She had been able to get scholarships so that she could put herself through college, but she could not accept them because she had to stay home to care for her siblings. She had to take unrewarding jobs to support her family, and she was expected to devote her after-work time to housework and cooking. Even after her parents had died, she found herself looking after her siblings, an obligation she maintained until she became incapacitated by her agitated depression. Although she had spoken of her exploitive background early in treatment, she was now expressing an intense resentment and rage that had been pent up for years. In contrast to the amorphous disruption of the past, her anger was now organized.

She still cried a good deal during these angry sessions, but she was not wailing or moaning as she so often had in the past. She was expressing grief, and I continued to think in terms of mourning. This was reinforced when she began recounting memories of good and tender experiences as well with various members of her family. The therapeutic atmosphere was saturated with ambivalence, and it was both painful and poignant.

She stopped manipulating appointments and began to express in an organized fashion her longing for me to care for her, to have tender feelings toward her, and to give her warmth and love. She felt very sad that she had not accepted herself as having any right to expect that others should be concerned about her welfare, and she was angry at herself for having throught so little of herself. She classified her behavior as masochistic and vented her rage toward herself and toward others who had exploited her masochism.

She remained in treatment for nearly seven years. The last year or so was devoted to completing her mourning reaction, using me as a representative of one or the other parent and occasionally a sibling. The emphasis during the termination phase of the treatment was on her love for and dependence on her family. She did not have any great affection for her mother, but she was willing to forgive her as she became increasingly aware of her basic inability to nurture. She saw this as a defect rather than a crime.

It was interesting to note the paucity of sexual material. Neither in her dreams nor in her associations was there any indications of erotic feelings toward me or anyone else. She had stated that her husband was impotent, but this did not matter. She saw it as his inability to become emotionally involved or to give of himself, but she could tolerate him. After all, this was the story of her life. Whether she was repressing sexual feelings or had not attained an oedipal level of development remains an unanswered question.

She finally saw me as a life-sustaining support, one that she eventually had to relinquish in order to stand on her own. She had been able to display her longing for me to care for her, but she was not able to express such feelings openly; they appeared in dreams with very little disguise.

She is far from well. She still has periods of profound depression but never to the degree that she cannot function. Most of the time she is fairly comfortable, but there are limitations to her capacity to be happy. Her marriage is far from satisfactory, and she would like to leave her husband because there is no basic rapport or understanding between them, but she does not blame him. She is grateful for the fact that he tolerated and survived the great misery she caused.

She has reconciled herself to her current situation. During the latter part of her analysis, she read Freud and applied to herself his statement that the aim of analysis is to convert neurotic suffering to common, everyday, ordinary misery (Breuer and Freud 1895). Some aspects of her life have turned out well. She takes pride in her relationship with her children. She remarked that she should have done better, but that when they show up on an analyst's doorstep, they will be good therapeutic risks.

* * *

Although some depression is part of the human condition, it is still difficult to understand and cope with when encountered in certain clinical situations. It is a well-known feeling and yet, in the context of psychopathology, it is a difficult feeling to fathom and to empathize with. Despite the familiarity of the feelings, the patient's behavior seems strange, alien, and paradoxical. To have experienced an emotional state oneself and then to be puzzled or confused when encountering the same feeling in a patient causes countertransference problems.

In specific contexts, certain affects are easily understood. Anxiety as a reaction to danger and depression as a response to disappointment, separation, and tragedy are ordinary, common responses. They are signs of psychopathology when we cannot recognize a stimulus, a precipitant. The further he is from recognizing a reality-based reason for an affective response, the more apt the therapist is to experience countertransference problems (Brenner 1985).

Some types of depression involve more than an apparently inappropriate or exaggerated response. Certain qualitative factors present clinicians with paradoxes, such as being wrecked by success (Freud 1916) or the negative therapeutic reaction (Freud 1923). Freud explained these paradoxes in the context of conflicting instinctual forces, based on gratifying a punitive superego. An analyst without a punitive superego might find it difficult to understand patients with inner-directed sadism, but they can develop some capacity to empathize because their superegos can occasionally become severe.

When structural problems occur, countertransference disruption can intensify. Specific disorders of the self-representation can lead to paradoxical defensive adaptations that dominate the clinical picture and determine the therapeutic course. I have emphasized good and bad internal objects and hated and valued parts of the self when discussing my patient. These are, in a sense, metaphorical descriptions of the depressive process, in which the patient is consumed with hatred and self-hatred, and the self-representation is submerged in misery and hopelessness, to which the patient tenaciously clings. The analyst often cannot understand such desperate tenacity, a confusion that becomes the nidus of countertransference turmoil. It is the particular way in which depressed patients use feelings that can be disconcerting and perplexing.

Feelings can serve an organizing function. Anger, anxiety, and sexual feelings, for example, can lead to the structuralization of inchoate and amorphous psychic states (see Chapter 6). I have specifically discussed how anxiety, or at least an affect that is phenomenologically similar to anxiety, maintains cohesion of the self-representation (Giovacchini 1958). When the synthesizing function of anxiety fails, the patient experiences terror.

I am distinguishing two types of regressive continuums. First, when signal anxiety, as a response to intrapsychic conflict, loses its synthesizing potential by producing defenses, the patient experiences panic. Second, when the anxiety that leads to cohesion of the self-representation becomes, for whatever reason, inoperative, the patient is overcome by a type of terror that is characteristic of patients suffering from agitated depressions (Silbermann 1983).

Terror is too painful a mental state to be tolerated indefinitely. In order to ensure psychic survival, the ego must somehow restore integrity to the self-representation. However, the patient is faced with the difficult task of trying to reestablish a psychically painful self-representation. Hatred and self-hatred have to be reintegrated into the identity sense and directed toward internal self and object representations. Again, the impact of a sadistically primitive superego has to be felt. Terror, on the other hand, is the outcome of the splitting off of rageful feelings in all directions and is unbearable as it accompanies the patient on the path to psychic dissolution and collapse. Unfortunately, the cohesive self-representation of the depressed patient is characterized by misery and hopelessness.

It is difficult for analysts to accept that the ultimate state of psychic equilibrium is composed of misery and hopelessness. They are more apt to view such disturbing and disruptive affective states as signs of structural disintegration and decompensation rather than as an effort to achieve psychic equilibrium. The countertransference is associated with a confusion of values, which is a reflection of the depressed patient's basic ambivalence and of the sadistic dominance of the superego.

I have emphasized the synthesizing qualities of misery and hopelessness. To be absolutely precise, I do not mean that such feelings achieve stability of the self-representation. By themselves, they achieve nothing. They are, however, the psychically felt manifestations of mental processes that promote equilibrium, processes that organize rage and self-hatred.

Again, misery and hopelessness are unbearable affects, but they are more bearable than terror, which if left unchecked, would destroy the identity sense and result in extreme fragmentation and perhaps suicide. Nevertheless, one would expect that the patient would not want to continue to feel miserable and hopeless. It is difficult for therapists to believe otherwise, and this only intensifies countertransference problems. To some extent, patients want relief from their oppressive feelings, but another part of the mind knows that relinquishing such feelings will engender the accompanying loss of the minimal stability of the identity sense. In a sense, misery and hopelessness function as a defense against the fundamental terror of psychic dissolution. These patients present us with extremely intense ambivalence, which, because of its tenacity, is experienced as maddening by the therapist. The analyst, feeling as hopeless as the patient does, may then seek organic explanations and psychopharmacologic treatment.

Nothing can be allowed into the self-representation that would upset its tenuous organization, which is anchored around rage and self-hatred. These patients suffer from anhedonia. Their egos cannot support anything that might be felt as joyous, as my patient repeatedly demonstrated. It is as though all their energies are concentrated on holding themselves together, and to allow a gratifying experience to intrude upon what is, at best, a precarious adjustment could be disastrous. Feeling hopeless and miserable, paradoxically, may help define the identity sense of some depressed patients.

If depressed patients represent, among patients suffering from structural problems, relatively higher levels of ego integration, why do they have to use such painful defense adaptations? This clinical phenomenon presents us with another paradox. To feel acute pain, at least in the psychic realm, requires considerable sensitivity and psychic integration. For example, these patients have a well-structured superego. Although it is generally acknowledged that the superego begins to emerge early on the developmental timetable, rather than simply being the "heir of the Oedipus complex" (Freud 1923), it is still a fairly advanced psychic structure. In the depressed patient, it is maldeveloped and psychopathologically distorted, but it is still part of a psychic apparatus that has reached fairly high levels of integration and sophistication. The pain generated by depressed patients is the outcome of having attained relatively well-structured developmental levels; it is not associated, as might be expected, with primitive, amorphous ego states.

Many clinicians are consciously or unconsciously aware of what is perceived as a discrepancy between behavior and psychic structure. The intensity of some depressed patients' reactions, such as the agitation my patient displayed, seems to be out of keeping with their capacity to function. I had had very few expectations about therapeutic progress with this patient at the beginning of treatment. Once I became aware of what she had achieved, and once I began to feel that she had considerable potential and capacity for insight, I developed a degree of impatience with her self-defeating behavior and self-depreciation. Despite many stormy sessions, I expected that she would make progress and relinquish her miserable and hopeless stance. I believe, in retrospect, that my countertransference was partially determined by my striving to bring good internal objects—that is, valued parts of the self—to the surface. I was aware of her need to keep them hidden because of her fear of destroying or losing them. I understood that she was afraid of my envy and greed. I did not realize, however, that she held her self-representation together by feeling miserable and hopeless, feelings that somehow kept good and bad internal objects separated. My countertransference was clashing with a vital adaptation.

As expected, my patient was re-creating aspects of her infantile environment in the treatment. She had done this elsewhere too, but the transference enabled us to see how she was reacting to specific aspects of her infantile past. Mainly, she was structuring our relationship so that I could do nothing but fail her. This situation was different in some respects from those transference–countertransference relationships, discussed earlier, in which the patient casts the therapist in the role of the inadequate caretaker and thus relives the helplessness experienced as a child. These factors were operating, but more was involved that contributed to particular facets of the countertransference. She was not simply reliving infantile traumatic failures. Because of her fairly high level of ego integration, her reactions were considerably more complex than just a passive reexperience of inadequate nurturing and deprivation in the treatment relationship. She was reacting to her frustration by exacting revenge.

Knowing that her attempts to gain succor from the family were doomed to fail, she had to master the bitter disappointment of her childhood, in much the same fashion Freud (1920) described for overcoming the anxiety of abandonment by acting out the compulsion to repeat. The chaotic and even violent atmosphere that dominated the early phases of treatment also represented an attempt to relive the traumatic failure of her infantile environment. She had to experience painful deprivation and rage and, if possible, seek revenge for her exploitation.

From a countertransference viewpoint, the deprived, helpless patient that I discussed previously causes the analyst to feel helpless and inadequate. Unless the therapist understands his reactions as repetitions of past failures, treatment can be disrupted. My patient caused me to feel more than frustration and helplessness.

I confess that it was hard to recognize the adaptive significance of her behavior when she was making impossible and futile demands of me. I felt attacked, and although in reality she posed no physical threat, I found myself at times fearing that she would attack and hurt me. This was a strange feeling in view of her diminutiveness and panic about destructive feelings and actions.

I have found that when patients who suffer from character-ological psychopathology try to acquire further ego integration, they seldom draw upon their historical past; that is, genetic reconstructions are not coined in terms of the infantile environ-ment (Gill 1979, 1983). Early object relationships are not at all neglected, but the patient is inclined to put the actual relation-ship in the background and to deal with that relationship as it is transferred to the therapist. The transference becomes the dom-inant, overriding theme.

* * *

During the last eighteen months of treatment, the patient discussed in considerable detail the various events and orienta-tion that had occurred during the course of therapy. She reviewed, for example, what she had been trying to accomplish during the beginning, explosive phases of analysis. She was, in effect, emphasizing that even the most seemingly disorganized and purposeless behavior has some adaptive significance. A person oriented around endless paradoxes, she was trying hard to work out her problems by having me fail her. Having felt rebuffed as a child, she would spitefully rebuff any attempt to help her. This childish attempt at revenge was aimed at frus-trating a parent who is trying to make amends. It was as if she were saying that because the mother was not there when she wanted her, she would have nothing more to do with her, no matter how hard she might try to make up for her negligence. The mother or father, for that matter, had no inclinations to make amends. In part, the patient's fantasied refusal of overtures and its reenactment in treatment also represented a wish-fulfillment, a wish that caretakers would approach and seek her so that she could reject them.

As Freud (1920) stressed, the aim of such repetitions is to convert a situation of passive vulnerability into one of active mastery. I was astonished when she informed me that she had been attempting to dominate the treatment from the beginning. This seemed to be the ultimate paradox, in that she had seemed to be totally out of control and vociferously helpless and vulnerable. She seemed to be as far from mastery as one could get. Still, when I recall our exchange during the first session, I could understand how the sequence of our interaction could be viewed as an attempt to frustrate me; I thought of her asking me to react to her in a nonanalytic fashion and of her resisting my interpretations. She emphasized how important it was for her to defeat me, and she teasingly thanked me for not trying too hard to help her.

Just as depressed patients present many paradoxes, so do patients suffering from primitive mental states. Paradoxes, as I will discuss specifically in Part III, present therapeutic problems. The countertransference toward depressed patients has many complex elements. The paradoxes produced by such patients are particularly significant because they create considerable confusion. Traditional orientations are reversed. They seek mastery and control by appearing weak and helpless; they seek power by producing weakness; they create chaos and disorder to achieve meaning and purpose.

Countertransference confusion is intensified because the therapist may be able to see neither meaning nor purpose in the patient's material and behavior. There are patients whose chaos possesses very little adaptive significance (see Chapter 6), but this is generally not true of depressions, although it is sometimes hard to keep that in mind.

The difficulties involved in understanding these patients are associated with the paradoxical aspects of the self-representation. As discussed, misery and hopelessness are reactions to the maintenance of a cohesive self-representation. They are manifestations of adaptations that are designed to protect the identity sense from collapsing into a state of terror and the psyche from falling into existential nihilism.

Therapists find it difficult to work within the context of such paradoxes, especially when they are connected to psychic structure. It is much easier to deal with drives because we are accustomed to polarities when dealing with instinctual forces as Freud (1915b) defined them. He discussed sadism and masochism and scopophilia and exhibitionism in the frame of reference of drive vicissitudes and polarities of mental life. The oppositional relationship between the id and the ego is a familiar phenomenon in the study of the psychoneuroses. However, similar polarities within a particular psychic structure, such as the self-representation and the superego, are difficult to comprehend and to integrate with our usual concepts about emotional disorders.

I believe that depressive disorders will cause us to revise many of our current attitudes about psychopathology and treatment. Throughout the years, it has generally been assumed that patients who have well-integrated egos are the easiest group to treat and cause the least homogeneous countertransference difficulties. This simple dictum is called into question if we accept that depressions belong to a group that has advanced relatively far on the scale of emotional development.

First, some clinicians have doubted whether the severity of psychopathology can be hierarchically ordered on the basis of our nosologic system, which distinguishes various neuroses and correlates them with specific levels of psychosexual development (Giovacchini 1979a, Reichard 1956). The cases that Freud (1904, 1909) described as examples of hysterical neuroses were later discussed as examples of character disorders (Meissner 1984–1985). This diagnostic shift might help explain why hysterics are very difficult to treat and tend to create disruptive countertransference problems. Here, if we question diagnosis, we are still asserting that difficulties in treatment cannot be equated with the severity of psychopathology.

Perhaps certain types of severe emotional disorders respond well to the psychoanalytic method because of its nonjudgmental and nonintrusive qualities, whereas a better-integrated patient may not feel as vulnerable and may want the analyst to make judgments and evaluations to help him deal with the external world.

Unanswered questions remain, but standard clichés about treatment will be more frequently challenged as we become increasingly aware of the subtle and unique transference–countertransference interactions that are encountered in the therapy of depressed patients. These patients test our capacities as analysts, but if we can survive as therapists and carry on treatment, we will have had a rewarding and clinically enriching experience.

PART III

TECHNICAL
TREATMENT PROBLEMS

8

Countertransference, the Psychoanalytic Paradox, and the Treatment Process

Having discussed various types of countertransference responses within the context of different forms of psychopathology, I believe it would be useful now to explore the psychoanalytic process in general and some peculiarities that occur because of specific developmental antecedents. The infantile environment, as it is re-created in the consultation room, and because of its similarities to the treatment setting, may create therapeutic impasses.

The analyst who has developed a particular style and mode of relating may find that his usual perspective hinders rather than enhances the treatment process.

As discussed earlier, the analyst may feel that his professional identity is being challenged, but there is the added confusion that follows the realization that his usual modus operandi is inappropriate. It is as if what the therapist has learned about the psychoanalytic process is no longer valid—at least not for a particular patient.

Working with patients who suffer from primitive mental states has taught clinicians the value of flexibility. Many years ago, Eissler (1953) coined the term *parameter* to describe modifications of treatment—that is, deviations of analysis—that might be temporarily required so that treatment can continue. Parameters are temporary, however, and they are relinquished as soon as it is appropriate so that analysis can be resumed. The modifications of techniques to which I will refer, on the other hand, are not given up. They are intrinsic to and essential for the analytic process.

Some analysts experience discomfort and resistance to permanent modifications of technique. This discomfort may lead to disruptive countertransference problems that may preclude the continuation of analysis. This does not mean that the patient is unanalyzable, however. If the therapist understands how the patient's past has become imbricated into the treatment interaction, it is possible to weather the countertransference storm, and therapy can proceed in the direction of further psychic integration.

THE PSYCHOANALYTIC PARADOX
   AND RESISTANCE

The psychoanalytic paradox is a situation that occasionally occurs in treatment, usually of patients suffering from characterological problems, in which some of the formal elements of the psychoanalytic method are experienced as a repetition of the traumatic past. By *formal elements*, I am referring to the use of the couch, the frequency of appointments, and the analyst's low-keyed responses. The latter may be a manifestation of analytic neutrality, but some patients are unable to tolerate such an attitude.

Certain types of psychoanalytic paradoxes simply have to be transcended. I recall a patient who correctly asserted that she had to experience her fundamental loneliness, but she was unable to do so as long as I was there beside her. She felt my presence and could not really feel alone, as she had in childhood. Yet she had to repeat these burdensome experiences of the past in treatment.

This patient's reactions were also the outcome of a structural defect. She lacked the capacity for evocative memory, as Fraiberg (1969) described, or for object permanency and object constancy, as Piaget (1952) discussed. She could not form and hold a mental representation without the actual presence of the external object. Her mental representations had to be periodically reinforced. Similarly, she could not abolish or decathect a mental representation if the external object were within her sensory field. She could not shut me out unless I was away from her. Consequently, she could not experience loneliness in the analytic setting.

There was no particular technical maneuver to enable me to deal with this problem. The patient eventually developed some capacity for evocative memory and was finally able to reproduce a traumatic element of her past in my presence. It was as if psychic structure had to keep up with the development of the repetition compulsion.

Another patient complained about his inability to experience anxiety in the treatment setting. The calm, interpretive, explanatory atmosphere characteristic of the analytic interaction did not permit him to feel anxious. He could not face the irrational within him, because once it was interpreted, it became rational. It might be suggested that the analyst's interpretations should have been withheld until the patient could mobilize some anxiety. This would have made little difference, however, because it was the supportive, holding aspects of the analytic ambience that provided the rational structure that prevented the experiencing of anxiety. Verbal interpretation contributed to, but was not a necessary condition for, a calm environment. Again, the presence of the analyst drove the irrational into the background.

The repetition compulsion component of the patient's reactions eventually became evident. Forced into premature adulthood, the patient had been denied his childhood. He was not allowed to be childish or dependent; rather, his parents were dependent on him. Since he was intellectually precocious, they relied on his intelligence and his ability to approach problems rationally. As so often happens with the repetition compulsion, he was reversing roles; he was treating me as he had been treated. Until we could detect this focus in treatment, we both felt stymied as to how the analytic method was seemingly interfering with the unfolding of his psychopathology.

There are other treatment situations in which the psychoanalytic paradox becomes unmanageable, and this is usually due to the analyst's resistance, which reinforces the patient's resistance, until a vicious circle, a negative feedback, is created. For example, narcissistic patients in particular complain of the analyst's lack of participation and silence. They may demand responses to their material, frequently to a dream. The analyst, in turn, feels that his professional autonomy is threatened; he wants to decide when and whether he will respond. As happened to me with my lawyer patient (see Chapter 2), the treatment may degenerate into a power struggle as the therapist "resists" the patient's demands. This form of analyst participation prevents the establishment of an observational platform and an intrapsychic focus. Needy patients insist that they have to have feedback. The emotional responses that they desire are precluded if the analyst insists on remaining neutral.

Many clinicians would assert that if an analyst abandons the neutral stance, he then has abandoned analysis. This is a classical viewpoint, but we have to examine exactly what constitutes analytic neutrality. It is usually defined in terms of what the analyst should *not* do—namely, responding to the patient's material at the level of content. This could mean not volunteering information, not answering questions, especially personal questions, or not responding to the patient's request for advice and guidance. The less classical analyst might permit some response, but only after the material has been analyzed. Thus, the technique to preserve neutrality consists of maintaining analytic silence or of questioning the patient about the motivations behind his material or protests. If the patient becomes uncooperative or otherwise disruptive, he may be told that he is resisting. From another viewpoint, however, the analyst is resisting the patient's material by treating it as if it should not have been brought into the treatment setting. This situation can be conceptualized as a disruptive crescendo of resistance and counterresistance.

Loewald (1960, 1986) has a somewhat different concept of the analytic relationship and of analytic neutrality. He states that the analyst, because of his capacity to understand and to perceive better than the patient can, is at a higher psychic level than the patient. Within the treatment situation, this differential can be structure-promoting. Loewald emphasizes the similarities between analyst and analysand and mother and child, the former dyad promoting psychic growth and the latter both psychic and physical growth. The structure-promoting aspects of the analytic relationship do not necessitate any particular techniques other than interpretations, but these are more acceptable and more easily integrated if a comfortable holding environment has been established.

There is nothing sacred about neutrality, especially if it is defined phenomenologically—that is, determined by the analyst's overt behavior and attitudes (Greenberg 1986, Shapiro 1984). To me, this level of definition seems ritualized and inflexible, especially when facing needy patients, for neutrality need not dictate specific reactions to the patient's material. Rather, neutrality is an attitude, one designed to create an objective, nonjudgmental setting that stresses the principle of psychic determinism. Analysts are neutral about their patient's associations; they neither make value judgments nor take sides in their patients' ambivalence. They give equal weight to each current of ambivalence (Modell 1968).

This attitude of neutrality can be achieved in various ways. Therapists' responses are determined by each patient's psychopathology, and what may be supportive of the analytic framework of one patient may be disastrous for another.

Certain types of patients require a style of involvement that will stand in stark contrast to the lack of feeling they experienced in childhood; otherwise, the transference–countertransference axis will become disruptive as a psychoanalytic paradox is created. The unique nature of the analytic relationship is highlighted, especially in the treatment of patients suffering from character disorders. From a behavioral viewpoint, the therapist is similar to the nonresponsive mother. The analyst's observational focus is experienced by the patient as a recapitulation of the suffering of the traumatic infantile past. The analyst is equated to the mother who never smiled, lacked radiance, and felt no pride or pleasure in her motherhood. Transference projections and the creation of the infantile ambience in the consultation room are virtually impossible to interpret effectively, because the patient is convinced that the therapist is really reacting as the mother did. The situation becomes even more complicated when analysts relentlessly cling to what they consider to be analytic decorum as their patient's dissatisfaction escalates (McDougall 1979).

Is analysis contraindicated for patients with this type of background and character pathology? In many instances, these patients have vigorously sought analysis, but they believe that they need analysts who will reveal their feelings, as opposed to analysts who strive to be no more than reflecting mirrors. They assert that analytic functioning can occur with more personal involvement. I believe that the creation of a psychoanalytic paradox by patients who received only minimal acknowledgment during childhood forces us to consider our concepts of treatability and of the techniques comprised by the analytic method.

For example, is it possible to conduct analysis at a "higher decibel level" than the traditional low-keyed analytic neutrality and still strive for the resolution of basic conflicts and traumas and the acquisition of further psychic structure? To reverse the question, is it possible to achieve analytic resolution without the therapist's becoming somewhat involved at an emotional level?

Psychoanalysts do not attempt to gratify infantile impulses. To do so would interfere with the maintenance of an intrapsychic focus and force therapists to become participants in the patient's external reality. Under these circumstances, they would no longer be transference objects and products of the patient's psychic creations and projections. I doubt, however, that anyone can actually gratify infantile impulses. What might have been appropriate nurturance in infancy will not suffice for adults, even if their egos are fixated at primitive developmental levels. Giving them breast milk will not gratify currently felt dependency needs. Their adult egos will have acquired elements of later developmental phases, resulting in a variety of adaptive techniques and regulatory mechanisms that make requirements for sustenance much more complex than those that were appropriate at the level of fixation. Furthermore, when the ego regresses to the point of fixation, many later adaptations are not lost. Most patients can still walk, talk, and remain continent.

Undoing the effects of infantile trauma is not the same as gratifying infantile needs. Rather than being concerned about the substance of nurturance, clinicians today are dealing with modes of relating that are pertinent to emotional development and to the acquisition of psychic structure. Analysts can furnish patients with a relationship that is different from the traumatic mother–infant interaction. This mode of relating transcends the psychoanalytic paradox and leads to emotional development.

I believe that the analyst's mode of relating can be a corrective experience, but it should not be confused with Alexander's (1961) corrective emotional experience. What I am discussing does not involve role playing in a transference context. The analyst's responses are natural, spontaneous reactions to the patient's specific psychopathology. Although some of the responses that I am about to discuss may differ from what is customarily accepted as analytic behavior, they are not, in my opinion, deviations from analysis. Rather, they are the outcome of optimal countertransference responses that involve a personal concern for the patient that goes beyond a benign clinical regard and a conscious or unconscious reaction to deficiencies in the quality of past object relations. I can best illustrate these concepts about the therapeutic interaction with a clinical example that I have described in greater detail elsewhere (Giovacchini 1979a).

* * *

The patient, a freshman college student, was referred to me by a university health department psychiatrist because he had had what was initially diagnosed as an acute schizophrenic episode. He had withdrawn to his dormitory room and was not sleeping, bathing, or eating. He had completely deteriorated both physically and emotionally. Finally, his classmates literally carried him to the student health clinic, whereupon he was immediately hospitalized. The diagnosis was changed to identity-diffusion syndrome (Erikson 1959) when he suddenly became alert and somewhat reality oriented after a visit from his parents. It was recommended to them that he remain in school and seek psychotherapy on an outpatient basis. Thus, he was referred to me.

He was withdrawn and silent when I first saw him. He appeared to be painfully shy. He offered nothing spontaneously and was guarded and cryptic in his replies to my questions. I soon reached the conclusion that his monosyllabic answers indicated that he found my questions intrusive and irritating, so I told him I did not want to keep bothering him with my curiosity. I said it might be better if he lay down; then he could be alone with his thoughts if he wanted to be. I would be nearby, however, and if he wanted to share anything with me, I would be there. He was visibly relieved as he lay down on the couch, saying nothing for the remainder of the session. He continued in this fashion for a month or so, and then tentatively started asking questions about pedestrian matters.

With some patients, I am irritated by being bombarded with questions, and I ordinarily do not answer them. I tend to deal with each statement as if it were a declarative sentence, regardless of its actual grammatical form. With this adolescent, my attitude was entirely different. I could not *not* have answered his questions. It would have been unthinkable and out of character to remain silent or to resort to the frequently used ploy of throwing the question back to the patient and asking him the reason for asking the question. I have used this strategy on other occasions, but with this patient it would have been impossible, and it felt wrong.

He spent many sessions asking me how to conduct himself in the external world. He would ask what kind of clothes were appropriate for specific occasions, and how to get to certain locations in the city. He even asked me how to make a telephone call to a girl for a date. These exchanges were calm and comfortable.

One day, he appeared extremely upset. He was disturbed about what turned out to be an insignificant change in the schedule of the train he took to commute to my office. I immediately felt as agitated as he did, and we began having an intense, anxious discussion about it. If outsiders had been able to see us, perhaps through a one-way mirror, without hearing the content of our discussion, they would have concluded that a nuclear bomb was about to be dropped in the next few minutes. The change in schedule turned out to cause no difficulties, however. In fact, it made matters more convenient for both of us.

This patient's analysis lasted many years and had many stormy moments (Giovacchini 1979a). I wish to emphasize that much more occurred between us than our initial intense involvement. The patient experienced considerable anxiety and rage, which he was capable of directing at me. The establishment and analysis of the transference would not have been possible, however, had we not formed a relationship through such interchanges.

His background made him particularly sensitive to certain issues. He described his mother as apparently concerned with his welfare, but cold and intellectual. He did not recall her ever smiling spontaneously at him or just casually talking or playing with him. His father was seldom at home, and he did not remember his attending any of the school activities at which parents would ordinarily be present.

My spontaneous "high-decibel" reactions were quite different from anything he had encountered in the past. He was not consciously aware that this involvement was an entirely new experience for him, and he did not openly recognize that he was beginning to feel that someone was interested in his potential for experiencing life and defining his boundaries. Nevertheless, he began to discover that he had needs of his own and that there was someone in the external world who shared and encouraged such a recognition.

My method of relating was not planned, nor, to my mind, was it an extra-analytic maneuver, in the sense of its being a parameter, as Eissler (1953) described. Rather, I regarded it as a unique aspect of the holding environment required for patients with particular infantile backgrounds. It was part of the analytic decorum, which, to a degree, must be tailored to the patient's needs.

This patient needed to be acknowledged. He had to make his presence felt. When he was a child, no one had related to what could have been his emerging sense of aliveness. As he gradually recognized that he was worthwhile and interesting, a realization that had been sadly lacking during his vulnerable years of emotional development, he also began to become introspective and to seek instructions about coping with external reality.

I believe that analysis is impossible for some patients who suffer from character disorders unless the therapist takes measures to avoid the unwitting recapitulation of the traumatic or abandoning infantile environment—even if the resemblance

would be only superficial. The modalities employed must acknowledge the patient's existence and express the analyst's
concern for further emotional development and autonomy. As
stated, the therapist does not deliberately plan a strategy.
Rather, for some analysts, their reactions are natural responses
of which they may or may not be particularly aware. They are
compelled to react as they do, and, in many instances, they have
a special interest in the patient.

For some reason, these analysts have a dedication to the
treatment of especially needy patients, a dedication that may be
difficult to understand (Chapter 7). The efforts required are
sometimes above and beyond the therapeutic gain that can be
achieved. It often seems that therapists experience very little
satisfaction compared to the abuse they have to suffer.

It may be that therapists who are able to persist in the
treatment of very difficult patients have special needs of their
own. This ability to persevere could well be the outcome of
idiosyncratic countertransference elements, as has been asserted
by classical analysts who limit their selection of patients to those
who have fairly well-integrated egos. I believe, however, that
other analysts find a special fascination with primitive mental
processes and adaptations, and understand that if they are able
to survive patients' deep regressions, then they will have been
enriched by a learning experience that will help them understand a wide variety of clinical states. They find that they are
able both to get in touch with the primitive parts of themselves
and to develop a respect and tolerance for the deepest levels of
the personality. Their sense that there are creative elements to
the most primitive layers of the unconscious will help them to
maintain comfort and equanimity in the face of psychic turmoil
and disorganization.

With patients who are less disturbed, the formal elements
of analysis do not create any particular problems. The low-

keyed, low-decibel analyst does not resemble an abandoning mother, because such patients have not been neglected or rejected in childhood. Their sense of security is sufficient to allow them to take it for granted that the analyst will maintain an interest in them.

Often included in the analyst's countertransference responses is the expectation of a cure. With better-integrated patients, this is usually not a problem. With patients who are more vulnerable, however, such an expectation is perceived as an intrusive assault and an attack on autonomy. With some schizophrenic patients, the slightest anticipation that they will change can be catastrophic. These patients will feel submerged and manipulated by such an expectation because they believe that they are changing for the analyst's benefit, not their own, and that they are being forced to relinquish their psychic adaptations.

COUNTERTRANSFERENCE AND PSYCHOPHARMACOLOGY

Inasmuch as the purpose of psychoanalytic treatment is to understand how the mind works, and not necessarily to achieve symptomatic improvement, analysts do not try to change the behavioral or subjective manifestations of ego states. The non-analytic psychiatrist is not concerned with the patient's getting in touch with various parts of the self; instead, he wishes to help the patient to get rid of disruptive and painful symptomatic psychic states, and he uses drugs to achieve that purpose. Making patients feel better or making them less troublesome to society is the dominant therapeutic goal.

This goal may be helpful for the patient, but, from an

analytic viewpoint, it may involve a subtle and deceptive interaction, which, insofar as it appears to be helpful, may actually be
destructive. Clinicians usually like to achieve a state of therapeutic security, a balanced, equilibrated countertransference
that is based on the attitude that they know what they are
doing. This is an understandable and reasonable endeavor for
therapists, but I have heard many discussions about patients in
which such knowledge, implicitly or explicitly, was considered
superfluous. Psychoanalysts, on the other hand, have to suffer
the pangs of uncertainty and ambiguity, and their ultimate
purpose is to know the patient in terms of psychic processes
rather than to achieve behavioral control.

To know the patient seems simple enough. There are,
however, various therapeutic philosophies and treatment approaches. Still, if they adhere to the medical model—this in itself
being a debatable issue—then therapists have to determine the
most appropriate approach to the emotional disorders they are
confronting. It is not the patient's choice. Therapists supposedly
have the expertise and experience to conduct rational treatment. Patients cannot decide what type of treatment is required
because they are constricted by their illness and by their lack of
knowledge. The decision is not their responsibility. Even in
general medicine, however, there are exceptions to this rule.
Patients sometimes decide what kind of treatment they will
receive by seeking a particular type of practitioner, such as a
naturopath or a chiropractor, rather than an internist or an
orthopedist.

With emotional disorders, the choice of practitioner wid-
ens. The patient usually does not need to make a treatment
decision based on diagnosis. The patient picks a therapist with a
certain orientation; he may choose an Adlerian, Jungian, or
Freudian analyst, or a behavioral, cognitive, or Gestalt therapist. The fact that the patient has made a choice as to the

orientation of the therapist is often the crucial determinant for believing that that is a feasible approach, and the decision frequently proves to be a sound one.

This may be especially true for psychoanalysis. If a patient wants to be analyzed, for whatever reason, his opinion must be respected. At the least, it usually means that the patient has an intrapsychic focus and is interested in psychic processes. Many of these patients are psychologically minded. I have occasionally consulted with patients who have been dissatisfied with a treatment that relies primarily on drugs and ignores underlying emotional factors. Analysts, in general, welcome such patients, who may not be particularly easy to treat, but who at least respect psychological processes.

Outside pressure may create countertransference dilemmas for analysts who do not want to include drugs in their treatment scheme. The problem intensifies if the patient acts out or is otherwise disruptive. Relatives, teachers, and others may demand some control of the patient's aberrant behavior. For some analysts, the dilemma becomes particularly thorny when psychiatric colleagues criticize them or accuse them of neglect and malpractice if they do not use neuroleptic drugs. The analyst himself may feel the need for some tranquility, but this can work against the patient's getting in touch with ego states that are, in a sense, abolished by drugs. Countertransference confusion escalates as the analyst struggles with moral and ethical issues that conflict with his basic therapeutic orientation. The added threat of malpractice litigation can also be destructive to the construction of a calm, tranquil holding environment. Analysts cannot work effectively with the threat of a malpractice suit hanging over their heads.

Countertransference reactions become further complicated when analysts make value judgments, not primarily about patients, but about treatment approaches. As much as possible, analysts try to avoid becoming involved with such issues, but they are sometimes unavoidable when dealing with questions of medication. A judgment about a treatment method will ultimately influence our opinion about the patient, and this creates more problems in the transference–countertransference relationship. When drugs are an essential feature of the therapeutic plan, many analysts have lesser expectations regarding what the patient will accomplish. Consciously or unconsciously, analysts may modify their goals for patients who are receiving such psychopharmacologic agents as antidepressants or antipsychotics. They lower their sights and expect less of their patients.

With schizophrenic or other severely regressed patients, custodial and behavioral management may be the direction that the therapist is forced to follow. Some of these patients are considered to be beyond hope, as was the case with the depressed patient discussed in the previous chapter. They represent a hopeless segment of the patient population that can only be contained in a custodial setting, and there is very little likelihood that analysis will be successful. In some instances it can be no other way, but there are other clinical situations that are not quite so clear-cut. Therapists are taking tremendous risks when they make an omnipotent judgment that excludes the possibility of the patient's ever returning to the external world and adapting at some functional level.

Clinicians have learned that some very sick and disruptive patients are able to engage in an interpersonal relationship based on the understanding of mental processes (see Chapter 7). Medication can be used to help maintain the patient in treatment, rather than being an end in itself; it can be used to help the patient behave to the extent that he does not threaten his caretakers or otherwise disturb the milieu. At times the situation truly is hopeless, but it is unfair to our patients and an abnegation of our professional identity to reach such a conclusion without first trying to become engaged in a meaningful relationship that engenders hope, and such an endeavor may require the use of medication.

Drugs can carry a variety of meanings. The effects may range from negative and destructive to beneficial and soothing, enabling the potential for character growth and the resolution of intrapsychic conflict. The soothing, tranquilizing effects of drugs on certain patients can facilitate the construction of the holding environment, but the analyst will still have to participate actively as he continues to stress an intrapsychic focus. Unfortunately, many patients who have been sustained by psychopharmacologic regimens are ignored from the interpersonal perspective, because the therapist has abandoned even the prospect of analysis.

In other instances, rather than working against it, medication can be an ally of the therapeutic process. The infantile holding environment provided by the mother may include the administration of drugs to alleviate pain. The mother responds to all aspects of her infant's needs, including those that arise from organic dysfunctions. For an adult patient, medication can represent that aspect of the mother–child relationship that led to soothing and relief, and it can thus become a focus of communication between therapist and patient within the context of the transference–countertransference interaction.

Some patients are so needy and concretely oriented that they can neither engage in an introspective process nor tolerate the frustration engendered by what they perceive to be a withholding or emotionally distant analyst. Their tension may be so intense that they demand immediate relief. Their misery is often expressed in somatic terms, however, and they are extremely difficult to soothe. They are so concretely oriented that they lack the capacity for symbolic gratification.

With this particular group of patients, we may have to

expand our professional self-representation to include some aspects of our medical orientation. Frequently, the only way we can relate to these patients is at the concrete level, and this may mean that we have to respond to their painful symptoms. We have to adapt to a caregiving role as we attempt to relieve their inner disruption. Thus, medication becomes an adjunct that soothes the patient.

Appealing for help may be the only way these patients can communicate to another person. Medication, in addition to its pharmacologic effects, can represent the mode by which an object relationship can be established. This concrete mode of relating is at a somatic rather than a mentational level. As discussed in Chapter 6, these patients' psyches are fixated at prementational levels. Thus, medication, in addition to helping to establish emotional equilibrium, may help promote a bond between patient and therapist that can become increasingly psychologically sophisticated, eventually enabling the therapist to enter the realm of the patient's mind.

Medication is involved in the primitive and dynamic interplay that characterizes the transference–countertransference axis of primitively fixated patients and is symbolically equated, or becomes equated, with infantile nurturing. Medication represents both the substance of nurturance and its soothing elements.

In terms of the two components of the nurturing experience—that is, soothing and nurturing (see Chapter 6)—various classes of drugs have different effects. Some drugs, such as the tranquilizers, both major and minor, help to establish both a nurturing and soothing matrix. Similarly, antidepressants can promote a sense of aliveness, but these effects occur optimally in the context of a treatment relationship, and they are most constructive when achieved without drugs. As I have stressed, there need not be absolute polarities between psychopharmacologic and psychoanalytic treatment. Strict adherence to such polarities seems least indicated when treating severely disturbed patients. Well-integrated patients, of course, would be less likely to be taking drugs, especially antipsychotic agents.

In treating severely disturbed patients, therapists might feel uncomfortable and find it difficult to maintain an intrapsychic focus if they themselves prescribe medication. When they do prescribe medication, they have assumed the responsibility of monitoring psychic states, and this interferes with analyzing them. Relatively well-integrated patients can relate to their analysts in different contexts, but patients suffering from primitive mental states are constricted and rigid, and can only deal with their surroundings and external objects in a limited fashion. They do not have the flexibility to move from one frame of reference to another. Parts of their psyches want to use their therapists as caregivers, a role that would include the prescription of medication. In many instances, however, the assumption of such a role by the therapist destroys him as an analyst, as a benign observer interested in psychic processes. To avoid such impasses, I find it useful to refer patients who require or feel they need medication to a colleague, who can evaluate the patient and prescribe drugs if they are indicated. The colleague also monitors medication's effects, titrating the dose according to the patient's responses. Meanwhile, the analyst can direct his attention to the nuances of the transference–countertransference relationship.

COUNTERTRANSFERENCE
AND THE REPETITION COMPULSION

Interpretation is the analyst's most important therapeutic tool. But there is much more operating in the interpretative interaction than just verbal communication. Various levels of the therapist's and patient's personality become interwoven, and the analyst's character structure largely determines the insights that will be integrated into the patient's psyche (Masterson 1976).

Sooner or later, the analyst will become involved with some facet of the patient's repetition compulsion. The recognition of the repetition compulsion and its role in determining the qualities of the transference–countertransference axis expands our concepts of the psychoanalytic treatment process. It also extends our concepts of interpretation beyond the interpretation of hidden instinctual impulses, defenses, and resistance. Although the "compulsion to repeat" (Freud 1920) is an intrinsic quality of an instinctual impulse, the repetition compulsion is a much broader process that describes an infantile frame of reference. Patients have developed certain defenses and adaptive techniques to deal with the traumatic infantile environment. In later life, they re-create the trauma in order to master it. If the total environment resembles the early dangerous and threatening relationships (usually assaultive or abandoning), then the patient has managed to externalize a milieu. The repetition compulsion is the motivating force behind externalization.

The purpose of the repetition compulsion, although it often seems to be a repetition of a self-defeating sequence, is to master trauma and to convert a state of passive vulnerability to active mastery. It represents an attempt at self-regulation and an effort to establish psychic equilibrium. When the infantile trauma has become part of the transference, in that the analyst has been assigned the threatening role, the patient can shift his attitude, now manifested as negative transference, as he recognizes the extent of his projections. He can also use the therapist as an ally to help him actively master the dangerous infantile past, which is being reenacted in the present.

Interpretation in this context deals with this reenactment.

The analyst reveals the patient's view of the analyst as a person of the traumatic past, a role that has been projected into him. Patients use their therapists in various ways. As previously discussed, roles can be reversed so that they traumatize their analysts as they themselves were traumatized by their caretakers. Nevertheless, the patient externalizes the infantile environment. He is trying to achieve some resolution of a painful early orientation.

Without the help of treatment, the patient would continue to repeat the traumatic past in the same self-defeating fashion. He might be able to make a minimal adaptation, but only at the cost of achieving more satisfying, autonomous levels of psychic integration. During treatment, the analyst interprets the scenario that the patient has created—not all at once, of course, but the eventual therapeutic purpose is to understand the patient's perception of the world in terms of early traumatic constellations and his use of infantile adaptations and outmoded defenses that are inappropriate and self-destructive in the current setting. The insights acquired pertain to the patient's maladaptive relationships to the external world rather than to forbidden instinctual wishes and intrapsychic conflicts.

The patient is then free to acquire more efficient, effective reality-attuned adaptations. Patients develop a capacity to make use of helpful sectors of their external world that were unavailable to them when they were operating under the pressure of the repetition compulsion. They learn new techniques that can now be incorporated into the ego's executive system. This often occurs through identification with, or sometimes incorporation of, the analyst's values.

At this juncture in treatment, analysts must be particularly vigilant about their countertransference attitudes. Many of the examples I have given of disruptive countertransference reactions referred to the therapist's feeling shut out and narcissisti-

cally injured. The situations I am now describing are the antith-
eses of these treatment situations. In order to gain autonomy
and mastery over their infantile environments, patients are
prone to identify with their therapist's values and adaptive
modes. Therapists, in turn, may feel narcissistically enhanced.

Such narcissistic gratification need not be harmful to the
therapeutic process if the analyst does not try to set himself up as
a model. It is easy to step out of the analytic role and into the role
of educator and participant in the patient's external world.
Inasmuch as patients might encourage this type of participation,
analysts might easily be lured into maneuvering their patients
into accepting their viewpoints and values. This is often facili-
tated by the frequently encountered situation in which there are
actually many similarities between analyst and patient.

The distinction between interpretations dealing with psychodynamic vectors and the scenario of the repetition compulsion is not as clear as I have implied. Within the context of the
repetition compulsion, we often encounter conflicting destructive feelings and considerable ambivalence, as well as helpful
identifications. Superego restrictions may also play a prominent
role, as may forbidden incestuous impulses. Still, with many
patients, the analyst has to demonstrate the involvement of all
these elements in their general misery and alienation from the
external world. Simply identifying conflicting feelings is not
enough.

For patients suffering from character disorders, interpretation cannot be separated from countertransference attitudes.
Countertransference may interfere with the interpretative process, because, as mentioned, neither the patient nor the analyst
may be aware of participating in the repetition compulsion
scenario. The analyst is not aware of being a participant precisely because he is a participant, and he is therefore unable to
help the patient understand what is happening.

As noted, the analyst is more prone to participating in the repetition compulsion when his narcissism is enhanced. What I will now describe concerns a type of countertransference in which the therapist feels frustrated. The therapist absorbs the patient's projections by assuming the role assigned to him, and then acts it out in the context of the repetition compulsion. He becomes either the persecutor (the parental imago) or the victim (the patient). I will briefly present a patient who illustrated the involvement of the repetition compulsion in the treatment interaction.

* * *

A 20-year-old college student was repeating a pattern of failure both in his daily life and in treatment. He sought therapy because nothing in life had ever turned out well for him. Although of superior intelligence, he did poorly in school, and now at the university he was receiving very poor grades or failing his courses. He had also been rejected by a fraternity and was continually turned down when he tried to date or asked a girl for a dance. He stated that his whole life had been one constant failure, but as a child, his failures had not bothered him much. Now, however, he was aware of how much pain and misery he felt because he could not get along in the world.

The patient had learned how to live in an environment punctuated by failure. His parents were intellectuals and they held high aspirations for their children. His father had pushed him to learn since he was 2 years old, and by the age of 4, he was able to read and write and had mastered addition, subtraction, and some multiplication.

Despite his achievements, his family gave him very little attention. Instead, they were devoted to his brother, four years older than the patient, upon whom they lavished all their admiration and concern. The brother was also considered very

bright, and the mother, especially, enjoyed basking in his limelight. He also had a delicate constitution and was frequently
sick. He had suffered most of the contagious diseases of childhood and had been diagnosed as having a rare congenital
muscular disease. The patient felt that he had been rejected and
abandoned, and he saw no point in being successful.

His negative attitude about success was discovered during
his therapy, where he repeated with me his feelings toward his
parents. Somehow he managed to make me feel concerned
about his academic progress. My concern was partially related to
the preservation of the treatment, because if he failed all his
courses, he would not be allowed to return to school; he would
have to return home and leave the city. I became aware of such
concerns later in treatment. He would start a course with
considerable promise and report to me his successes. He might
even get an A on a midterm examination. Then his work would
precipitously deteriorate and he would either fail or nearly fail
the course. I was extremely frustrated, and my feelings vacillated
between wanting to urge him to try harder and wanting to
reprimand him for what, at times, I believed were attempts to
sabotage his academic career and future ambitions. He was
planning on applying to law school and he needed a superior
academic record to gain admission. His father, a lawyer, was
very anxious that he be accepted to a prestigious law school.

I finally realized that my reactions were similar to his
father's. I would start out with hope and perhaps even move on
to complacency, since it seemed that his superior intelligence
would gain him success. I would then experience shock at his
first failure, followed by concern, frustration, and finally indignation. This progression was repeated several times, and although I should have been familiar with this sequence, I nevertheless continued to react.

While writing a summary of this patient for a seminar in

which the participants discussed what they considered to be their problem patients, I was impressed by the persistence of my reactions after so many identical episodes. I was also struck by how, for a while, I regularly felt complacent and recalled that the patient bitterly complained about it. He remonstrated that he was needy and that I was not responding to his needs. His complaints seemed to usher in his series of failures.

Although I did not understand as fully as I would have liked the significance and manipulative aspects of the patient's destructive and self-destructive behavior, I recognized that I was somehow allowing myself to be pulled into his infantile frame of reference. I had lost analytic objectivity and had moved away from the observational position as I reacted to the content of his material. I became aware of my misdirected involvement after I wrote the summary of the clinical material for the seminar.

During the next session, the patient began the litany of his failures. He had reached the stage at which his previous successes had suddenly crashed as he sought the road to failure. Because I had reached some conclusions, tentative though they were, as to what was happening, I felt considerably more detached than I had in the past. The patient sensed that something was different, and he asked me about my reactions to his current failure. Spontaneously, I replied that I found it interesting that he had to build up hope and expectations and then suddenly dash them. I added that this was a hostile pattern that had to be understood and, as far as I was personally concerned, it no longer mattered whether he failed or succeeded. I was simply interested in how his mind worked and in what he was trying to accomplish by his behavior. I also acknowledged that, in the past, I had been concerned to the extent that I had lost my analytic focus, but that now my viewpoint about what he was doing had changed. The patient was bemused and replied, "Man, you're playing it cool." I felt considerably relieved. The patient's demeanor also lost some of its edginess, and he gradually developed an interest in learning more about his motivations and manipulations.

My reply does not seem to be an interpretation. It is a countertransferrnce admission, disclosing my feelings and reactions rather than being designed to evoke insights about the patient's self-defeating behavior. Reflecting further on this interaction, I concluded that it was an example of a definition of the analytic setting. I was covertly pointing out that the patient had been trying to make me part of his infantile environment, and he had succeeded in doing so. Later, I related his behavior to the repetition compulsion. Our relationship had submerged our purpose of analytic inquiry and, in a sense, obliterated the therapeutic setting. I was trying to reestablish it, and by acknowledging my countertransference participation, I was also emphasizing his transference projections. I must have succeeded in doing this in a noncritical fashion, as evidenced by his response, "Man, you're playing it cool."

The course of analysis took on a different focus after this exchange. The crucial factor involved my feeling of complacency after the patient had demonstrated his intellectual capabilities. It was then that his family had taken him for granted and, from the patient's viewpoint, abandoned him as they turned their attention toward the needy, sickly older brother. In treatment, I had been content to rest on his laurels: I felt complacent about his achievements, taking them for granted as his family had done. He, in turn, had to recapture his parents' and now my, interest and concern. He also wanted revenge, so if he could not be loved for achieving, he would make an impact by failing and thus shattering our complacency. He was competing with his brother, but not on the basis of winning. Losing was his aim because, paradoxically, it meant victory. It was a Pyrrhic victory, however, and it made life difficult and unrewarding.

We were eventually able to understand his "compulsion to repeat," or more precisely, his "compulsion to fail," as a reaction to the terrifying fear of abandonment. Furthermore, his rage became overwhelming as he faced the oxymoron that "to be strong is to be weak," which, when carried to its extreme, became "to be alive is to be dead." His brother, in fact, had died when the patient was 16, and the patient believed that his parents regretted that he had not died instead of his brother. He was furious at them but, at the same time, he felt intense guilt about being the survivor. This combination forced him to choose a self-defeating life pattern that incorporated both his need for revenge and his guilt.

Over the next several years, the analysis dealt with various facets of the patient's infantile orientation and with how, through the repetition compulsion, he had re-created it, or externalized it, in both the academic and treatment settings. As he began to see me more in the role of observer than participant, succeeding and failing meant less to him, as it did to me. He gave up his ambition to enter law school and settled for a liberal arts degree. He then found a position in an advertising agency, a setting in which his creative talents have flourished.

* * *

As is true of any analysis, there were many facets to the transference that involved id impulses and projections of inner feelings. Nevertheless, these particular processes, in order to be understood, had to be fit into the broader framework of the infantile setting, which was characterized by idiosyncratic attitudes about success and failure, strength and weakness, and life and death.

I believe that Freud (1937) was referring to a similar situation when he discussed how he formulated the wider gestalt

of constructions in analysis as various interpretations are integrated with one another. Freud was interested in lifting infantile amnesia and reconstructing the past. This task can be achieved by putting together bits and pieces of insight derived from transference–countertransference interactions. The recognition of the reenactment of the infantile environment in the transference is, for patients suffering from character disorders, equivalent to the lifting of infantile amnesia, which Freud felt was the goal of treatment for patients suffering from the psychoneuroses.

The patient I have just discussed had a fairly intact ego, although he had a somewhat unstable self-representation. His confusion about life and death, and success and failure, hampered the development of a consistent ego ideal that would have given him a sanguine outlook and the ability to set worthwhile, gratifying goals. To be fixated on his concern about abandonment and survival narrowed his focus and interfered with the development of satisfying adaptive techniques. Still, his self-representation and his ego's integrative capacities were sufficiently structured so that he was able both to retain a coherent representation of the infantile environment and to externalize it in the analytic setting. Interpreting the scenario of the repetition compulsion, as it was reenacted in the analysis, freed him from the constricting adaptations and defenses against the trauma of rejection, abandonment, and, later, crushing guilt.

The patient's acquired freedom is related to inner structural changes. He had always had the capacity to be a successful student, but he had not carried his abilities into his relationships with the outer world. His executive techniques were hindered and underdeveloped because of his need to inhibit progression whenever he achieved a modicum of academic success. Thus he restricted himself to the academic area and did not develop any interpersonal skills. Analysis permitted him to pursue an autonomous scholastic program—autonomous in that he had no particular compulsion to excel, to gain admiration, or to fear rejection. He took pride in his work, but he felt that he was doing it for himself. The self-confidence he gained helped him to develop effective modes of relating to both male and female peers. He has reached a higher level of integration of the ego's executive system and now perceives the external world on its own terms rather than those of infancy and childhood.

Placing the gestalt of the repetition compulsion in an interpretative interaction can lead to the lifting of infantile constrictions that interfere with or distort the developmental process. Thus, such interactions are particularly apt for patients suffering from structural problems. The college student I have described can be considered an example of a patient suffering from a character neurosis with some structural deficiencies. Similar interactions in treatment can also be useful for patients who have very few structural problems, whose psychopathology is primarily the outcome of intrapsychic conflict. More severely disturbed patients, such as those with borderline disorders, can also benefit from interpretations aimed at understanding the extent of the patient's externalization of the infantile environment and the definition of the analytic setting.

BACKGROUND AND FOREGROUND ELEMENTS OF INTERPRETATION

Insofar as interpretation leads to the acquisition of further psychic structure, it bears some similarities to the mother–infant nurturing relationship. The infant grows both physically and emotionally because he has been properly nurtured. An effective interpretation has been compared to a good feed indicating that it is directed toward the gratification of basic needs.

As previously discussed, both interpretation and the nurturing relationship can be divided into two components: a foreground of nurturing and a background of soothing. The nurturing element refers to the satisfaction of needs, such as those for food and shelter, the removal of irritants, and other caretaking activities. In addition, the mother soothes her child by holding him with warmth and tenderness. She constructs a calm, pleasant atmosphere in which optimal nurturing can occur. The analytic process, through interpretation, provides nurturance in the context of a soothing, holding background environment. As I have noted, the construction of the holding environment is also part of the interpretative process.

The college student patient illustrates the way in which the repetition compulsion was an impediment to the development of psychic structure and executive ego functions that would have permitted him to deal effectively with the external world. Other patients remain fixated at primitive developmental stages because they have not received adequate soothing. The creation of a holding environment in the analytic setting can be a structure-promoting experience. In these instances, improvement is not the outcome of a specific intervention; rather, the therapist's interest and exploratory, nonjudgmental approach create a calm, objective environment that helps soothe the patient's disruption. I recall a middle-aged woman who no longer needed to drink vodka to calm what had been constant agitation. Her analytic sessions achieved the same effect, so she no longer needed to drink.

A supervisee reported how his patient, a disturbed, agitated 24-year-old woman with a marked tendency to act out, reported that the water in her aquarium had become murky. She bought a new filter, and the water once again became clear. The therapist saw himself as a filter that had the potential of clearing up the murkiness within the patient. The patient had calmed down considerably and her life became better organized after she bought the new filter for the aquarium. The therapist discussed how he saw himself functioning as the filter did, and the patient agreed that she felt that the treatment had an organizing and cleansing effect. The patient had succeeded in attributing to the therapist the capacity to stabilize her. She had previously been unable to achieve inner regulation—that is, to clear up psychic murkiness.

How did this soothing relationship develop? I raised the same question in Chapter 6. In the past, the patient had not been able to find a person who could help her regulate her inner turmoil, and she had seen several other therapists. My supervisee was obviously different from the therapists she had seen in the past, but it is difficult to understand precisely what he did to exert such a beneficial influence on her.

Like the patients discussed in Chapter 6, this patient had the capacity to create chaos and provoke anxiety in persons who were involved with her. She could be intrusive to the point of disrupting treatment. For example, she often threatened to remain in the consultation room at the end of a session. Her therapist was an exceptionally stable person who was not easily provoked or frightened. Regardless of the turmoil the patient tried to create, he could maintain a therapeutic focus and deal, for the most part, with her behavior in a calm, nonjudgmental fashion. He would not allow her to be destructive or physically abusive, however, and he would have picked her up, and ejected her from his office if she tried to carry out her threat not to leave at the end of a session. His nonanxious matter-of-fact approach was no doubt reassuring and calming. Taming disruption—that is, the background soothing element of the therapeutic interaction—creates a situation in which the patient can strive for higher levels of psychic integration.

This clinical vignette is the antithesis of the situations

described in Chapter 6, in which the therapists had absorbed their patients' inner prementational disruption. My supervisee was apparently able to soothe his patient without absorbing her agitation. He acted as a purifying filter but somehow did not retain the murky elements of his patient's personality. He filtered them through, or, in terms of psychic structure, he organized inner chaos by giving it form and structure, which caused the patient to feel soothed.

This relationship was no doubt the outcome of positive countertransference attitudes. The therapist provided structure and solid boundaries because of his firm ego organization. Therefore, he was able to superimpose those integrated parts of himself on the patient's primary process–organized chaos. Furthermore, he was able to get in touch with the maternal elements of his personality, which enabled him to soothe his patient.

Other disturbed patients emphasize features of the treatment process that involve specific forms of patient–analyst interactions, such as fusion. The therapist may internalize elements of the patient's psychic structure that evoke specific countertransference reactions.

THE THERAPIST'S INTROJECTION
OF THE PATIENT'S EGO DEFECT

In some instances, the therapist introjects the patient's ego defect. The absorption of the patient's projections is a well-known phenomenon, but clinicians usually think in terms of projections of impulses or parts of the self, such as the superego. The introjection of an ego defect is a phenomenon different from that which occurs in the usual introjective–projective interaction. Nevertheless, in the treatment of some patients who have serious structural problems, it can become the basis for a helpful therapeutic relationship that involves both the foreground and background elements of the interpretative interaction.

The patients to whom I am referring do not exactly project. They do not have enough psychic structure to achieve a psychic organization sufficient to allow them to do so. Still, the analyst is able to take on certain of the patient's structural configurations and then rearrange them in a more integrated fashion, thereby helping the patient. This is what my supervisee did. On the surface, this process sounds similar to projective identification. It is different, however, in that the patient does not project, and in that the final interaction is the outcome of fusion rather than of the more complex process of identification.

For example, I once again refer to the patient who, at the beginning of treatment, gave me a wooden statuette to care for (see Chapter 5). I have discussed this patient several times in various contexts (Giovacchini 1979a, 1986); here, I wish to emphasize a specific ego defect that I, after a fashion, absorbed. The patient set it up by giving me the statuette.

The statuette represented the patient's view of herself. It was her self-representation: primitive, amorphous, jagged, with hard angles and without arms to embrace. At first, I thought she had given it to me because she wanted me to understand her. This was true, but she also wanted me to have it so that I could keep her in my mind, so that I would not forget or lose her. Whatever reluctance I may have had in accepting her offer of the statuette must have quickly vanished, because I was certain that there would be no treatment if I refused.

As I have discussed, the patient would periodically get angry at me, usually when she felt I was threatening to wander beyond her psychic range. In a rage, she would grab the statuette and break it. I felt anxious and upset at such moments, but my tension would quickly subside after I glued the statuette back together. The patient would usually have these outbursts at the end of sessions.

After eight years of treatment, and after not having threatened the integrity of the statuette for several years, she once again became angry. I do not recall the reason, but it was not the same anger she had previously felt. Nevertheless, she started to reach for the statuette, but, to my surprise, I had no feelings about her actions. She immediately noticed my lack of reaction and suddenly put her arm down. Startled, she asked me how I felt, and without deliberation I said, "It's okay. I don't need her anymore." She nodded and took the statuette, but did not break it, and I have not seen it since.

The patient, over the course of treatment, had developed the capacity to hold a mental representation without external reinforcement. She no longer questioned me about my trips and sometimes even felt enthusiasm if she thought I was attending a worthwhile and exciting conference.

Apparently, within the context of treatment, I was also unable to hold a mental representation of the patient without external reinforcement—in this case, the statuette. I was uneasy and upset every time she broke it and would regain my composure only after I had mended it. At the beginning of treatment, the patient assumed that I would have the same difficulty she had when she entrusted the statuette to my care.

I do not actually have any problems with evocative memory, but in terms of our relationship, I adopted an orientation toward her that reflected her ego defect. This was evidenced by my concern for the statuette as well as by my having forgotten on one occasion to tell the patient that I would be out of town. I forgot to cancel her appointment. In fact, I did not remember her at all when I left. This was partly my revenge for the anticipated attack about my leaving, but I believe that, for the moment, I had also lost her mental representation.

Although it is difficult to be certain, I doubt that the patient's projections played much of a role in my reactions. Unlike the college student, she lacked the psychic structure and organization to sustain even such a primitive mechanism as projection. Again, this is a question of degree because, to some extent, she used many defensive adaptations; compared to persons with more well-structured personalities, however, she made only minimal use of projective defenses. When she gave me the statuette, she simply assumed that everyone was like her—unable to form and hold a mental representation. She could not appreciate the fact that there were minds different from her own that could relate to her at higher levels of psychic organization.

Nevertheless, even if the patient was unable to project effectively, I still managed to "absorb" her ego defect during certain periods of our relationship, in the same way that analysts internalize prementational agitation. Although she had not projected, I was able to introject certain aspects of her lack of psychic structure. The mechanism I used, introjection, was at a higher level of ego integration than were the modalities she used to maintain emotional balance. Still, re-creating a similar psychic state within myself enabled me to be in resonance with many of her feelings. I understood, and at times could feel, the anguish she experienced in many situations that would otherwise have seemed trivial. I could also finally appreciate her need to have me constantly present, although I could, at the same time, obliterate her from my mind. What began as a difference in levels of relating—my introjecting despite her inability to project—had now reached an equilibrium in which we were participating in somewhat similar functional modes.

The resonance of our ego states seemed to be an essential

feature of her eventual acquisition of psychic structure. It was not an active interpretative interaction, but it became a type of bonding that stabilized our relationship and that gradually evolved into a soothing holding environment. The patient had many moments of regression and affective volatility, but despite her disruption, she was attached to the treatment. I offered many interpretations about the way she related to people and about the way in which her inability to hold mental representations created panic and forced her to be demanding of her friends and of me. We were able to relate her current feelings to their genetic antecedents, but I believe that the soothing bond we had established created sufficient structure so that she could now fuse with me—that is, with the more integrated aspects of my psyche.

This patient presented many paradoxical features that were the manifestations of psychic discontinuity. I have emphasized the primitive aspects of her personality because that was how she generally presented herself. I also knew, however, that she could occasionally function in a highly competent manner. She had a remarkable memory for music and was able to recognize various compositions and to identify the orchestra and often the soloists. She could also be very adept socially, bringing people together, introducing them, and easily remembering names. The patient lamented that this part of her personality was seldom available to her. She could behave like an adult, but she did not believe that this was her true self.

Like some other patients I have discussed, she did not view herself as having connecting bridges between the primitive and advanced levels of the psyche. Unlike many psychoneurotic patients, she had no problem in getting in touch with the primitive self; rather, she had difficulty in maintaining contact with higher levels. I apparently juxtaposed myself with her unstructured orientation and, as she fused with me, helped her develop connecting bridges to establish more reality-adapted ego orientations. I had incorporated her lack of structure to some extent, but I was simultaneously able to function at higher levels of analytic functioning and integration. Her spectrum of psychic functioning expanded because of her fusion with me, and she gradually incorporated, or superimposed, higher levels of psychic structure and connecting bridges that enabled her to remain in touch with her capacity to function effectively. We eventually discussed these processes, which enabled her to register the interaction indelibly in her mind. Our interaction had then become clearly interpretative, as it led to lasting, effective insight.

FUSION, PROJECTION, AND EXTERNALITY

In the treatment of patients with structural defects, fusion with the healthier aspects of the analyst's personality leads to structure-promoting identifications. These identifications lead to changes in psychic structure that are similar to the effects produced by mutative interpretations (Strachey 1934).

Borderline patients, and others who have characterological problems, often have difficulty fusing with potentially helpful external objects. They cannot avail themselves of beneficial experiences in the outside world, as dramatically illustrated by my depressed patient (see Chapter 7). They have similar problems in the treatment setting in that they cannot internalize various aspects of the analytic process that would help them to achieve ego integration and resolution of intrapsychic conflicts. The fear of fusion and the inability to fuse are equivalent to resistance, generally to a meaningful interpretation. As discussed, this can lead to disruptive countertransference reactions.

Patients who view fusion as destructive often demonstrate a discontinuity of psychic structure and of the construction of hierarchies. Their characterological configurations lead them to view the world in a concrete fashion and to be isolated from the primitive parts of their personalities. They may relate to the world on the basis of a false-self compliance (Winnicott 1960).

To continue with Winnicott's viewpoint, the true self, if it exists to any significant degree, is not connected to the false self. There is little continuity between higher and lower psychic levels. In other words, there is a lack of connection between the functioning, adaptive aspects of the psyche and the inner world of affects.

These patients are not aware—indeed, they vehemently deny—that they have any control over their destinies. Inasmuch as they are constantly involved with the surrounding world and blame it for all their mishaps, they seem to be constantly projecting. This is not projection in the ordinary sense, however, and, as noted earlier, patients with such primitive orientations have not yet achieved the capacity to project.

The ability to project requires the capacity to distinguish between external reality and the inner world of the psyche. It also requires that the patient be able to place some aspects of the inner world (psychic structure, feelings, id impulses) into the outer world. The patients I am describing have no access, relatively speaking, to the inner world and therefore cannot project it.

Still, many of these patients demonstrate all the features of paranoid characters. They are querulous, suspicious, and often immersed in a litany of complaints, constantly blaming others for their endless misfortunes. Rather than projecting in the classic sense, these patients are demonstrating the consequences of an ego defect, psychic discontinuity, that renders them incapable of getting in touch with the deeper recesses of the psyche. Consequently, all understanding and explanation, all etiologic sources, are confined to only one frame of reference: the superficial context of visible phenomena. They have little or no concept of psychic reality.

Understandably, this lack of connection to the psyche would make psychoanalysis difficult, if not impossible. Inasmuch as interpretations are directed toward understanding psychic reality, they would be meaningless to these patients. In some instances, however, therapists can work with them, although, from what I have described, the situation seems impossible — and it often is.

Clinicians are familiar with the rigidity of the paranoid patient, and the patients I am describing may appear to be extremely rigid. It is a rigidity, however, that is founded on a lack of options and an inability to make connections. These patients can only connect external events and conscious reactions, and the resulting connection frequently seems to be of a paranoid nature. Nevertheless, it is the only way they can relate and maintain psychic synthesis.

The synthesis is precarious at best, however. Because the larger portion of their psyches operates on the basis of a false self, they do not feel that they are whole persons; in extreme instances they do not have any assurance that they even exist. We are sometimes aware of the poignant nature of their adaptations, which are based on self-effacement and constriction. On other occasions, therapists become intensely confused because although they can perceive certain aspects of the patient's inner life as it is revealed to them, they feel at the same time that the patient is very rigid and concrete. The fact that these patients are disconnected from the unconscious, so to speak, differentiates them from the concrete patients discussed earlier. Thus,

rather than simply feeling overwhelmed by frustration, as usually occurs with inaccessible patients, the therapist experiences
countertransference reactions that are mixed and complex.

Some novelists intuitively appreciate the dilemma posed by
such constrictions. I turn to an unlikely source of data, a mystery
novel written with unprecedented sensitivity. The main character is a writer who pretends to be a certain detective so that he
can continue his mission of following a person who is wandering
the streets of New York in an apparently senseless fashion,
collecting all sorts of meaningless items and junk. It is interesting
that the writer in the novel must assume the identity of another
so that he can function effectively. The author of the novel
writes:

> By flooding himself with externals, by drowning himself
> out of himself, he had managed to exert some small degree
> of control over his fits of despair. Wandering, therefore,
> was a kind of mindlessness . . . he was obliged now to
> concentrate on what he was doing, even if it was next to
> nothing. Time and again his thoughts would begin to drift,
> and soon thereafter his steps would follow suit. This meant
> that he was constantly in danger of quickening his pace and
> crashing into [the person he was following] . . . to guard
> against this mishap he devised several methods of deceler-
> ation. The first was to tell himself that he was no longer
> Daniel Quinn. He was Paul Auster now, and with each step
> he took he tried to fit more comfortably into the strictures
> of that transformation. Auster was no more than a name to
> him, a *husk without content*. To be Auster meant being a
> man with no interior, a man with no thoughts. And if there
> were no thoughts available to him, if his own inner life had
> been made inaccessible, then there was no place for him to
> retreat to. As Auster, he could not summon up any mem-
> ories of fears, any dreams of joys, for all these things as they
> pertained to Auster, were a blank to him. *He consequently*

had to remain solely on his own surface, looking outward for
sustenance. [Auster 1985, pp. 98–99; emphasis mine]

This quote stresses the adaptive nature of this type of externality and of the lack of inner connections. The outcome of this adaptation is not always a paranoid outlook. Some patients find this "husk without content"—the state of being a "mindless zombie," as one patient described himself, intolerably painful. Their misery causes them to seek therapy and makes treatment possible, despite the inaccessibility to the inner life.

Again, we can ask how a transference can be established if the primitive parts of the patient cannot be projected. A transference can develop, but it will be based on fusion rather than projection. Ordinarily, we view the mechanisms of projection and fusion as interrelated, as Klein (1946), Ogden (1982), Grotstein (1981), and others have written in their descriptions of projective identification. But this does not mean that fusion cannot occur with only minimal projection. Fusion does not require that all levels of two personalities merge with each other. The patient can feel that only the surface layers of his character are incorporated by his therapist; he can then internalize, in a limited fashion, the superficial elements of the analyst's psychic structure. As discussed in the previous section, The Therapist's Introjection of the Patient's Ego Defect, the patient who gave me the statuette, could not project, whereas I could introject her ego defect of being unable to maintain mental representations. Eventually, however, the patient was able to merge with the healthier surface elements of my personality. Projective identification includes superficial as well as deeper elements of the psyche. Inasmuch as the patient has to remain solely on his *own surface, looking outward for sustenance*, there is a potential for fusion, at least of surface levels of the psyche. This fusion can then lead to the patient's structuring a transference, which in turn helps to establish a connection with the inner world. This connection makes interpretative discourse possible.

The concrete personality has achieved a certain amount of psychic stability. Other persons are aware to some extent of the lack of connections with their inner world, and they lament their false-self status (Boyer 1983). They revile themselves for "lacking character" as they constantly mold themselves to the contours of the surrounding reality – in itself, a fusion. They are disturbed by their lack of identity, their "as-if" qualities (Deutsch 1942).

The former therapist of a patient currently in treatment with another analyst compared his patient to the main character in Anton Chekhov's short story "The Darling." The story contained a remarkable description of the as-if character. The patient agreed that, at that time, she did not have a distinct personality; she stated that she had no mind of her own and that she had had an intense need to please her first therapist. She also indicated that she had fused with him, and there was considerable evidence that the therapist had also fused with her. Gradually, the patient began to believe that she was developing feelings of her own. The general impression was that, within the context of fusion, the patient had begun to consolidate her own identity; that is, there was an emerging inner core. For extraneous reasons, however, the treatment relationship had to terminate, and some years later she sought further therapy.

In her second course of treatment, she reached the startling conclusion that what she had viewed as an emerging sense of self based on newly felt feelings was an illusion. She now knew that she was not experiencing her own feelings; rather, her reactions were the feelings that her therapist had put into her. She had believed that she was both "the darling" and, later, a distinct person. Her therapist believed that she had achieved autonomy, and his belief became hers when they fused with each other.

Nevertheless, she did not experience much vitality in her "autonomy." I believe that her former therapist was exhibiting an idiosyncratic type of countertransference. He had reported to her that her transference need to fuse with him was a progressive step in the direction of autonomy. It became apparent that her therapist had reasons of his own for fusing with her. He had viewed their interaction as one that would facilitate the integration of his interpretations and, for a while, the patient felt the same way. As she reviewed this material with her second analyst, she gained the conviction that her first therapist, because of some countertransference difficulty, was compelled to believe that she was acquiring psychic structure. Perhaps the absorption of her feeling of emptiness was too painful for him.

One of the most impressive moments in her former treatment was the analysis of a dream. Briefly, the dream involved frogs, which, to her therapist, indicated that childish patterns were surfacing and being released so that they could be integrated by the ego, thereby enabling her to achieve higher levels of psychic organization. She told her second therapist that, as a young child, she had been impressed by her mother's bathrobe, which was covered with pictures of tiny frogs. In her associations, she felt that she would be smothered by this bathrobe, and her dream was, in fact, a nightmare. Apparently the therapist was unaware of her fear of being devoured by the frogs of her internal world, and the patient outwardly accepted his attributing a sense of identity to the logo of the frog. True, she had made some connections with the inner world that were lacking when she felt like an "as-if" character. But despite some accessibility to deeper levels of her personality, she was still reacting, at least toward her therapist, in an as-if fashion. She was adapting herself to his viewpoint and, on a surface level, was fusing with him.

* * *

When discussing the treatment of patients suffering from character disorders, processes such as projection and fusion must be understood as thoroughly as possible. The part and level of psychic structure that is being projected or merged with must be identified, and the therapist's contributions have to be evaluated. What appears to be an interpretation is frequently a disruptive countertransference reaction.

The various examples of countertransference cited throughout this book have many characteristics in common. I have just discussed reactions to the patient–analyst fusion, but various degrees of fusion will inevitably occur in any psychoanalytic treatment relationship. Even projection is a type of fusion that is experienced by both therapist and patient. Patients cannot project feelings, and especially parts of the self, unless the analyst is willing to accept these projections. If the analyst is unwilling to receive them, then therapy with that particular analyst may be impossible.

The degree to which the analyst allows himself to internalize the patient, and it may be minimal, represents a countertransference element that is an intrinsic part of the therapeutic interaction. Inasmuch as an effective interpretation requires the patient to fuse with the therapist, all interpretations occur within a transference–countertransference context. This formulation is in accord with the recent emphasis that has been placed on empathy. But there is nothing mysterious or esoteric about empathy; it is simply another way of describing subtle and sometimes complex transference–countertransference interactions.

I have given countertransference reactions a central position in the therapeutic interaction and have viewed them as an integral part of any technical maneuver. They cause technical treatment problems, and they become a means of resolving them. Whether good or bad, countertransference reactions are ubiquitous.

Countertransference was ignored for many years. The recognition of its effects and its role in the therapeutic interaction has broadened the scope of psychoanalytic treatment and has made the analytic interaction a human and mutually enriching experience.

References

Abraham, K. (1927). Notes on the psychoanalytic investigation and treatment of manic depressive insanity and allied conditions. In *Selected Papers of Karl Abraham*, pp. 137–157. London: Hogarth Press, 1955.

Alexander, F. (1927). *Psychoanalysis of the Total Personality.* New York: Nervous and Mental Disease.

——— (1956). Two forms of regression and their therapeutic implications. *Psychoanalytic Quarterly* 25:178–196.

_____ (1961). *The Scope of Psychoanalysis.* New York: Basic Books.

Anzieu, D. (1987). Some alterations of the ego which make analysis interminable. *International Journal of Psycho-Analysis* 68:9–21.

Auster, P. (1985). *City of Glass.* Los Angeles: Sun and Moon Press.

Bertin, C. (1982). *Maria Bonaparte: A Life.* New York: Harcourt Brace Jovanovich.

Bleger, J. (1967). Psycho-analysis of the psychoanalytic frame. *International Journal of Psycho-Analysis* 48:511–519.

Blum, H. P. (1986). Countertransference and the theory of technique: discussion. *Journal of the American Psychoanalytic Association* 34:309–329.

Boesky, D. (1983). The problem of mental representation in self and object theory. *Psychoanalytic Quarterly* 52:564–583.

Boyer, L. B. (1961). Provisional evaluation of psycho-analysis with few parameters in the treatment of schizophrenia. *International Journal of Psycho-Analysis* 42:389–403.

_____ (1983). Analytic experiences in working with depressed patients. In *The Regressed Patient,* pp. 187–216. New York: Jason Aronson.

_____ (1983). *The Regressed Patient.* New York: Jason Aronson.

Boyer, L. B., and Giovacchini, P. (1980). *Psychoanalytic Treatment of Characterological, Borderline, and Schizophrenic Disorders.* New York: Jason Aronson.

Brazelton, T. B. (1980). New knowledge about the infant from current research: implications for psychoanalysis. Presented at the May meetings of the American Psychoanalytic Association, San Francisco.

Brenner, C. (1985). Countertransference as compromise formation. *Psychoanalytic Quarterly* 54:155–163.

Breuer, J., and Freud, S. (1895). Studies on hysteria. *Standard Edition* 2:1–307.

Brown, L. (1985). On concreteness. *Psychoanalytic Review* 72:379–402.

Davis, M., and Walbridge, D. (1981). *Boundary and Space: An Introduction to the Work of D. W. Winnicott.* New York: Brunner/Mazel.

Deutsch, H. (1942). Some forms of emotional disturbances and their relationship to schizophrenia. *Psychoanalytic Quarterly* 11: 301–321.

Ehrenberg, D. (1985). Countertransference resistance. *Contemporary Psychoanalysis* 21:563–576.

Eissler, K. (1953). The effects of the structuring of the ego on psycho-analytic technique. *Journal of the American Psychoanalytic Association* 1:104–143.

_____ (1958). Goethe and science: a contribution to the psychology of Goethe's psychosis. *Psychoanalysis and Social Sciences* 5:51–98.

Emde, R. (1980). Levels of meaning for infant emotions. In *Development of Cognition, Affect, and Social Relations*, ed. W. A. Collins, pp. 36–72. Hillsdale, New Jersey: Erlbaum.

Engel, G. (1954). Selection of clinical material in psychosomatic medicine. *Psychosomatic Medicine* 16:368–382.

_____ (1968). Follow-up on Monica. Paper presented at a meeting of the Chicago Psychoanalytic Society, October 22.

Engel, G., and Reichsman, F. (1956). Spontaneous and experimentally induced depressions in infants with gastric fistulas. *Journal of the American Psychoanalytic Association* 4:428–452.

Epstein, L., and Feiner, A. (1979). *Countertransference*. New York: Jason Aronson.

Erikson, E. H. (1959). *Identity and the Life Cycle*. New York: International Universities Press.

Esman, A. (1983). The "stimulus barrier": a review and reconsideration. *Psychoanalytic Study of the Child* 58:193–207.

Federn, P. (1952). *Ego Psychology and the Psychoses*. New York: Basic Books.

Fenichel, O. (1945). *The Psychoanalytic Theory of Neurosis*. New York: W. W. Norton.

Flarsheim, A. (1975). Therapist's collusion with the patient's wish for suicide. In *Tactics and Techniques in Psychoanalytic Therapy*, vol. 2, ed. P. Giovacchini, pp. 155–196. New York: Jason Aronson.

Fraiberg, S. (1969). Libidinal object constancy and mental representation. *Psychoanalytic Study of the Child* 24:9-47.

Freud, A. (1937). *The Ego and the Mechanisms of Defense*. New York: International Universities Press.

―――― (1965). *Normality and Pathology in Childhood*. New York: International Universities Press.

Freud, S. (1900). The interpretation of dreams. *Standard Edition* 4, 5.

―――― (1904). Fragment of an analysis of a case of hysteria. *Standard Edition* 7:1-123.

―――― (1905). Three essays on the theory of sexuality. *Standard Edition* 7:123-244.

―――― (1909). Analysis of a phobia in a five-year-old boy. *Standard Edition* 10:1-148.

―――― (1910). The future prospects of psychoanalytic therapy. *Standard Edition* 11:139-153.

―――― (1911-1915). Papers on technique. *Standard Edition* 12:85-172.

―――― (1912a). Recommendations to physicians practicing psychoanalysis. *Standard Edition* 12:109-121.

―――― (1912b). The dynamics of transference. *Standard Edition* 12:97-109.

―――― (1913). On beginning the treatment. *Standard Edition* 12:121-145.

―――― (1914a). Observations on transference love. *Standard Edition* 12:157-172.

―――― (1914b). Remembering, repeating, and working through. *Standard Edition* 12:145-157.

―――― (1915a). The unconscious. *Standard Edition* 14:159-205.

―――― (1915b). Instincts and their vicissitudes. *Standard Edition* 14:109-141.

―――― (1916). Some character types met with in psychoanalytic work. *Standard Edition* 14:309-337.

―――― (1917a). Mourning and melancholia. *Standard Edition* 14:237-261.

_____ (1917b). Introductory lectures on psycho-analysis. *Standard Edition* 16:241–478.

_____ (1918). From the history of an infantile neurosis. *Standard Edition* 17:1–123.

_____ (1919). Lines of advance in psycho-analytic therapy. *Standard Edition* 17:157–169.

_____ (1920). Beyond the pleasure principle. *Standard Edition* 18:3–66.

_____ (1923). The ego and the id. *Standard Edition* 14:1–60.

_____ (1925). An autobiographical study. *Standard Edition* 19:235–241.

_____ (1926). The problem of anxiety. *Standard Edition* 20:75–175.

_____ (1929). Civilization and its discontents. *Standard Edition* 23:255–271.

Gill, M. (1979). The analysis of the transference. *Journal of the American Psychoanalytic Association* 27:263–288.

_____ (1983). *Analysis of Transference.* Vol. 1. New York: International Universities Press.

_____ (1984–1985). The range of applicability of psychoanalytic technique. *International Journal of Psychoanalytic Psychotherapy* 10:109–116.

Giovacchini, P. (1958). Mutual adaptations in various object relationships. *International Journal of Psycho-Analysis* 39:1–8.

_____ (1972). *Tactics and Techniques in Psychoanalytic Treatment.* New York: Jason Aronson.

_____ (1975). *Tactics and Techniques in Psychoanalytic Treatment: Countertransference Issues.* Vol. 2. New York: Jason Aronson.

_____ (1979a). *Treatment of Primitive Mental States.* New York: Jason Aronson.

_____ (1979b). Countertransference in primitive mental states. In *Countertransference,* ed. L. Epstein and A. Feiner. New York: Jason Aronson.

_____ (1984). The blank self. In *Character Disorders and Adaptive Mechanisms,* pp. 79–92. New York: Jason Aronson.

_____ (1986). *Developmental Disorders: The Transitional Object in Mental Breakdown and Creative Integration.* Northvale, NJ: Jason Aronson.

_____ (1987). *A Narrative Textbook of Psychoanalysis.* Northvale, NJ: Jason Aronson.

Giovacchini, P., and Boyer, L. B. (1975). The psychoanalytic impasse. *International Journal of Psychoanalytic Psychotherapy* 4:25–47.

_____ (1982). *Technical Factors in the Treatment of the Severely Disturbed Patient.* New York: Jason Aronson.

Gitelson, M. (1952). The emotional position of the analyst in the psycho-analytic situation. *International Journal of Psycho-Analysis* 33:1–11.

Glover, E. (1931). The therapeutic effect of inexact interpretation. *International Journal of Psycho-Analysis* 12:397–411.

_____ (1955). *Technique of Psychoanalysis.* New York: International Universities Press.

Gorkin, M. (1985). Varieties of sexualized countertransference. *Psychoanalytic Review* 72:421–440.

Greenberg, J. R. (1986). The problem of analytic neutrality. *Contemporary Psychoanalysis* 22:76–86.

Greenson, R. (1960). Empathy and its vicissitudes. *International Journal of Psycho-Analysis* 41:418–424.

Grinberg, L. (1962). On a specific aspect of countertransference due to the patient's projective identification. *International Journal of Psycho-Analysis* 43:436–440.

_____ (1979). Countertransference and projective counteridentification. *Contemporary Psychoanalysis* 15:226–247.

Grosskurth, P. (1985). *Melanie Klein.* New York: Knopf.

Grotstein, J. (1981). *Splitting and Projective Identification.* New York: Jason Aronson.

Guttman, S., Jones, R., and Parrish, S. (1980). *Concordance to the Psychological Works of Sigmund Freud.* Boston: G. K. Hall.

Hartmann, H. (1939). *Ego Psychology and the Problem of Adaptation.* New York: International Universities Press.

Heiman, P. (1950). On countertransference. *International Journal of Psycho-Analysis* 31:81–84.

Hoyt, M., and Farrell, D. (1984–1985). Countertransference difficulties in a time-limited psychotherapy. *International Journal of Psychoanalytic Psychotherapy* 10:116–135.

Jacobs, T. J. (1986). On countertransference enactment. *Journal of the American Psychoanalytic Association* 34:298–308.

Jacobson, E. (1964). *The Self and the Object World*. New York: International Universities Press.

Jung, C. (1909). The psychology of dementia praecox. In *Collected Works of C. G. Jung*, vol. 3, ed. W. McGuire, pp. 3–151. Princeton, NJ: Princeton University Press.

Karidner, A. (1977). *My Analysis with Freud*. New York: W. W. Norton.

Kernberg, O. (1965). Notes on countertransference. *Journal of the American Psychoanalytic Association* 13:38–56.

Klaus, M., and Kennel, J. (1982). *Parent–Infant Bonding*. St. Louis: C. V. Mosby.

Klein, M. (1935). A contribution to the psychogenesis of manic-depressive states. *International Journal of Psycho-Analysis* 27:145–174.

_____ (1946). Notes on some schizoid mechanisms. *International Journal of Psycho-Analysis* 27:99–110.

_____ (1948). *Contributions to Psycho-Analysis*. London: Hogarth Press.

Kris, A. (1983). Determinants of free association in narcissistic phenomena. *Psychoanalytic Study of the Child* 38:439–458.

Lichtenberg, J. (1986). The tension between unrestricted personal revelation and circumscribed personal revelation. *Contemporary Psychoanalysis* 22:71–76.

Little, M. (1951). Countertransference and the patient's response to it. *International Journal of Psycho-Analysis* 32:32–40.

_____ (1981). *Transference and Countertransference*. New York: Jason Aronson.

Loewald, H. W. (1960). On the therapeutic action of psychoanalysis. *International Journal of Psycho-Analysis* 41:16–32.

_____ (1986). Transference–countertransference. *Journal of the American Psychoanalytic Association* 34:275–289.

Martin, P. (1975). The obnoxious patient. In *Tactics and Techniques in Psychoanalytic Treatment: Countertransference Issues*, vol. 2, ed. P. Giovacchini, pp. 196–205. New York: Jason Aronson.

Masterson, J. (1976). *Treatment of the Borderline Adult.* New York: Brunner/Mazel.

McDougall, J. (1979). Primitive communication and the use of countertransference. In *Countertransference*, ed. L. Epstein and A. Feiner, pp. 267–303. New York: Jason Aronson.

Meissner, W. W. (1984–1985). Studies on hysteria: Dora. *International Journal of Psychoanalytic Psychotherapy* 10:567–598.

Modell, A. (1968). *Object Love and Reality.* New York: International Universities Press.

Ogden, T. (1982). *Projective Identification: Psychotherapeutic Technique.* New York: Jason Aronson.

Piaget, J. (1952). *The Language and Thought of the Child.* London: Routledge and Kegan Paul.

Pick, I. B. (1985). Working through in the countertransference. *International Journal of Psycho-Analysis* 66:157–166.

Racker, H. (1953). A contribution to the problem of countertransference. *International Journal of Psycho-Analysis* 34:313–324.

_____ (1968). *Transference and Countertransference.* New York: International Universities Press.

Reich, A. (1951). On countertransference. *International Journal of Psycho-Analysis* 32:25–31.

Reichard, S. (1956). A re-examination of "Studies in Hysteria." *Psychoanalytic Quarterly* 25:155–177.

Sandler, J., and Rosenblatt, B. (1962). The concept of the representational world. *Psychoanalytic Study of the Child* 17:128–195.

Schafer, R. (1968). *Aspects of Internalization.* New York: International Universities Press.

Searles, H. F. (1953). Dependency processes in the therapy of schizophrenia. *Journal of the American Psychoanalytic Association* 1:19–60.

———— (1960). *The Non-Human Environment.* New York: International Universities Press.

———— (1963). Transference psychosis in the psychotherapy of schizophrenia. *International Journal of Psycho-Analysis* 44:249–291.

———— (1965). *Collected Papers on Schizophrenia and Related Subjects.* New York: International Universities Press.

———— (1975). The patient as therapist to his analyst. In *Tactics and Techniques in Psychoanalytic Treatment: Countertransference,* vol. 2, ed. P. Giovacchini, pp. 95–151. New York: Jason Aronson.

———— (1987). Countertransference as a path to understanding and helping the patient. In *Countertransference,* ed. E. Slakter, pp. 131–165. Northvale, NJ: Jason Aronson.

Shapiro, T. (1984). On neutrality. *Journal of the American Psychoanalytic Association* 32:269–282.

Sharpe, E. F. (1930). The technique of psycho-analysis. *International Journal of Psycho-Analysis* 11:361–386.

Silbermann, I. (1983). On anxiety and terror. *Psychoanalytic Study of the Child* 38:569–574.

Slakter, E. (1987). *Countertransference.* Northvale, NJ: Jason Aronson.

Spitz, R. (1941). On hospitalization. *Psychoanalytic Study of the Child* 1:53–74.

Stern, A. (1924). On the countertransference in psychoanalysis. *Psychoanalytic Review* 2:166–174.

Stern, D. (1985). *The Interpersonal World of the Infant.* New York: Basic Books.

Stone, L. (1963). *The Psychoanalytic Situation.* New York: International Universities Press.

Strachey, J. (1934). The nature of the therapeutic action of psychoanalysis. *International Journal of Psycho-Analysis* 15:127–160.

Thorner, H. (1985). On repetition: its relationship to the depressive position. *International Journal of Psycho-Analysis* 66:231–236.

Tower, L. (1956). Countertransference. *Journal of the American Psychoanalytic Association* 4:224–255.

Volkan, V. (1975). *Primitive Internalized Object Relations*. New York: International Universities Press.

_____ (1987). *Six Steps in the Treatment of Borderline Personality Organization*. Northvale, NJ: Jason Aronson.

Wachtel, P. (1986). On the limits of therapeutic neutrality. *Contemporary Psychoanalysis* 22:60–70.

Waelder, R. (1960). *Basic Theory of Psychoanalysis*. New York: International Universities Press.

Winnicott, D. W. (1949). Hate in the countertransference. *International Journal of Psycho-Analysis* 30:61–74.

_____ (1952). Psychosis and child care. In *Collected Papers: Through Paediatrics to Psycho-Analysis*, pp. 219–228. New York: Basic Books.

_____ (1956). Primary maternal preoccupation. In *Collected Papers: Through Paediatrics to Psycho-Analysis*, pp. 300–305. New York: Basic Books.

_____ (1960). Ego distortions in terms of the true and false self. In *Maturational Processes and the Facilitating Environment*, pp. 140–153. New York: International Universities Press.

_____ (1963a). The psychotherapy of character disorders. In *Maturational Processes and the Facilitating Environment*, pp. 203–217. New York: International Universities Press.

_____ (1963b). The mentally ill in your caseload. In *Maturational Processes and the Facilitating Environment*, pp. 217–230. New York: International Universities Press.

Index

paradoxical aspects of, in depressed
  patients, 286–287
of therapist, 54
unstable, versus intact ego, 318, 319
Sensory apparatus, defects in, 66
Setting, analytic
  concrete change in, intolerance of,
    104–110
  threats to, 112
Sexual feelings, organizing function of,
  280
Sexual involvement between therapist
  and patient, 198–201
Sexual material, lack of, in dreams of
  depressed patient, 278
Shapiro, T., 296
Sharpe, E. F., 14
Silbermann, I., 280
Silence
  analytic, as weapon, 88
  of patient, 261–262
Slakter, E., 5
Soothing, 82–83, 103, 136, 137, 180,
  183–185, 187, 188, 189, 190, 191,
  196–197, 198, 200, 201, 307–308,
  320–322, 326
  potential of anxiety for, 204
  of psychiatrists, 195, 201
Speaking, manner of, of depressed
  patient, 257–258, 260
Spitz, R., 205, 206
Standard Edition, 15
Stern, D., 178
Simuli, responses of depressed patient
  to, 246–247
Stimulus barrier, 82, 179
Stone, L., xii, 144, 215
Strachey, J., 327
Structural defect(s)
  fusion in, 327, 328
  lack of evocative memory and, 293
  specific, countertransference and,
    111–173
Structural problems
  intensification of countertransfer-
    ence with, 280, 281

interpretation with patients, with,
  319
introjection of ego defects in, 323
Structural psychopathology, spectrum
  of, 176
Structure, psychic
  discrepancy between behavior and,
    283
  paradoxes of self-representation and,
    287
Structured affect, anger as, 198,
  201–204, 280
Subjective viewpoint, toward intrusive
  patient, 58
Suicidal characteristics, of depressed
  patients, 228–229
Superego
  emergence of, in development,
    282–283
  self-representation and, 287
Survival, as main task of therapist, in
  dealing with primitive mental
  states, 70

Tape recorder fantasy, of therapist, 51
Telephone, talking to prospective pa-
  tients on, 243
Terror, toleration of, 281
Therapeutic process
  components of, 82
  disruption of, 27–54
Therapist
  contribution of, to course of ther-
    apy, 1–8
  introjection of patient's ego defect
    by, 322–327
  personal orientation of, threats to,
    135–159
Thorner, H., 238, 261
Tower, L., x, 17–18
Transference–countertransference
  axis, 135, 215, 226, 308, 310
Transference neurosis, 2
Transference psychosis, 117
Transitional object(s)
  analyst as, 125